D0120222

Understanding
Cry, the Beloved Country

The Greenwood Press "Literature in Context" Series
Student Casebooks to Issues, Sources, and Historical Documents

The Adventures of Huckleberry Finn
by Claudia Durst Johnson

Animal Farm
by John Rodden

Anne Frank's *The Diary of a Young Girl*
by Hedda Rosner Kopf

The Call of the Wild
by Claudia Durst Johnson

The Catcher in the Rye
by Sanford and Ann Pinsker

Ceremony
by Lynn Domina

The Crucible
by Claudia Durst Johnson
and Vernon E. Johnson

Death of a Salesman
by Brenda Murphy and
Susan C. W. Abbotson

The Grapes of Wrath
by Claudia Durst Johnson

Great Expectations
by George Newlin

The Great Gatsby
by Dalton Gross and MaryJean Gross

Hamlet
by Richard Corum

I Know Why the Caged Bird Sings
by Joanne Megna-Wallace

Jamaica Kincaid's *Annie John*
by Deborah Mistron

Jane Eyre
by Debra Teachman

King Lear
by Donna Woodford

The Literature of World War I
by James H. Meredith

The Literature of World War II
by James H. Meredith

Lord of the Flies
by Kirstin Olsen

Macbeth
by Faith Nostbakken

The Merchant of Venice
by Jay L. Halio

O Pioneers! and *My Ántonia*
by Sheryl L. Meyering

The Odyssey
by Claudia Durst Johnson and
Vernon Johnson

Of Mice and Men, The Red Pony, and
The Pearl
by Claudia Durst Johnson

The Old Man and the Sea
by Patricia Dunlavy Valenti

Othello
by Faith Nostbakken

Pride and Prejudice
by Debra Teachman

A Raisin in the Sun
by Lynn Domina

The Red Badge of Courage
by Claudia Durst Johnson

Richard Wright's *Black Boy*
by Robert Felgar

Romeo and Juliet
by Alan Hager

The Scarlet Letter
by Claudia Durst Johnson

A Separate Peace
by Hallman Bell Bryant

Shakespeare's *Julius Caesar*
by Thomas Derrick

A Tale of Two Cities
by George Newlin

The Tempest
by Faith Nostbakken

Things Fall Apart
by Kalu Ogbaa

To Kill a Mockingbird
by Claudia Durst Johnson

Zora Neale Hurston's *Their Eyes Were*
Watching God
by Neal A. Lester

Understanding *Cry, the Beloved Country*

A STUDENT CASEBOOK TO ISSUES, SOURCES, AND HISTORICAL DOCUMENTS

Ngwarsungu Chiwengo

The Greenwood Press
"Literature in Context" Series
Claudia Durst Johnson, Series Editor

GREENWOOD PRESS
Westport, Connecticut London

Library of Congress Cataloging-in-Publication Data

Ngwarsungu Chiwengo.

Understanding Cry, the beloved country: a student casebook to issues, sources, and historical documents / Ngwarsungu Chiwengo.

p. cm.—(The Greenwood Press "Literature in context" series, ISSN 1074–598X)

Includes bibliographical references and index.

ISBN 0–313–33508–7 (alk. paper)

1. Paton, Alan. Cry, the beloved country—Examinations—Study guides. 2. South Africa—In literature. 3. Race relations in literature. 4. Apartheid in literature. I. Title.

PR9369.3.P37C736 2007

823'.914—dc22 2006030388

British Library Cataloguing in Publication Data is available.

Library of Congress Catalog Card Number: 2006030388
ISBN–10: 0–313–33508–7
ISBN–13: 978–0–313–33508–2
ISSN: 1074–598X

First published in 2007

Greenwood Press, 88 Post Road West, Westport, CT 06881
An imprint of Greenwood Publishing Group, Inc.
www.greenwood.com

Printed in the United States of America

The paper used in this book complies with the Permanent Paper Standard issued by the National Information Standards Organization (Z39.48–1984).

10 9 8 7 6 5 4 3 2 1

Copyright Acknowledgment

Every reasonable effort has been made to trace the owners of copyright materials in this book, but in some instances this has proven impossible. The author and publisher will be glad to receive information leading to more complete acknowledgments in subsequent printings of the book, and in the meantime extend their apologies for any omissions.

Contents

Introduction

Alan Paton is South Africa's most renowned writer, one who had the courage to write about the plight of Africans at a time when they might not have been considered by some to be worthy of much consideration. He may have written *Cry, the Beloved Country* not so much to denounce the oppression of Africans as for fear of their impeding revolt; nonetheless, despite his failure to support international sanctions and embargoes against his country, he had the temerity to voice his opposition to the practices of his contemporaries and to expose the iniquity in his country. Alan Paton's own dealings with people of other races may not have always been exemplary—James Gubavu told him that he was a racist when he worked at the Diepkloof reformatory school—but he was, nonetheless, willing to listen and to change his attitude in his relations with Africans. It was his willingness to learn, to criticize, to observe, and to profoundly believe in the Christian tenet of brotherhood that empowered him to produce a novel that cried out for justice and elicited compassion for an oppressed people. South Africa and apartheid might not have been put on the world map had Paton not have written *Cry, the Beloved Country* at a time when the South African political system was increasingly coming under question. Regardless of the shortcomings in the representation of African characters, *Cry, the Beloved Country* put a face on the oppressive segregationist regime. If Paton failed to see the African without the evolutionary paradigms that justified segregation, nonetheless the empathy of the narrator and the novel's higher moral calling for justice humanized the simple native Reverend Kumalo. Paton's denunciation of the sordid and oppressive existence of Africans was hurled into the world and demanded that European South Africans and the rest of the world look into the mirror and see the reflected South African reality in a new light.

The action of Alan Paton's *Cry, the Beloved Country* takes place in the 1940s, but to provide the reader a better understanding of the historical consciousness that informs this novel, this casebook includes a chapter on the book's historical context that far exceeds the scope of the novel. One cannot fully understand the fears felt by the European characters and their transgressive, or subversive, actions and words if one does not have knowledge of the events that inform the historical moment of the novel. Paton's *Cry, the Beloved Country* also invites the reader to ponder the future consequences of the oppressive historical present in which the characters evolve. The narrator of the novel can only wonder what the future will bring, but his future is our present, so the historical context also covers the historical events that brought to an end the reign of fear.

This sourcebook consists of nine sections. The first chapter focuses on a literary analysis of the novel and contains a short analysis of the adaptations and films that have been based on the novel. The second chapter presents an overview of South African history. This is followed by seven other chapters that provide primary resources related to South Africa's population and cultures; the origin of apartheid; the work conditions endured by miners and the history of miners' revolts; socioeconomic conditions in urban areas in South Africa; socioeconomic conditions in rural areas in South Africa; the condition of South African women; and postapartheid South Africa. I have also used essays, interviews of South Africans, ANC historical documents, excerpts from diaries and autobiographies, and excerpts from novels to illuminate Alan Paton's *Cry, the Beloved Country.*

Although all South Africans are Africans, the words "black" and "African" are specifically utilized to refer to the indigenous people. The terms "white" and "European" are used to refer to Westerners in general; "Coloreds" refers to people of mixed races, and "Asians" to Indonesians, Malays, and Indonesians.

South Africa was a symbol of black oppression in the 1970s in Africa, and the Democratic Republic of Congo in particular. Ironically, South Africa has also become home for many Congolese refugees and other immigrants who have fled dictatorships, conflicts, and wars. It is thanks to singers such as Miriam Makeba; politicians such as Steve Biko, Nelson Mandela, Walter Sisulu, and Winnie Mandela; clergyman such as Bishop Desmond Tutu; and writers such as Peter Abrahams, Dennis Brutus, Es'kia Mphahlele, and Alan Paton that South Africa gained visibility and won the struggle against the apartheid regime. Alan Paton is rightly considered a major literary figure because, as Harriet Beecher Stowe, through *Uncle Tom's Cabin,* advanced the American abolitionist movement, so Paton, through *Cry, the Beloved Country,* contributed much to the dismantling of apartheid by making the world aware of the plight of Africans in South Africa.

I have incurred many debts in the process of writing this book. I would like to thank Claudia Johnson, who had faith in an African academic in the early days of southern desegregation, for carefully reading this manuscript, mentoring, and nurturing me. My sincere thanks also go to my spouse, Nyunda ya Rubango, and my three children, Aminatu, Kani, and Mudimbe, who exhorted me to write and to forgo the news and who willingly accepted their abandonment. I also thank the Creighton College of Arts and Sciences for funding my travel to do research in an Africana collection. Thanks, also, to my South African friend for his assistance with the interviews and comments and my colleague Ashton Welch, who has continuously listened, advised, read, and commented on the historical section.

Chronology of South African History

c. 1000 B.C.–200 A.D.	The Khoisan occupy the land.
300–1000 A.D.	Bantu-speaking people, ancestors of the majority modern Bantu population, begin to occupy the area.
1478	The Portuguese Bartholemeu Dias arrives at Mossel Bay.
1652	The Dutch East India Company establishes a refreshment station at the Cape of Good Hope.
1652–1795	The Dutch (later called Boers or Afrikaners) conquer the Khoisan; slaves are imported from Indonesia, India, Ceylon, Madagascar (Malagasy), and Mozambique.
1658	The first slaves are imported to the Cape.
1685	The first school for slaves is established.
1795	The British take over the Cape Colony from the Netherlands.
1799	The South African Missionary Society is created.
1803	The Dutch Batavian Republic regains the Cape Colony by treaty.
1806	The British retake the Cape Colony from the Netherlands.
1808	Britain abolishes the international slave trade in its empire.
1809	The government issues the "Hottentot Proclamation" to control Khoi "vagrancy."
1811–12	British and colonial forces expel Africans from the Fish River territory.

1812	Khoisan children are indentured on settler farms. The "Black Circuit" begins.
1816–28	Shaka's revolution and the Mfecane take place.
1820	A state-sponsored immigration scheme is put into operation. John Philip's arrives in South Africa to lead the London Missionary Society.
1828	The Pass Laws are repealed, and Ordinance 50 is promulgated.
1834	The Cape Colony Legislative Council is created.
1834–38	Cape Colonial slaves are emancipated across South Africa.
1834–35	British and colonial powers defeat the Xhosa.
1836–40	Voortrekkers undertake the Great Trek.
1838	Afrikaner defeat the Zulu at Blood River.
1842	Natal is annexed.
1852–54	The British recognize the Transvaal and the Orange Free State as Afrikaner republics.
1854	The Bloemfontein Convention is held.
1856–57	The Nongqawuse tragedy (Xhosa cattle-killing) takes place.
1858	War begins between Lesotho and the Orange Free State.
1860–1911	Indian indentured laborers are introduced in Natal.
1865–67	The Orange Free State defeats Lesotho.
1867	Diamonds are discovered in Bloemfontein.
1866	The British annex British Kaffraria.
1867	Diamond mines in Griqualand West are exploited.
1868	The British annex Lesotho, formerly known as "Basutholand."
1877	The British annex the Transvaal.
1878	The British defeat Thlaping (Tswana).
1879	The British conquer the Zulu after losing a regiment at Isandhlwana.
1880–81	The Boer agitation begins, and the Transvaal regains its independence following the Pretoria Convention.
1886	Gold is discovered in Witwatersrand.
1895–96	Leander Starr Jameson leads an unsuccessful raid into the Transvaal.

1898	Transvaal Europeans conquer the Venda, resulting in a total European conquest of Southern Africans.
1899–1902	Anglo-Boer wars, or the South African wars, take place.
1903	Alan Stuart Paton is born, at Pietermaritzburg, on January 11.
1904–07	Chinese workers are imported.
1906–07	The former republics are given parliamentary government. Whites alone are enfranchised.
1907	The Orange River Colony acquires self-government.
1910	The Act of Union is passed. The Union of South Africa is formed by the unification of the Cape Colony, Natal, the Transvaal, and the Orange Free State.
1911	The Mines and Works Act is passed.
1912	The South African Native National Congress (NNC), which becomes the African National Congress (ANC) in 1923, is founded.
1913	The Land Act limits African landownership to the reserves, 13 percent of South Africa.
1914	The Nationalist Party is founded.
1914–18	South Africa participates in World War I.
1917–20	Black labor militancy begins at Witwaterstand.
1917	The Anglo-American Corporation of South Africa is founded.
1918	Broederbond, an exclusive Afrikaner cultural and economic society, is formed, and municipal workers strike.
1921	The Communist South African Party is formed, and the massacre of the "Israelites" takes place.
1922	White miners' strike, known as the Rand Revolt, takes place in the Witwatersrand gold mining area. Native Urban Areas Act is passed.
1923	The Industrial Conciliation Act gives workers, except for Africans, collective bargaining power. The Natives (Urban Areas) Act is passed.
1924–36	Legislation establishes nationwide segregation.
1928–30	The Industrial and Commercial Workers' Union of Africa (ICU) collapses.
1930	White women are enfranchised.

1932	The Native Service Contract Act restricts black labor tenants on farms. The Slums Act allows municipalities to move inhabitants of lower-grade housing.
1933	The United Party is founded.
1935	The South African National Congress renamed the African National Congress.
1936	The Native Trust and Land Act and the Representation of Natives Act are passed. The All-African Convention (AAC) is formed, and Africans placed on separate voters' rolls.
1939–45	General Smuts becomes president of the coalition government, and South Africa participates in World War II (on the Allied side).
1942	Black industrial workers strike.
1943	The Non-European Unity Movement (NEUM) is formed.
1944	The ANC Youth League is formed.
1944–50	Squatter campaigns on Witwatersrand increase.
1946	African gold-mine workers strike. Alan Paton travels to Europe, the United States, and Canada. He begins writing *Cry, the Beloved Country.*
1948	Alan Paton's *Cry, the Beloved Country* is published.
1948	The Afrikaner Nationalist Party wins the parliamentary election and begins the implementation of apartheid policies. Dr. Malan becomes the president.
1949	The Prohibition of Mixed Marriages Act passes. The ANC adopts the more militant program of action of the Youth League.
1950	The Immorality Act and the Suppression of Communism Act are passed. Racial classification of the population and racially zoned residential areas are established. The Communist Party is banned. Maxwell Anderson and Kurt Weill's *Lost in the Stars* is published.
1951	Zoltan Korda films *Cry, the Beloved Country.*
1952	The ANC and its allies mount a passive-resistance campaign against the Pass Laws, the Group Areas Act, the Voter Representation Act, the Suppression of Communism Act, and the Bantu Authority Act.

1953	Nationalists increase their majority in general elections. The government controls education through the Bantu Education Act. The Criminal Law (amendment) Act and the Native Labor (settlement of disputes) Act are passed. Alan Paton forms the South African Liberal Party.
1955	The South African Congress of Trade Unions (SACTU) is held. The ANC adopts the Freedom Charter.
1956	Colored parliamentary voters are placed on different voting rolls, and 156 members of the Congress Alliance are charged with treason. The Riotous Assemblies Act is passed.
1956–58	Women campaign against the extension of the pass laws to include women.
1958	The Nationalist Party increases its majority once again.
1957	The Alexandra bus boycotts take place.
1958–66	Dr. Hendrik Frensch Verwoerd becomes prime minister.
1959	The Pan-Africanist Congress (PAC) is founded.
1960	White representation of Africans and Coloreds in Parliament ends. The Sharpeville massacre takes place, and the first republican constitution is written.
1961	South Africa leaves the Commonwealth and becomes the Republic of South Africa. The ANC forms the underground militant wing *Umkhonto we Sizwe* ("Spear of the Nation"). Albert Luthuli becomes president of the ANC. The territorial authority of the Transkei asks for self-government.
1962	The United Nations General Assembly imposes economic and diplomatic sanctions against South Africa. Britain and the United States continue to invest in South Africa, which they believe can be persuaded to decrease the oppression of blacks through constructive engagement.
1964	Nelson Mandela, Walter Sisulu, and other ANC members and PAC leaders are sentenced to life imprisonment during the Rivonia trials. Winnie Mandela is detained.

1966–68	Lesotho, Botswana, and Swaziland attain independence.
1966	Prime Minister Verwoerd is assassinated.
1969	The Black Consciousness student movement leads to the creation of the South African Students Organization (SASO), led by Steve Biko.
1973	The black labor movement re-emerges.
1974	The Inkatha National Cultural Liberation Movement is created by Mangosuthu Buthelezi.
1976–77	Soweto and other township endure massacres.
1976–81	The Transkei, Bophuthatswana, Venda, and Ciskei homelands become independent.
1977	The U.N. Security Council imposes a mandatory embargo on arms supply to South Africa. Steve Biko, the Black Consciousness leader, is killed, and Black Consciousness organizations are banned.
1978–89	Pieter Willem Botha's tenure as prime minister begins.
1979	The Federation of South African Trade Unions (FOSATU) and the Azanian People's Organization (AZAPO) are formed.
1980	Zimbabwe becomes independent.
1983	The United Democratic Front (UDF) and the National Forum (NF) are formed.
1984	A new constitution gives Asians and Coloreds (Africans are excluded) limited participation in the central government.
1984–86	Black South African townships' resistance to the South African regime elicits a violent government response. Desmond Tutu is awarded the Nobel Peace Prize.
1986	The Pass Laws are repealed; a nationwide state of emergency is declared. The U.S. Senate passes the comprehensive Anti-Apartheid Act.
1987	African mineworkers engage in a three-week strike.
1987–90	Squatter communities spread around the main cities.
1988	The UDF is banned, and the Congress of South African Trade Unions (COSATU) creates an alliance with the local UDF and creates the Mass Democratic Movement (MDM). Alan Paton dies.

1989	F. W. de Klerk succeeds Pieter Botha as leader of the National Party and subsequently becomes president of South Africa.
1990	De Klerk lifts the bans on the ANC, the PAC, and the SACP and releases Mandela and other prisoners. The ANC also suspends armed struggle. The Inkatha Freedom Party is formed, on July 14, with Mangosuthu Buthelezi as its president.
1990–91	The 1913 and 1936 Land Acts, the Group Areas Act, the Population Registration Act, and the Separate Amenities Act are repealed. Bans on political organizations are lifted, and the state of emergency is revoked.
1992	White voters support the negotiation process in a referendum, but the conflict between Inkatha and the ANC intensifies.
1993	De Klerk, Mandela, and the leaders of 18 other parties endorse an interim constitution. F. W. de Klerk and Mandela receive the Nobel Peace Prize.
1994	The governments of Bophuthatswana and Ciskei collapse. May 27–30. ANC is victorious in the country's first nonracial election. May 10. Nelson Mandela is sworn in as president, and a Government of National Unity is created. Foreign governments lift sanctions in response, and South Africa becomes a member of the Commonwealth once again.
1995	The Constitutional Court is inaugurated; disturbances occur in the universities; Inkatha withdraws from the Constituent Assembly, the constitution of the Commission for the Restitution of Land Rights, and the Truth and Reconciliation Commission, headed by Archbishop Desmond Tutu. Darrell James Roodt films *Cry, the Beloved Country.*
1996	The permanent constitution is enacted. The National Party withdraws from the Government of National Unity.
1998	The report of the Truth and Reconciliation Commission (TRC) is published.

1997	De Klerk retires from politics.
1999	General elections are held, and the ANC triumphs, with 66 percent of the vote. The Democratic Party becomes the official party of the opposition. Mandela is succeeded by Thabo Mbeki.
2000	A large-scale industrial strike takes place, and the Zimbabwe crisis has repercussions in South Africa. The National and Democratic parties merge.
2002	The Federal Alliance Party and the Democratic Party merge, forming the Democratic Alliance.
2004	The Democratic Alliance forms an alliance with Inkatha against ANC during the 2004 elections. ANC is victorious in parliamentary elections, and Mbeki is re-elected.
2005	The new National Party disbands and merges with the ANC.

List of Abbreviations and Acronyms

AAC	All-African Convention
ADP	African Democratic Party
ANC	African National Congress
ANCYL	African National Congress Youth League
APO	African People's Organization
AZAPO	Azanian People's Organization
COSATU	Congress of South African Trade Unions
DP	Democratic Party
FOSATU	Federation of South African Trade Unions
GEAR	Growth Employment and Redistribution
ICU	Industrial and Commercial Workers' Union
IFP	Inkatha Freedom Party
LPSA	Liberal Party of South Africa
MDM	Mass Democratic Movement
MK	Mkhonto we Sizwe
NCWA	Native and Coloured Women's Organization
NEUM	Non-European Unity Movement
NF	National Forum
NGK	Nederdutse Gereformeerde Kerek
NP	Nationalist Party
NUM	National Union of Mineworkers
ORCNC	Orange River Colony Native Congress
PAC	Pan-African Congress
SACP	South African Communist Party
SACPO	South African Coloured People's Organization

SACTU	South African Congress of Trade Unions
SANNC	South African Native National Congress
TINA	There is no alternative
TRC	Truth and Reconciliation Commission
UDF	United Democratic Front
UNESCO	United Nations Educational, Scientific, and Cultural Organization

1

Cry, the Beloved Country: A Literary Analysis

The majority of works written in recent years about South Africa are generally labeled "post-apartheid" or are referred to as being about the new South Africa. Alan Paton, the author of *Cry, the Beloved Country* (1948), is among the first South African writers to have exposed the racial tensions, the ethnic conflicts, and the social and economic exploitation of blacks within South Africa to the international community. Although he did not call for the dismantling of segregation and the total integration of non-Western racial groups, he did, however, support a society free from racial prejudice. While the sordid oppression of Africans is not directly developed in the novel, their fate and social conditions are presented with much empathy. Reading *Cry, the Beloved Country,* writes Alan Paton's biographer Peter F. Alexander, is "like listening to a story of deep sorrow and love told by the Recording Angel" (xv). This politicized novel—published in more than 20 languages and read in Asia, Europe, North America, Latin America, and Africa—won for Paton the great admiration of the international community and threatened the position of South African conservatives.

Cry, the Beloved Country takes place just after World War II, and the book itself was published in 1948, the year apartheid, a political concept promoting official or state-sanctioned segregation and discrimination, was officially endorsed. It was written during the period of Afrikaner nationalism, a movement that viewed Afrikaners as a distinct ethnic and cultural group and separate from other English-speaking Europeans. Afrikaner nationalists believed that people were entitled, on the basis of their color or race, to different social statuses and also, on the basis of their Calvinist religion, that they were God's chosen people who were ordained to rule the country. The novel is also historically contextualized during the Alexandra township bus boycotts and the 1944 campaign against pass laws. According to Jack Simons and Ray Simons, between 40,000 and 60,000 Africans and Coloreds lived in Alexandra Township, about nine miles from the center of Johannesburg, and thousands of the inhabitants walked about 18 miles a day to work in August 1943 rather than pay the increased bus fares (547). The novel also takes place during the time when black workers who were dissatisfied with their two-shillings-a-shift wage went on strike and when African families, against the will of the government, took possession of the vacant land next to the township of Orlando and built shelters with whatever materials they could get. When the government failed to stop African settlement in towns, a squatter leader claimed, "The Government is beaten, because even the government of England could not stop the people from squatting. . . . The Government sends its policemen to chase us away and we move off and occupy another spot" (Stadler 93).

Alan Paton began writing *Cry, the Beloved Country* while traveling in Norway and when he was homesick because Swedish and Norwegian, the languages of the countries he was visiting, were Germanic languages similar to Afrikaans. Writing *Cry, the Beloved Country* was, hence, therapeutic for the author. It is a novel about a humble, rural pastor, Reverend Stephen Kumalo, who goes to Johannesburg to assist his sister and to find his brother and his son. While there, he encounters his white neighbor, James Jarvis, whose son was killed by Reverend Kumalo's son, Absalom. Once both the pastor, Kumalo, and his neighbor, James Jarvis, return home, they reconcile, and Jarvis works for the betterment of the living conditions of the Ndotsheni African community. This novel, according to Alexander, was inspired by Paton's readings of Hamsun's (pseudonym of Knut Petersen) *Growth of the Soil* (originally titled *Markens Grøde*), Richard Wright's *Black Boy,* and John Steinbeck's *The Grapes of Wrath.* In addition to these contemporary literary works, he also read John Bunyan's *The Pilgrim's Progress.*

THE SETTING OF *CRY, THE BELOVED COUNTRY*

The novel unfolds with a lyrical juxtaposition of two landscapes: lush hills and a sterile valley. The hills are covered with grass and bracken. Birds, especially the titihoyo, sing in this veld. The grass is well tended and is infrequently burnt; it is a land for which man has much respect, for it is the source of life. The valley below, on the other hand, is red and bare. The grass there, unlike that on the hills, does not "hold rain and mist, and the streams are dry in the kloofs" (3). The land in the valley is depleted of nutrients, having been used to feed too many cattle and having had too many fires on it. This untended land is sharp and coarse, and no titihoyas cry there. It is a dying land that, despite the efforts of nature to water it, yields no food. The population, primarily old men and women, cannot, like the land on which they live, promise hope and life, so the young leave for Johannesburg.

The juxtaposition of the lush hill and the sterile valley—suggesting the know-how and the hegemony of the Western world and the ignorance and inferiority of the African community—is also evident in the description of the city and the rural settings. The African rural world is replete with "illness" and suffers from food scarcity. The European urban world is associated with technology—trains, stations, cars, and great buildings—while the African is full of squalor, poverty, and crime.

These contrasting spaces, at the beginning of the novel, metaphorically represent a racially hierarchized society. The setting reinforces the image of Africans as children who are incapable of providing for their minimum needs and who lack the intelligence to understand the working of nature. The green color of the hills also reinforces the idea of growth, wealth, and abundance whereas the red color of the valley conveys a sense of death and violence. While the hills, "full of the red blood of the earth," are full of life, the languishing valleys of Ndotsheni barely have sufficient soil for women to cultivate and water to feed the soil.

While the setting establishes the economic and social conditions of the characters and the racial segregation of the rural South African community, the racial divide is not as easy to maintain within urban areas. Hence, when Reverend Stephen Kumalo sees the skyscraper in Johannesburg, he sees both "red and green lights on them. . . . Water comes out of a bottle, till the glass is full. Then the lights go out. And when they come back on again, lo the bottle is full and upright, and the glass is empty. . . . Black and white, it says, black and white, though it is red and green" (17). Reverend Kumalo has difficulties deciphering the color images, but it is evident that the urban space brings blacks and whites together in the same space. The economic status of blacks, determined by race, in the urban area is worse than in the village, where communal ways of life guarantee one a meal and where there is a benevolent environment. The rural area may be poor, but the Africans have at least a land to call home; in the urban areas, where they have no land, they become squatters, living in a "village of sack, plank, and iron" (56) where nothing truly grows.

Once the novel establishes the racialized economic setting in both Ndotsheni (inspired, according to Alexander, by the actual location Nokweja) and Johannesburg, the action of the novel takes place in various other locations—Ixopo, Johannesburg, Sophiatown, Claremont, Doornfontein, Alexandra, Orlando, Shanty Town, Parkwold, and Ezenzeleni—where the main hero, Reverend Kumalo, journeys to find his sister, son, and brother and runs an errand for a Dotsheni village fellow. It ultimately ends in Ndotsheni, with Reverend Kumalo sitting on top of a mountain, an indication of his empowerment and his growth in wisdom. His elevation to the mountaintop puts him on the same level as James Jarvis; both men, by grappling with the fates of their sons, come to a deeper understanding of the human experience.

THE STRUCTURE OF THE NOVEL

Cry, the Beloved Country is divided into three parts. Book one delineates Reverend Stephen Kumalo's journey to Johannesburg to assist his sister and to find his son and brother, who left the village but never returned. The second part of the novel depicts James Jarvis's journey to Johannesburg to attend his son's funeral and his emotional and intellectual experience as he deals with his son's murder by Reverend Kumalo's son, Absalom. This second section focuses on the murder trial, Arthur Jarvis's ideals, and the encounter between James Jarvis and Reverend Kumalo in Parkwold. The third and last part of the book covers Reverend Kumalo's return and both James Jarvis's and Kumalo's conversions and reconciliation.

Cry, the Beloved Country is, moreover, built around two epic journey structures. It begins with a call to journey when Reverend Kumalo receives a letter from Reverend Theophilus Msimangu inviting him to go to Johannesburg to assist his ailing sister. The story thus begins with a personal conflict to be resolved by Reverend Kumalo, yet the collective racial conflict is depicted at the very beginning of the narrative through the description of the setting. Reverend Kumalo's journey is, hence, a quest to find a resolution to both the collective and the personal. In the city, he undergoes numerous tests while attempting to find his sister and his son. The epic hero generally battles monsters, but Reverend Kumalo confronts the hurdles of urban life, which displace and destabilize individuals, in his quest to find his sister and his son. After visiting numerous locations—Sophiatown, Claremont, Doornfontein, Alexandra—he finally finds his sister and his son, only to discover that they are, respectively, a prostitute and a murderer. He overcomes physical obstacles but must, in addition, overcome psychological hurdles, pain, disappointment, and humiliation. Finally, he is able, at the end the novel, to find reconciliation, peace, and freedom from poverty through his individual action, his sense of communal responsibility, and his newly acquired knowledge of pain and learned compassion for James Jarvis.

The subepic journey structure within the novel delineates James Jarvis's travel, mirroring that of his neighbor Reverend Kumalo, to Johannesburg, where his son, Arthur Jarvis, has been murdered by Absalom Kumalo. James Jarvis must overcome his emotions, his anger and hatred over the murder of his son, and learn to have sympathy and compassion for Reverend Kumalo and his community. Once he learns the nature of compassion by reading his son's essays, influenced by Abraham Lincoln's "The Famous Speech at Gettysburg and the Second Inaugural Address," Jarvis is able, upon his return home, to demonstrate compassion for the struggling Africans living at the bottom of his hill and to initiate social actions, such as building a new church for Reverend Kumalo's parishioners, providing milk for children, and bringing an agricultural demonstrator to Ndotsheni to teach the villagers how to farm. Through these social actions, his conversion, and his newly developed understanding with Reverend Kumalo, the ecological and social plagues that are described at the beginning of the novel are overcome and the fear that haunts the European community is replaced by love.

The structure of the book initially posed a problem for both Paton and his publisher. Alexander claims that Paton criticized the loose structure of *Cry, the Beloved Country* and vowed to write "a perfectly constructed" novel (258). The chief editor of the book, Maxwell Perkins, on the other hand, disliked the fact that the novel dragged on after the climax in book two (Alexander 215). Despite its problematic ending, *Cry, the Beloved Country* was published without modifications, and rightly so, because the third part of the book—the return home of the main protagonist and antagonist of the novel—resolves the collective plague introduced at the beginning of the novel through the description of the setting.

CHARACTERIZATION

Alan Paton's *Cry, the Beloved Country* is a thesis novel, more interested in ideas than in the development of characters. The characters in this novel are representative types rather than individuals. They represent racial, cultural, and class categories. The white characters are depicted as able, technologically competent, and knowledgeable, whereas the blacks are depicted as humble children, unaware of the workings of nature, corrupted by urban life, and incapable of fending for themselves. The European characters are also ethnically and culturally divided into groups: Afrikaners and English. Evolving in a racialized society, the characters of *Cry, the Beloved Country* embody the racial conflicts and tensions that riddled South Africa in the 1940s. They embody the various ideological positions of their time, as well as their societal perceptions of gender differences.

The main protagonist, Reverend Stephen Kumalo, is depicted at the beginning of the novel as a poor, disillusioned man who is upset by the silence of his son, Absalom, his sister, Gertrude, and his brother, John Kumalo, who went to the city; he complains that they all go to Johannesburg and never write or return. Angered and hurt by their lack of concern for those who have remained in the village, he tells his spouse to ask the white man if they have sent letters. "Perhaps," he writes, "they have fallen under the counter, or been hidden amongst the food. Look there in the trees, perhaps they have been blown there by the wind" (9).

Although Kumalo is described as a humble and religious man at the beginning of his journey, his vanity is quickly apparent when he ensures that other passengers hear how busy he will be in Johannesburg and looks around the train for people of a certain class with whom he can interact. Yet, behind this vanity, there is man who is afraid of his new urban environment, for his knees are weak and his Bible is the only certain world. Before Reverend Kumalo returns home, his vanity and nonpastoral behavior are, once again, exposed in Johannesburg when he purposely misleads his activist brother into believing that he is being watched and deceived by a friend. He loses his faith in Johannesburg and sees himself as the victim of his sister's promiscuous behavior. His cruelty and arrogance are also evident when he humiliates his son's pregnant mistress by asking her about her sexual life (a transgressive act in African culture) and whether she would desire him as a fourth husband.

Reverend Kumalo is portrayed, throughout *Cry, the Beloved Country,* as a dignified old man who does not know his way around the city but through whom the sordid living conditions of blacks in South Africa are presented. The pain and suffering he feels in losing his son, who has murdered James Jarvis's son, enables him to mature into a man more aware of the suffering within his environment. At the beginning of the novel, before his trip to Johannesburg, he never questions his social conditions. But, after his stay in Johannesburg, he returns to Ndotsheni with a better understanding of his environment and his condition, "greater humility," and thoughts of rebuilding. He develops in Johannesburg a sense of communal responsibility for the younger generation and a new understanding of the white community through James Jarvis.

James Jarvis, on the other hand, embodies the British community, which is insensitive to the fate of the black community and hostile to Afrikaners. The racial tensions within South Africa are also represented through his character.

Through his interactions with the family of his son's in-laws, the Harrisons, the nationalist sentiments of South African whites are revealed. Hence, John Harrison, emphasizing the role mines play in the South African economy, vents his anger against the Afrikaners who consider the British mining people foreigners "to the country, and . . . sucking the blood out of it, ready to clear out when the goose stops laying the eggs" (151). Yet, his son's manuscripts and Abraham Lincoln's "The Famous Speech at Gettysburg" address give Jarvis a different understanding of South African racial relationships. Although he had taught his son integrity, honesty, honor, religion, and charity, he, according to his son, had taught him nothing about South Africa. James Jarvis's son's and, indirectly, Abraham Lincoln's writings teach Jarvis compassion, love, and forgiveness; when he returns to Ndotsheni, he becomes a social reformer who believes in helping less privileged others. However, despite his new perspective on racial relations, Jarvis fails to espouse a philosophy of universal brotherhood and racial equality; he remains superior to the Africans who rely on him for their welfare, for social reform is achieved solely through his individual actions.

While Jarvis and Kumalo are the two major protagonists in the novel, a third important character, Msimangu, a caring minister in *Cry, the Beloved Country* is Reverend Kumalo's guide in Johannesburg. Although he is aware of the dire conditions in which his people live in Alexandra, Shanty Town, and Johannesburg, he feels impotent and incapable of bringing a resolution to their social crises. Overwhelmed by the social problems of Africans in Johannesburg, he tells Reverend Kumalo, when the Reverend is moved to compassion by his son's mistress, "Have you not troubles enough of your own? I tell you there are thousands such in Johannesburg. And were your back as broad as heaven, and your purse full of gold, and did your compassion reach from here to hell itself, there is nothing you can do" (68). While Msimangu is a great minister, he is no revolutionary because, according to the narrator, he is good for the government. His words move people to seek the spiritual and not the material world by preaching "of a world not made by hands, while in the streets about him men suffer and struggle to die. . . . And how fools listen to him, silent, enrapt, sighing when he is done, feeding their empty bellies on his empty words" (92). Theophilus Msimangu is an educated African who philosophizes about life but dwells solely in the world of ideas. He is truly a lover of the spiritual world, as his name Theophilus, "lover of God" in Greek, so well conveys. He is no social reformer, for his words, which could galvanize the community, do not translate into social action.

Another important character who embodies radical Afrikaner nationalism is Mr. Harrison. His speech is full of radical chauvinist clichés about natives and Afrikaners. He also expounds clichéd ideas concerning the decent lodgings of natives and stereotypical ideas about their dependency. He contends that Afrikaners have "some fool notion that the mining people are foreign to the country, and are sucking the blood out of it, ready to clear out when the goose stops laying the eggs" (151) and expostulates, "Republic! Where would we be if we ever got a republic?" (151). His radical social and political ideologies are contrasted with those of his son John, a great admirer of Arthur Jarvis, who understands that it is time to adapt to the changing political climate, even though his father and James Jarvis are incapable of understanding the ongoing changes.

Finally, women do not play a major role in *Cry, the Beloved Country.* Apart from Mrs. Lithebe, the majority of the women have minor roles; they are classified as good married or widowed women, like Mrs. Kumalo and Lithebe, or as loose single women, such as Gertrude and Absalom's wife. Whether they are good or bad, all the women in the novel are oppressed and subservient to men. Thus, when Reverend Kumalo leaves his wife after recognizing that he has hurt her during a discussion, she is described as sitting "at his table, and put[ting] her head on it, and [being] silent, with the patient suffering of the black women, with the suffering of oxen, with the suffering of any that are mute" (10).

Cry, the Beloved Country calls for the dismantling of racial oppression; it does not, however, call for racial equality. Even though it can be inferred from the idealized Arthur Trevelyn Jarvis's letters, funeral homily, social actions, books, and manuscripts that truth and the freedom of all individuals are fundamental, ethical rights, the novel itself does not advocate social equality. It only intimates hope for a new South Africa that will free Ndotsheni and the South African community at large from fear. Neither does the characterization of the novel suggest racial equality, since James Jarvis's conversion and empathy for his needy African neighbors do not result in egalitarian relationships. The boundaries erected by the segregation system of South Africa continue to dictate racial relationships. The characters are frequently said to behave in accordance with the diktat of their social categories, and when they behave in opposition to the expectations of their society, for example, when Jarvis hesitates to assist Reverend Kumalo, the narrator stresses that "it is not lightly done" (178).

The absence of racial equality is also shown through the characterization of African characters, whites' perception of blacks, and the racialization of crime. The cultural differences between white and black characters are established through the romantic association of rural blacks with nature and innocence and urban blacks with violence. Kumalo associates Ndotsheni with innocence and the slowness of living "in the slow tribal rhythm" (111). James Jarvis also refers to them as "these" people. They are considered idle and worthless. Moreover, theft and crime are associated with blacks, who are the perpetuators of most of the crimes reported in newspapers. Black miners are also described as simple, illiterate people easily manipulated and incapable of thinking for themselves. This stereotypical representation of blacks is reinforced in the very resolution of the novel. Whereas Reverend Kumalo has understood the need to effect change within his community during his stay in Johannesburg, his action is limited solely to his rhetoric. He speaks of his vision to the chief and his counselors and to the school headmaster, but when he realizes they are powerless, he submits the fate of his people to God. His blessings are for the most part passively received. The very resolution to the village plague comes not from his meditation and action but from Mr. Jarvis's action. Even the young, agricultural demonstrator, moved by a new desire for independence and nationalist will to work for South Africa, has inherited his vision from "a white man who taught [him] . . . that we do not work for men, that we work for the land and the people. We do not even work for money" (268).

Alan Paton had difficulties, like other South African writers such as Peter Abrahams, rendering the speech of non-English-speaking African characters in *Cry, the Beloved Country.* The biblical speech of his African characters is stilted and archaic, like that of characters in Peter Abrahams's *Wild Conquest.* Some critics claim that this biblical language, which attempts to render the polite speech of traditional African communities, affects Zulu speech patterns and conveys the obsoleteness of African culture, which is decaying and dying.

In addition to this language technique, Alan Paton uses character contrast and parallelism. Reverend Stephen Kumalo and James Jarvis are contrasted White and black characters who undergo different cultural and racial experiences, yet they are parallel characters because, as fathers, they both deal with the pain of losing their sons. Pastor Msimangu and John Kumalo are also contrasted in their aspirations: Msimangu is interested in the spiritual and Kumalo in the political worlds. Yet, they are similar in that they both utter empty words: Msimangu's words are empty, and Kumalo's are incapable of bringing about a revolution because of his attachment to material possessions.

CRY, THE BELOVED COUNTRY AS SOCIAL AND POLITICAL NOVEL

Cry, the Beloved Country is a social and political novel that combines, as Peter Alexander claims, both fictional and factual information in its analysis of the social and political South African systems. Even though Alan Paton declares in the "Author's Note" that the characters are all fictional with the exception of two, Professor Hoernlé and Sir Earnest Oppenheimer, Alexander suggests that other characters in the novel are also modeled on actual historical individuals. Stephen Kumalo is said to be based on an old clergyman at Diepkloof Reformatory; Gertrude, Kumalo's sister is inspired by Jacky, a boy at Diepkloof; and Father Vincent is modeled on Father Trevel Huddleston, of the Rosetten Ville Mission House (31). In addition to real individuals, Paton integrates actual historical events, such as the mine strike, World War II, and the bus strike, into his fictional work. While he claims to have adopted only John Steinbeck's technique of dialogue in *The Grapes of Wrath,* which he read in Stockholm, he has also been influenced by his social narrative of suffering.

Cry, the Beloved Country is a social novel, influenced by Abraham Lincoln's writing, which advocates a Christian, race-free South Africa. It is a Christian narrative of love, compassion, and forgiveness. Direct scriptural allusions, such as "though I walk through the valley of the shadow of death, I shall fear no evil, if Thou art with me" (62), and direct invocations of God and Christian love convey the Christian perspective and the main theme of the novel. This Christian ideology (a way of making sense of the world) is also present in the novel through images of Christ, the sacrifice of sons, and the biblical discourse and the role of religion.

Cry, the Beloved Country denounces the inhumane South African segregation system and calls for a more humane and compassionate order that respects Africans, supports their development and integration, and provides them access to the wealth of the country. This social-justice novel falls short, however, in its call for racial equality. The Christian call for love is the result of fear, just as it is this very same fear that calls for incorruptible law, for "in a land of fear this incorruptibility is like a lamp set upon a stand, giving light to all that are in the house" (158). It is fear, as is often repeated in the novel and in Nadine Gordimer's *July's People,* of revenge and losing one's social privilege that maintains these barriers. Despite the European community's fear of an eventual uprising by black South Africans, they consider this eventuality a frightening fantasy. "Blacks," according to them, "are not organized for it, they would suffer untold hardships, they would die of starvation. Yet, the thought of so fantastic a thing is terrifying, and white people realize how dependent they are on the labour of the black people" (189). Yet, as Arthur Jarvis, the spokesperson for the author, contends, South Africa is a Christian nation and should hence be led by morality. Consequently, Africans should not be economically exploited but should benefit from education, decent wages, and a new cultural order.

The period during which this story evolves in South African history is said to be a time of anxiety, because "strange things are happening in the world, and the world has never let South Africa alone" (189). These strange things—increasing call for autonomy in African colonies and increasing criticism of South African racial politics—are not, however, only external to South Africa but also internal, because this desire for freedom is stirring in South African black hearts, as shown in the fiery speeches of John Kumalo, the activist and the brother of the pastor. His call for better wages and equal access to South Africa's wealth questions the status of blacks in South Africa. But his vision is limited because, despite his lion-like qualities, he fails to seek "equality and the franchise and the removal of the color-bar" (185) for fear of losing his personal material privileges. Likewise, the Europeans fear equality because privilege is possible only if the Africans are disenfranchised. Is equality a possibility when the fear of losing one's possessions, superiority, and whiteness is at stake, even if it means hedging one's life with "safety and precaution" (79)? Unfortunately, when the white community is ready to love, according to Msimangu, it will discover that blacks have turned to hating (40).

Change in *Cry, the Beloved Country* is motivated by Europeans' fear that black resentment and hatred might reverse the situation. Indeed, the narrator implores God to "save [them] from the fear that is afraid of justice" (225). While the Europeans might control blacks now, the fear of an African rebellion that may not be forever arrested perpetually haunts them. This threat is frequently invoked in the novel through imagery; for example, it is likened to a deserted harbor, which has "water that laps against the quays. In the dark and silent forest there is a leaf that falls. Behind the polished panelling the white ant eats away the wood. Nothing is ever quiet, except for fools" (190). The metaphoric imagery of lapping water, falling leaves, and ants eating away at the wood eloquently alludes to this threat. If love alone is incapable of engendering whites' compassion, the white population should embrace love at least for the sake of the unborn child, the inheritor of the consequences of their actions, as revealed in the "Cry" in the title of the book—lest Africans revert to hatred, with the terrible consequence that the Europeans will lose their land and become foreigners in their own adopted country. Even though Europeans are afraid of the consequences of their segregation policies, they don't know how to resolve their long history of racial injustice. "Which do we prefer, a law-abiding, industrious and purposeful native people, or a lawless, idle and purposeless people? The truth is that we do not know, for we fear them both. And so long as we vacillate, so long will we pay dearly for the dubious pleasure of not having to make up our minds. And the answer does not lie, except temporarily, in more police and more protections" (76). Despite this political impasse, the novel suggests, through the conversions of both James Jarvis and Reverend Kumalo, that there remains hope for social change. Yet, the ultimate resolution of this fear and the ongoing sociopolitical crises remains unknown, for the dawn "of [their] emancipation, from the fear of bondage, and the bondage of fear, why, that is a secret" (277).

THEMES

In addition to the social and political background against which the quest of Kumalo takes place, *Cry, the Beloved Country* expounds on themes of love, loss, Christian forgiveness, individual social responsibility, the disintegration of the family and the clan, urban corruption, and father-son relationships. Since some of these themes are developed indirectly in other subsections, only those that need to be discussed in depth are elaborated in this section.

Love of the Other and One's Country

The theme of love is associated primarily with the political and religious ideas foregrounded in the novel. *Cry, the Beloved Country* speaks of love of one's neighbor and love of country. These two elements are inextricably interconnected, since there is no South Africa without racial harmony. Through Arthur Jarvis, the novel demonstrates the necessity of loving and sharing the country's wealth with the African majority. It denounces the oppressive segregation system of South Africa and advocates a new South Africa that upholds all human rights. Love, moreover, is dramatized through Stephen Kumalo's journey to Johannesburg to assist his sister and to search for his son. What motivates him to offer the wife of his son and his unborn grandchild shelter is love. Similarly, it is love for the other that is manifested through Mrs. Jarvis's renovation of the Ndotsheni church, James Jarvis's club donations, and Arthur Jarvis's son's indirect gift of milk to the Ndotsheni community. Love, kindness, and the desire to effect change are what also motivate Msimangu's present of 33 pounds 4 shillings and 5 pence to Reverend Kumalo. The salvation of the entire community depends on its ability to love. "Yet men," according to the narrator, "were afraid, with a fear that was deep, deep in the heart, a fear so deep that they hid their kindness, or brought it out with fierceness and anger, and hid it behind fierce and frowning eyes. They were afraid because they were so few. And such fear could not be cast out, but by love" (276). At the end of the novel, it is love and understanding that prevail, since Reverend Kumalo and James Jarvis establish a mutual affectionate relationship, as evinced in their reciprocal gift giving. Moreover, it is solely in the abnegation of self in an act of love that South Africa itself, according to the novel, can be saved from bloodshed. As shown by the Truth and Reconciliation Commission (TRC), love is the ultimate solution to the South African problem, because love alone, which engenders forgiveness and tolerance, can avert violence.

Loss

Loss is another major theme in *Cry, the Beloved Country.* Reverend Stephen Kumalo loses his son, Absalom, his sister, Gertrude, and his brother, John, to the city, while James Jarvis loses his son, Arthur, and his wife, Mary. The journeys of both men are quests to understand South Africa's racial problems and to achieve racial reconciliation through their losses. Although James Jarvis and Reverend Stephen Kumalo use formal titles when they address each other, they call each other friend at the end of the novel. This friendship is fashioned through their pain of loss; having lost his sister and his son again after finding them, Reverend Kumalo informs one of his friends who asked him to inquire in Johannesburg about the lost daughter of a friend that she too is lost but that, despite all the worldly problems he had encountered, he still believed. "I believe, he said, but I have learned that it is a secret. Pain and suffering, they are a secret. Kindness and love, they are a secret. But I have learned that kindness and love can pay for pain and suffering" (226). Indeed, through the loss of his son, Absalom, Reverend Kumalo gets closer to James Jarvis and develops a profound understanding of forgiveness. Both Reverend Kumalo and James Jarvis are able, through their loss, to transcend their grief and, through their pain and suffering, to reach out to others. Their losses and pain empower them to grow spiritually.

Father-Son Relationships

The theme of father-son relationships emanates from that of loss. Both James Jarvis and Stephen Kumalo are patriarchal figures, although Kumalo holds a lower position in the novel. The geographical positions they hold well convey their social positions: James Jarvis's abode is on top of the hill and looks down on the valley of Ndotsheni, and this is why Harnett P. Connor considers this novel a parable, with Jarvis as God. Even though Reverend Stephen Kumalo also sits at the top of mountain Emoyeni at the end of the novel, he nonetheless acknowledges that he is incapable of conceiving a revolution that would put him on a par with James Jarvis. He is too old, he claims, to absorb the revolutionary words of the young agricultural demonstrator, for "they struck at the grave silent man at High Place, who after such deep hurt, had shown such deep compassion. He was too old for new and disturbing thoughts. A white man's dog, that is what they called him and his kind" (269). Even though James Jarvis holds a higher position in society than Kumalo, they both sacrifice their sons—one murdered and the other executed—for the benefit of the communal well-being that arises from their suffering.

It is through the sacrifices of both Reverend Kumalo and James Jarvis that they bond and gain a better understanding of their children. Jarvis, who had expected his son to follow in his footsteps, had little understanding of the ideals that drove the younger man. Little did he know how spiritual, compassionate, his son was, and how critical of his South African society. It is only when the father reads his son's correspondence and lecture notes that he is able to understand the man his son had become. Likewise, Reverend Kumalo is embittered because his son has not gone to St. Chad to acquire the learning that would have enabled him to succeed in their new world. Instead, he commits a crime that alienates him even further from his father. "He is a stranger, he said, I cannot reach him. I see no shame in him, no pity for those he has hurt. Tears come out of his eyes, but it seems that he weeps only for himself, he who has made two children fatherless" (109). Although the novel highlights Reverend Kumalo's shame, and that of his wife, at having raised a murderer, the questions he raises and his prayers for his son at the end of the novel are testimony to his new-found understanding of his son.

Disintegration and Unification of the Family

The disintegration and restoration of the family and the nation are also major themes of *Cry, the Beloved Country.* Reverend Kumalo's quest to find his son and his sister, Gertrude, is a quest for family unification. He is able to find his son, sister, and brother, but Kumalo is not able to totally unite the family, for Gertrude runs away, he quarrels with his brother, and his son ends up on death row. Even though Reverend Kumalo successfully returns his son's wife and unborn child and his sister's son to the healing pastures of Ndotsheni, this family reunification is incomplete and temporary, for, as the agricultural demonstrator states, "We can restore the valley for those who are here, but when the children grow up, there will again be too many. Some will have to go still" (268). Despite the restoration and fertilization of the dry valley of Ndotsheni, Johannesburg will continue to attract the villagers, since all roads are said to lead to Johannesburg. Johannesburg has solutions to all human woes because jobs and anonymity can be gotten there. Whether you are "white or if you are black they [roads] lead to Johannesburg. If the crops fail, if you are black they lead to Johannesburg. If there are taxes to be paid, there is work in Johannesburg. If the farm is too small to be divided further, some must go to Johannesburg. If there is a child to be born that must be delivered in secret, it can be delivered in Johannesburg" (52).

Reverend Kumalo's failure to reunify the family is a microcosm of the gradual decay of South African traditional society per se. The departure of the many young people of Ndotsheni who leave for Johannesburg affects the overall quality of life of the village because, as Reverend Kumalo admits to himself, "The tribe was broken, and would be mended no more. . . . The tribe was broken, and would be mended no more. The tribe that had nurtured him, and his father and his father's father, was broken. For the men were away, and the young men and the girls were away, and the maize hardly reached to the height of a man" (88). Traditional Africa's contact with Europeans resulted in the weakening of its traditional structure and morality. Arthur Jarvis, the spokesperson for Paton, claims, "The old tribal system was, for all its violence and savagery, for all its superstition and witchcraft, a moral system. Our natives produce criminals and prostitutes and drunkards, not because it is their nature to do so, but because their simple system of order and tradition and convention has been destroyed. It was destroyed by the impact of our civilization" (146).

Not only does traditional African society lose its moral fabric, it also loses the power of its chiefs and their legitimacy. The Ndotsheni chief and counselors have most certainly lost their power, their legitimacy, their control over their environment, and their knowledge. They have become mere ignorant and uneducated pawns of Western power. They have become irrelevant and serve only as props for the European South African government, since Reverend Kumalo, who had awakened to the condition of Africans during his journey to Johannesburg, asserts that South African chiefs have become "a thing the white men had done, knocked these chiefs down, and put them up again, to hold the pieces together. But the white man had taken most of the pieces away. And some chiefs sat with arrogant and blood-shot eyes, rulers of pitiful kingdoms that had no meaning at all" (230). Technologically challenged, they are clueless about the nature of the discussion and the ongoing operation when James Jarvis and some other white men plant stick and flags into the ground at the early stages of the conception of the dam. The chief is incapable of making decisions since he and his counselors have no advice to give, the chief having become, according to John Kumalo, "an old and ignorant man, who is nothing but a white man's dog. He is a trick, a trick to hold together something that the white man desires to hold together" (37).

The healing of traditional society, according to the novel, can be achieved not by the helpless, leaderless Africans but only by Europeans. After he visits the chief and the headmaster of the school, both being repositories of knowledge and power, it becomes apparent to Reverend Kumalo that the Ndotsheni educational and administrative powers have no solution to their predicament. He commends Ndotsheni to God, and miraculously, after his prayer, he sees before his eyes a young child, Jarvis's grandchild, representing Europeans, sitting on a horse, like his father several years ago. Thanks to the grandchild, Jarvis provides milk and life to the Ndotsheni children and spearheads other charitable projects in honor of his son, Arthur. Not only can the living conditions of Africans but also their morality can be improved solely by Europeans, because, as the narrator of *Cry, the Beloved Country* frequently reminds the reader, the source of urban crime is the erosion of traditional values, which must be replaced by a new order. Both the narrator and Arthur Jarvis call for the education of natives and their Westernization. Traditional African culture, considered tribal, tyrannical, constricting, and closed, must be replaced by Western culture.

Ironically, the South African Europeans who are called upon to save their country are themselves as ideologically and culturally divided as the Afrikaners and the British. While the disintegration of African culture is important in the story, the alienation and tensions between British and Afrikaners are also major themes. This rift between the two communities is evinced early in part two when James Jarvis states that there are an increasing number of Afrikaners in the area and that some, locally and nationally, have even married English-speaking women. This was not the case in the past, since his father had sworn that he would "disinherit any child of his who married an Afrikaner, but times had changed. The war had put things back a bit, for some of the Afrikaners had joined the army, and some were for the war but didn't join the army, and some were just for neutrality" (132). This division is once again expressed through the British distaste of bilingualism, through Afrikaners' perception of the British as foreigners, and in the racial and ethnic issues that define South African politics and economics. The theme of reconciliation and restoration of morality and the family in *Cry, the Beloved Country* thus metaphorically extends to the entire nation.

Black-on-Black Crime

Black-on-black crime and the racialization of crime are two of the major themes of *Cry, the Beloved Country.* The novel dedicates much space to the discussion of this problem. The bored and unoccupied youth of the cities are constant perpetuators of crimes, and the African slums themselves are to be feared. Numerous newspaper headlines remind the reader of the rampant nature of black crime in Johannesburg. When these young people or blacks of any age are not assaulting Europeans or stealing, they are murdering someone.

Arthur Jarvis, who is said to have waded in stranger waters than his parents, devotes his life to understanding native crime and fighting for the improvement of native living and labor conditions. Native crime also preoccupies John Harrison and the entire Johannesburg community. The latter claims, "There are too many of these murders and robberies and brutal attacks. I tell you we don't go to bed without barricading our houses" (140). This crime trend, according to Jarvis, is the result of the disintegration of African traditional values. But this theory is not much heeded because even before the trial of Arthur Jarvis ends, another murder of a European by a native hits the headlines and inflames the white community. Whites also commit crimes—a white man rapes a white woman—but their crimes are not foregrounded to the same degree as those of natives. The defense makes a strong case for Absalom Kumalo, arguing that his criminal behavior is the product of the segregationist policies of his country, which do not allow him to fulfill himself, yet the novel, in its association of crime with the disintegration of traditional African values, does not delve sufficiently into the social problems that are at the origin of this social problem, thus making crime race-specific.

Conversion

The chief editor of, *Cry, the Beloved Country,* Maxwell Perkins, had a problem with the third part of the novel because of its anticlimactic nature, but he decided to publish it as it was. Jan Hendrik Hofmeyer, to whom Paton had sent a copy, was equally critical of the structure, which, according to him, "suffered from the anti-climax of having Kumalo part from his son and go back to Ndotsheni several chapters before the boy is hanged in Johannesburg" (Alexander 215). Indeed, the climax does take place in the second book, but the third section of the book is the resolution to the epic-like quest of Reverend Kumalo. It delineates the resolution to the plague, poverty, desolation, and loss enunciated at the beginning of the journey and is also the response to the thesis of the book about white South Africans' fear. The third book speaks of forgiveness, transcendence of pain, and conversion and clearly shows the possibility that good can triumph over evil. Mr. Jarvis's willingness to consider the welfare of the Ndotsheni Africans, despite the fact that Reverend Kumalo's son, Absalom, killed his son, Arthur, is a manifestation of his conversion. It is also a manifestation of his will to transcend his pain and to understand that of others. Even after learning that Absalom Kumalo killed his son, he still has the strength and compassion to tell the murderer's father, "I have heard you. . . . I understand what I did not understand. There is no anger in me" (181).

Jarvis is able to forgive only after he has undergone a spiritual journey of growth. Through his exploration of his son's ideas, he is able to gain a better understanding of him and of his South African world, one of which his son had claimed to have "learned nothing at all" (174). Arthur's writings question the nature of South African Christianity and address the incongruity between Christian dogma and European South Africans' actions. "The truth," he writes, "is that our civilization is not Christian; it is a tragic compound of great ideal and fearful practice, of high assurance and desperate anxiety, of loving charity and fearful clutching of possessions" (155). As the father works through his emotional pain of loss, he converses with his "missionary" son through his papers. Upholding ideals, the son claims, is what is essential, and not possessions. "It would be exciting, exhilarating, a matter for thanksgiving" if his children, he writes, could think as he and his wife do. "But it can not be bargained for. It must be given or withheld, and whether the one or the other, it must not alter the course that is right" (175). The will to do right is an individual commitment, he says. He hopes his children will espouse his views, but he need not wait long to see his father do so, for, as he embarks for home, James Jarvis begins, after much intellectual thinking about his son's principles and his closer encounters with the Ndotsheni community, to divest himself of his worldly possessions to bring hope and equity in his world. Ultimately, when Reverend Kumalo seeks to thank him for all his humanitarian acts, James Jarvis does not see his achievements as individual acts; rather, he sees his actions as a calling and the result of his spiritual conversion. "—I have seen a man, said Jarvis with a kind of grim gaiety, who was in darkness till you found him. If that is what you do, I give it willingly" (272). It is love and spiritual growth that empowers Jarvis to transcend his anger and to create a profound relationship with Kumalo and to eventually transform his community.

Likewise, Reverend Kumalo undergoes a conversion through the pain he experiences during his stay in Johannesburg. His trip results in his maturation and his awakening to his social condition. His sadness is changed into happiness, but he also understands that a racially equal South Africa lies in the future because Europeans are afraid of Africans. Kumalo wonders:

> And what was there evil in their desires, in their hunger? That men should walk upright in the land where they were born, and be free to use the fruits of the earth, what was their evil in it? Yet men were afraid, with a fear that was deep, deep in the heart, a fear so deep that they hid their kindness, or brought it out with fierceness and anger, and hid it behind fierce and frowning eyes. They were afraid because they were so few. And such fear could not be cast out, but by love. (276)

Before his journey, Reverend Kumalo did not have an in-depth understanding of the condition of Africans in South Africa; however, his journey through the hells of Sophiatown, Alexandra, Shanty Town, and Orlando empowers him to discover the economic, political, and social struggles of his people.

Upon his return to Ndotsheni, Reverend Kumalo claims that his journey has opened his eyes and affirmed his faith. He, moreover, discovers that prayer alone is not sufficient in his ministry but that he is called to act to change the world. "Somewhere down here upon the earth," he claims, "men must come together, think something, do something" (229). Through his indirect and sometimes insignificant actions, such as raising the issue of the conditions of the population with the chief and the headmaster, he is able to bring about changes. Finally, Reverend Kumalo feels, at the end of his journey, an increased faith in God and an awareness of the good in humanity as he ponders how a human can have his pain changed into joy and how some people are given a strong awareness of God. These reflections and his engagement to effect change within his community are all the result of his conversion; it is his awareness of his social condition, his mortality, and his unconditional belief in God that transcends pain and suffering that enable him to act, albeit through Jarvis's good will.

Christianity and Individual Action

A central theme of *Cry, the Beloved Country,* especially with its Christian values, is the individual responsibility of South African Christians. The entire section dealing with Arthur Jarvis is about the individual responsibility of Christians when they are faced with injustice. Arthur Jarvis, chastises, in his writings, Christians' complicity in the oppression of Africans and the prevailing injustice. Christian civilization, according to Jarvis, is "riddled with dilemma." Men are willing to accept the brotherhood tenets of Christianity, but they are incapable of putting them into practice. Consequently, humans are willing to assist underdogs but ultimately desire to keep them under. In order to obliterate the discrepancies between religious ideals and human actions, Europeans are ready to ascribe human intentions to God and to assume that He blesses their devious schemes to oppress Africans and supports them in their drive by depriving them of means to better their existence and to be noteworthy. He concludes, in his paper, that the truth about Western civilization is that it "is not Christian; it is a tragic compound of great ideal and fearful patience, of high assurance and desperate anxiety, of loving charity and fearful clutching of possessions" (155). Responsible Christians are not swayed by the opinion of others; rather, it is their consciences that should determine their actions. They should not ask themselves "If this . . . is expedient, but only if it is right. I shall do this, not because I am noble or unselfish, but . . . because I need for the rest of my journey a star that will not play false to me, a compass that will not lie.

I shall do this, not because I am a negrophile and a hater of my own, but because I cannot find it in me to do anything else. . . . Therefore I shall try to do what is right, and to speak what is true" (175). It is this individual stance that stems from a religious power that must be maintained in one's quest for truth.

POINT OF VIEW AND STYLE OF THE NOVEL

Cry, the Beloved Country unfolds with a poetic lyrical prose description of nature, which shifts to narrative and dramatic methods of presentations. The language of the text is simple, and the dialogues are generally short but effective. This lyrical and prophetic voice, recalling that of a storyteller, has its source in orality, as evinced by the parallelism and repetitions within the text.

Cry, the Beloved Country also presents the South African experience from a multiplicity of point of views. It begins with the point of view of an omniscient, lyrical, editorial narrator who frequently expresses his moral perspective on the South African social situation, ponders the nature of South African events, actions, and sociopolitical ideologies, and prophesies on the political future of the country. The grim reality of Johannesburg should not exist, he claims, and should never be duplicated. When he discusses South African chauvinism, he also warns the reader about the impeding threat represented by the exploited blacks.

But this omniscient European editorial narrator of chapter 1 is transformed in the subsequent chapters into the subjective first-person female perspective of a Shanty Town landlady and dweller, Mrs. Seme, the father and mother of an ailing child, and Mr. Dabula. Various first-person voices are embedded in the narrative of the omniscient narrator. He also introduces the first-person voices of the legislators, Mr. McLaren and Mr. de Villiers. The omniscient voice becomes a collective "we" at one point, only to espouse the limited perspective of the Afrikaner, Jarvis James, and the Africans, Reverend Kumalo, Mrs. Lithebe, and Msimangu. The third, limited, subjective narrators look at the unfolding events through their limited perspectives and then frequently shift to dialogue. Thus, we hear about Shanty Town from the perspective of a community member who explains the nature of a squatter and how photographers go to Shanty Town to take their pictures. The reader eavesdrops on the inhabitants of Shanty Town as they converse about getting a doctor or obtaining lodging.

While the omniscient narrator's voice is compassionate and most certainly biased toward Africans, he does not identify with them. This narrator remains an outsider who cannot understand the call of a Zulu even if he speaks the language and who perceives Africans as Others. He fails to identify with his subject because, despite the novel's call for universal equality, his gaze from the highest mountain in the land continues to reveal only a humble, unfathomable African. This liberal narrator, akin to the liberals that Alan Paton speaks of in *Towards the Mountain,* "clung to the irrational idea that one could maintain white supremacy and yet be just. [He] had not yet learned to understand that justice might be no more than the interest of the stronger" (240).

CRITICAL REVIEW

Alan Paton's *Cry, the Beloved Country* was published on February 1, 1948, in New York City. Even before its release, Paton was counting on the earnings from the book to resign from his job at Diepkloof Reformatory. Early American reviews of his novel surpassed his expectations. The *New York Times* lauded the rhetoric of the novel and the in-depth treatment of the subject matter. The *New York Herald Tribune,* according to Alexander, praised the quality of the style, which had "a new cadence, derived from the native languages." According to Margaret Hubbard, who did not speak any of the native languages, Paton's English was influenced by the cadence of native languages. Ironically, the author did not speak Zulu fluently and had to resort to Ben Moloi to edit the little Zulu he included in the novel. The novel was highly praised by other reviewers for its "biblical simplicity," its "passion for humankind," its radiance, amazing deft fusion of realistic detail and symbolical synthesis of various points of view," and its brilliance (220). Moreover, even though Charles Scribner did not invest much in advertising the novel, it went through six reprints in three months.

The Scribner publication was soon followed by the British and South African Jonathan Cape editions in September 1948. Although Paton felt that some of the South African reviews were more reserved than the American, the majority, according to Alexander, gave him glowing reviews. The *Daily Herald* claimed that it was better than Harriet Beecher Stowe's *Uncle Tom's Cabin,* and other British newspapers said that *Cry, the Beloved Country* was simply enthralling, moving, and the work of a genius (Alexander 228). The success of the novel ultimately resulted in the production of Zoltan Korda's film *Cry, the Beloved Country* (1951) and Maxwell Anderson's musical *Lost in the Stars* (1948). Alan Paton, who disliked criticism and was oblivious to the pedantic criticism, enjoyed the praise.

Cry, the Beloved Country caught the attention of the world, but it did not always get rave reviews from some of Paton's South African friends, such as

Jan Hofmeyr and Railton Dent. Unfortunately, their constructive criticism of the novel resulted in strained relationships with Paton. But they were not the only South Africans to criticize the novel; it was also unfavorably received by those who did not share the author's liberal Christian humanistic vision. For some, the book was too propagandistic and sentimental to have literary value, and for others, it depicted white South Africans negatively. The wife of a nationalist Afrikaner politician, according to Carol Iannone, is reported to have remarked, after viewing the 1951 film version, "Surely, Mr. Paton, you don't really think things are like that" (447)? The novel was banned in South Africa, like those of other South African writers such as Peter Abrahams, because of its political and critical stance.

Cry, the Beloved Country was considered dangerous propaganda by some, and other, more radical Africans criticized it for its demeaning characterization of blacks. Even though African authors acknowledged the impact of the novel, many blacks, such as Ezekiel Mphahlele, decried the flat characterization of Stephen Kumalo and all the other characters and the liberal ideas of the novel, which Mphahlele claims are "thickly laid." Others deplored Paton's lack of commitment to the liberation of South Africa, because, even though he believed in social justice, he nonetheless desired gradual changes and rejected embargoes as a tool of political pressure, thus failing to support the revolution. Despite its supposed literary limitations, *Cry, the Beloved Country* has proven to be an artistic work that has had the ability to move readers around the world and to put South African literature on the world map. *Cry, the Beloved Country* also began worldwide conversation on morality and social justice in South Africa.

TOPICS FOR ORAL OR WRITTEN EXPLORATION

1. How is the setting described at the beginning of Alan Paton's *Cry, the Beloved Country?* What can we conclude about the lives of the people who live in the setting described by the narrator?

2. In what ways is Reverend Stephen Kumalo's journey to Johannesburg similar to that of the country bumpkin who goes to the city?

3. What types of color symbolisms are used in *Cry, the Beloved Country?* Are these colors associated with specific places and people? If this is the case, what can we infer about the lives of these people and the living conditions in these places?

4. What kind of person is *Cry, the Beloved Country*'s Reverend Kumalo? Is he a good pastor, or is he also tempted by worldly vanity? And in what ways is he similar to or different from James Jarvis?

5. *Cry, the Beloved Country* is about generational conflicts. Describe the relationships between sons and fathers, between older women and girls, and between brothers and sisters.

6. Some critics believe that the African characters in *Cry, the Beloved Country* are negatively depicted. Do you agree with this position? If not, use the text to show why you believe they are portrayed positively.

7. Trace Reverend Kumalo's journey to Johannesburg and other townships in *Cry, the Beloved Country.* What political and social facts are covered during his meanderings?

8. What political solution to the South African racial problem does Alan Paton advocate in *Cry, the Beloved Country?* Study the history of South Africa before and after the dismantling of apartheid. Do you believe that Alan Paton's vision was a solution to the racial tensions in South Africa?

9. Examine the relationships among the characters of *Cry, the Beloved Country.* Do you believe that friendship is a major theme in the novel? And is there equality in these relationships?

10. What roles do women have in *Cry, the Beloved Country?* On the basis of their roles, what is their social status? Are they part of the brotherhood that the novel seeks to establish?

11. Who is telling the story, and how is this story told? Do we see events constantly through the same point of view throughout *Cry, the Beloved Country?*

12. Examine the relationship between Reverend Kumalo and Arthur Jarvis's son. Is it similar to Reverend Kumalo's relationship with the other children in his community? What explains these differences?

13. Read Abraham Lincoln's Gettysburg Address, and then write an essay explaining why this American figure is so important for Arthur Jarvis.

14. Watch a *Cry, the Beloved Country* film and compare it to the novel. Does the film change or reinforce the message of the book? Write a paper explaining the differences or similarities and how the film reinforces or distorts the author's message.

15. On the basis of your contemporary knowledge, write a letter to Alan Paton arguing that *Cry, the Beloved Country* does not address in-depth South African land, farming, and social issues.

16. Alan Paton wrote *Cry, the Beloved Country* with the United States in mind. There are several references to the United States, which has had its own racial problems. What is the importance of the United States in the novel? Since the author refers to the state of Tennessee, research the Jim Crow concept and compare it to apartheid.

SUGGESTIONS FOR FURTHER READING

Abrahams, Peter. *Mine Boy.* Portsmouth, NH: Heineman, 1975.

———. *Wild Conquest.* London: Faber and Faber, 1951.

Baker, Sheridan. "Paton's Beloved Country and the Morality of Geography." *College English* 19 (1957): 56–60.

Black, Michael. "Alan Paton and the Rule of Law." *African Affairs* 91, no. 362 (1992): 52–72.

Callan, Edward. *Cry, the Beloved Country: A Novel of South Africa.* Boston: Twayne, 1991.

———. *Alan Paton* (rev. ed.). Ed. Bernth Lindfors. Boston: Twayne, 1982.

Collins, Harold R. "*Cry, the Beloved Country* and the Broken Tribe." *College English* 14, no. 7 (April 1953): 379–385.

Gailey, Harry A. "Sheridan Baker's 'Paton's Beloved Country.'" *College English* 20 (1958): 143–144.

Gannett, Lewis. Introduction to *Cry, the Beloved Country,* by Alan Paton. New York: Collier Books, 1986.

Hartnett, Connor, P. *Paton's* Cry, the Beloved Country. New York: Monarch Press, 1965.

Watson, Stephen. "*Cry, the Beloved Country* and the Failure of Liberal Vision." *English in Africa* 9 (1982): 29–44.

WEB SITES

Gulvin, L. F. " Cry, the Beloved Country." <http://www.bookwolf.com/free_booknotes/Cry_the_Beloved_Country_/Cry_the_Beloved_Country_html>

Paton, Alan. "Cry the Beloved Country." <http://www.bookrags.com/notes/cbc>

FILMS

Alan Paton: A Profile. Prod. Meyburgh Catherine. Videocassette. Films for the Humanities and Sciences, 1997.

Cry, the Beloved Country. Dir. Darrell James Roodt. Prod. Anant Singh. Perf. Earl James Jones and Richard Harris. Videocassette. Miramax, 1996.

Cry, the Beloved Country. Dir. Zoltan Korda. Perf. Sidney Poitier and Canada Lee. Videocassette. Monterey, 1951.

WORKS CITED

Alexander, Peter F. *Alan Paton.* Oxford: Oxford University Press, 1994.

Gordimer, Nadine. *July's People.* New York: Penguin Books, 1982.

Iannone, Carol. "Alan Paton's Tragic Liberalism." *The American Scholar* 66 (1997): 442–451.

Simons, Jack, and Ray Simons. *Class and Color in South Africa 1850–1950.* London: Southern Africa, 1983.

Stadler, A. W. "Birds in the Cornfield: Squatter Movements in Johannesburg, 1944–1947." *Journal of Southern African Studies* 6:1 (1979): 93–123.

2

Cry, the Beloved Country: Historical Context

Alan Paton concludes *Cry, the Beloved Country* with the rising sun. "Ndotsheni," he writes, "is still in darkness, but the light will come there also. . . . But when that dawn will come, of our emancipation, from the fear of bondage and the bondage of fear, why that is a secret" (277). The conclusion of *Cry, the Beloved Country,* pondering the future of South Africa, clearly indicates that Paton's novel is not just delineating a fictional world, which Paton tellingly contends in the "Author's Note" of the Collier edition is nonexistent. It is a literary work that encapsulates both factual and fictional information in its will to truth. Hence, Paton claims that, even though the characters in the novel are fictional, "the accounts of the boycott of the buses, the erection of Shanty Town, the finding of gold at Odendaalsrust, and the miners' strike, are a compound of truth and fiction. In these respects therefore the story is not true, but considered as a social record it is the plain and simple truth" (vii).

In "*Cry, the Beloved Country* and the "Broken Tribe," Harold R. Collins claims that more historical information is needed to understand Paton's *Cry, the Beloved Country* than is provided in Lewis Gannett's "Introduction," in which Paton's speech providing the historical background to the novel at a book and author luncheon is quoted. Collins contends that "we need reliable information on race relations in South Africa and the rest of Africa, so we may confidentially demonstrate the novel's power and integrity in dramatizing racial problems in terms of human feelings—human hopes, aspirations, fears, and sorrows" (379).

Collins thus resorts to anthropological, historical, and scientific journals and to other colonial fictional works to validate Paton's representation of the "native problem" in *Cry, the Beloved Country.* After comparing Paton's novel to secondary sources, he concludes that the work ""does what no other discursive work in political science, sociology, economics, or anthropology could ever do; it makes us understand 'how it feels' to be a South African today; it gives us the 'form and pressure' of life in South Africa" (385).

Alan Paton's biographer, Peter Alexander, likewise invests much time demonstrating the autobiographical nature of the work and thus the historical veracity of the story. In *Alan Paton,* he, like Gannett, confirms how Paton's life experience shaped the narrative. He readily explains how Diepkloof reformatory entered the story and how various characters were based on real-life individuals the author had known or encountered. Hence, the young, idealistic, white character at the reformatory is modeled on "Lanky" de Lange, the reformatory supervisor, even though Alexander contends that this character is more likely the author's self-portrait. Other characters pulled out of the author's life are Father Beresford, modeled on Michael Scott, the activist priest Paton met while working on the Bishop Geoffrey Clayton's 1942 commission, referred to as the Bishop's Commission. Father Vincent is said to be based on Scott's fellow activist Trevor Huddleston and the character of Msimangu on the first black Anglican monk, Father Leo Rakale. Even names of characters, such as that of Father Vincent, are those of real individuals. Father Vincent's name is inspired by Father Vincent Wall, of Johannesburg (200). He further details how *Cry, the Beloved Country* is informed by historical events that occurred during Paton's life time, such as the miner's strike that began in 1940 and continued intermittently until 1945 (201).

The purpose of this chapter is not to validate either the lifelike quality of Alan Paton's *Cry, the Beloved Country* or its autobiographical nature, for, as Stephen Clingman asks, in "Literature and History in South Africa," what is the purpose of using fiction for historiographic reasons? Some critics define literature as an art that is an end unto itself, and others see no difference between literature and history because they are both only discourses among many and history is in its very nature similar to fiction. Yet, in the South African context, he contends, literature, in its fictive nature, provides historical evidence and delineates a certain kind of history. Literature, according to him, "does not just provide a kind of *documentary* evidence, nor is it supplementary to something else, more real, called actual history; nor is it *illustration* of any kind for historical shadow, but *substance;* it offers a specific kind of evidence within a domain of cultural history" (102).

Despite the difficulty of defining cultural history, Clingman contends that cultural history should be construed in its exclusive notion of literature being a specific cultural institution. Rather, the historical value of literature should be apprehended in its more inclusive ability to depict "ways of life, patterns of experience, and the structures of thought and feeling of communities and classes at large." Fiction, according to him, reveals concepts of identity, "definitions of other and self and other, projections of past, present, future, and of value, and appreciations of the varying problematic area of social life facing such classes and communities" (108). The historian, he writes, is interested in the observable or social history, which literature well embodies; but literature ultimately offers the "historical *consciousness* embedded in the work—its framework of reality, codes of thought, and structures of perception and vision which shape and add meaning to its observation. . . . In short, at this level one approaches a different kind of history through fiction—a *history of consciousness,* not only of individuals, but of groups, communities, classes, and societies at large" (109).

Literature, Clingman contends, is that site where individuals can write about what is happening in their lives, about what might happen in the future, and about individual responsibility in relationship to the human becoming. Through literature, writers are able to fill out, within the fictional context, the "complexities" and "perturbations" of society and their own personal position in relationship to their social realities. The South African writers Daniel P. Kunene, Njabulo S. Ndebele, Sheila Roberts, among others, corroborate this assertion in *Writers from South Africa.* According to Kunene, quoting Brian Bunting, South Africa's problems are so pressing that it is virtually impossible to ignore the political. Nadine Gordimer calls South African writers "testifiers" (18–19). Indeed, Alan Paton himself declares, in *Towards the Mountain,* that *Cry, the Beloved Country* is not about the beauty of the landscape but about "its men and women and about the inequalities that so disfigured our national life" (268). This work, considered, mostly by South Africans propagandistic, political, or polemical, is, he claims, a novel that South Africans disliked because "it revealed a picture of South Africa that they did not wish to look at." He claims, moreover, that the novel was engendered by powerful emotions and anger toward an unjust system. Indeed, Clingman corroborates that while there is no direct connection between the policies of the Liberal Party and *Cry, the Beloved Country,* it nonetheless spells out "some of the major codes and workings of white liberal consciousness in this period, its allegories of power and love, what it feared and what it desired" (116).

It is evident that, even as Paton writes about the issues that govern the present, he confronts the South African past, which shapes that historical moment. To understand the emotions, the interracial relations, and the vision of the future depicted in *Cry, the Beloved Country,* one must have an understanding of the political and historical forces that inform the reality depicted in his work. The dawn announcing a new South Africa was already on the horizon, he writes in his novel; while Paton did not know the nature of that day, history has spoken, as we now speak of post-apartheid South Africa.

AFRICAN INHABITANTS OF SOUTH AFRICA

Khoisan

When the Dutch came to South Africa, they did not occupy an uninhabited land, for they encountered natives, the San (the term used by Khoikhoi to refer to others) and the Khoikhoi ("men of men" or "real men"), referred to by earlier Europeans as "Bushmen" and "Hottentots," respectively. In addition to these hunters and gathers and pastoralist people, there were mixed farmers (pastoralists-farmers), called "Kaffirs" by the Dutch, who spoke Bantu languages. The San also occupied the territory that is currently known as Zimbabwe, northwestern Botswana, and the Drakensberg of Lesotho. Some of their descendants are said to currently live in the arid regions of Botswana, northern Namibia, and southern Angola. The Khoikhoi, on the other hand, occupy present-day Botswana, Namibia, and South Africa. Both groups were small in stature, but the San, who were barely five feet tall, were the smaller of the two. They both had yellowish-brown or olive complexions and what was described as peppercorn tufts of hair and spoke distinctive click languages (Thompson 6). Both groups, despite the claims of early Europeans, also had strong religious beliefs. However, the San were nomadic hunters and food-gatherers, while the Khoikhoi were pastoralists who raised fat-tailed sheep and long-horned cattle. (Analysts have yet to resolve the mystery of the origin of these animals; there is speculation that they may have come from East Africa.) Even though the Khoisan raised cattle, they continued to hunt and gather like the San. Some analysts contend that the subsequent differences that developed between the two groups—in lifestyle, worldview, social organization, and physical characteristics—were the result of the Khoikhoi's acquisition of livestock. Yet, Susan Newton-King contends that it was difficult to establish ethnic boundaries between the two groups because the names "did not always coincide with differences in lifeways: there were hunters who spoke Khoe languages and herders who considered themselves to be of 'Bushman' or San extraction" (28). The cultural, physical, and linguistic similarities between these two peoples clearly suggest a common ancestry and validate, despite the differences, the use of the term "Khoisan" to designate both groups.

The San lived in small clans of 20 to 300 people. These clans usually met annually with other bands to exchange news and techniques, settle disputes, or find marriage partners. During these encounters, disgruntled members had the opportunity to transfer to other bands. Within these communal bands, labor was gender specific (e.g., women gathered edible plants and nuts, and men hunted), but both groups were interdependent. These communities were somewhat egalitarian, so men were not considered superior to women, as evidenced, according to Marjorie Shostak, in the relationships between men and women among the San people's descendants, the Kung. In this ancient tradition, she claims, "men and women live together in a nonexploitative manner, displaying a striking degree of equality between the sexes. . . . Kungmen, however, do seem to have the upper hand" (237). Conversely, the Koikhoi lived in larger and more settled communities because they no longer depended on gathering and hunting for their livelihood. Some clan villages formed chiefdoms headed by a chief; as property became important, they organized cattle raids on other clans or chiefdoms, and, as cattle became increasingly a source of wealth controlled by men, the latter gradually began to dominate women. The pastoralist and hunter-gatherer ways of life were not, however, static but interchangeable, since some San acquired cattle and some Khoikhoi lost cattle; there was also intermixing between the two groups. Consequently, even though the Khoikhoi and the San are perceived as two different peoples by some historians and anthropologists, the real difference between these two groups is predicated on whether they were Khoisan pastoralists or Khoisan hunter-gatherers.

Bantu People (c. 300 A.D.)

In Cry, the Beloved Country, numerous references are made to the various populations that inhabit South Africa. Mrs. Kumalo is said to read like a Zulu (7); Mrs. Lithebe is said to be a Msutu who speaks Zulu well (21); a young conman assumes that Reverend Stephen Kumalo is a Xhosa when he arrives in Johannesburg (18); and the men who work in the mines are said to come from Zululand, Bechunanaland, Sekukuniland, and countries outside Johannesburg (188). Indeed, when speaking of the lack of housing in Johannesburg, a speaker claims that the houses are full, "for everyone is coming to Johannesburg. From the Transkei and the Free State, from Zululand and Sekukuniland. Zulus and Swazis, Shangaans and Bavenda, Bapendi, and Basuto, Xhosas, and Tembos, Pandos and Fingos, they were all coming to Johannesburg" (53). South Africa thus is not occupied by a homogenous African population but has a heterogeneous population comprising numerous Bantu groups that speak Bantu languages derived from Sotho-Swana.

In addition to the earlier Khoisan population that inhabited Southern Africa, myth had it that the Bantu who lived in the area during the Iron Age, prior to the arrival of Europeans, came as immigrants. Archeologists, using carbon-14 dating techniques, have debunked this myth of Bantu immigrants; some claim that changes in the population were the result of a major cultural development rather than immigration, and others maintain that they filtered into the area in small groups. Leonard Thompson contends that their presence in Southern Africa continues to mystify scholars but that Khoisan gene is present in the Bantu group.

According to Kevin Shillington, by the sixteenth century there were three main language subdivisions in Southern Africa: "The Tswana in the central and western regions, northern Sotho in the northeast and southern Sotho south of the Vaal" (16). Conversely, T.R.H. Davenport and Christopher Saunders contend that there were numerous Southern Bantu cultures but that south of the Limpopo there were four main linguistically divided groups—the Sotho-Tswana, the Nguni, the Venda, and the Tsonga (11). According to them, it is not easy to identify original Sotho-speakers, but there were three settlement waves: the Fokeng, the Rolong (named after the name of the group's ancestor, Morolong), and the Tlhaping (thus named because the people ate fish during a severe drought). The Rolong, according to Shillington, split further into four groups: the Ratlou, the Rapulana, the Seleka, and the Tshidi, and during the reign of King Tau, another group of Rolong broke away and settled in lower Vaal and became known as the Tlhaping (17).

According to Shillington, east of the Rolong lived the Hurutshe, the Kwena, and the Kgatla. The Hurutshe were the senior group, whereas the Kwena, located in present-day Pretoria and extending to the Molepolole region, constituted the dominant lineage group. The Kwena who moved south of the Vaal formed the group in southern Lesotho. Further splintering in the Molelpolole gave rise to the Ngwaketse and the Ngwato, who moved to the Shoshong hills, and the Serowe of Botswana. The Kgatla, on the other hand, controlled the northeast Central Transvaal; they also splintered into numerous subgroups. The most powerful were the Kgafela-Kgatla. An important offshoot of the Kgatla was the Tlokwa, which also divided into numerous branches. Other important Kgatla subgroups were the Pedi and, in the northern Transvaal, the Venda and the Lobedu, but these two groups were not part of the Sotho-Swana group because they had Shona origins (16–18). The Nguni, on the other hand, according to Davenport and Saunders, lived in the southeastern region between Drakensberg and the sea. They were well established in the region when the Kgatla and the Kwena were spreading across the region. Nguni chiefdoms in the south were the Xhosa. The Tsongo, who occupied the coastal region between the Save river in Mozambique and St. Lucia Bay, were culturally different from the Nguni because they ate fish, although the earliest Nguni may have descended from them (11–13).

According to J. D. Omer-Cooper, the relationship between the Khoikhoi and the Bantu (mixed farmers or pastoralists-farmers) was anything but harmonious. The Khoikhoi resisted the Bantu when they realized that the latter wanted control of their land and resources. This encounter resulted in conflicts, expulsions, mutual attempts at elimination, and intermarriage; the San were often assimilated by the Bantu, but both groups dominated each other at different time (16).

As the pastoralists-farmers moved west, they encountered the pastoralist Khoikhoi. Since both groups were cattle owners, they mingled easily and created mixed communities, but, according to Jeffery Pieres, quoted by Leonard Thompson, the mixed farmers ultimately dominated the Khoikhoi. However, the integrated pastoralist Khoikhoi "[w]ere not expelled from their ancient homes, or relegated to a condition of hereditary servitude on the basis of colour. They became Xhosa with the full rights of any other Xhosa. The limits of Xhosadom were not ethnic or geographic but political: all persons or groups who accepted the rule of Tshawe thereby became Xhosa" (Thompson 29). By the time Europeans arrived at the Cape, the hunter-gatherers and the pastoralists occupied the western part, whereas the pastoralists-farmers lived in the eastern part of the country, except in the mountainous area occupied by the San. Because of intermarriages, the Bantu acquired Khoisan genes. The most genetically influenced groups are the Xhosa and the Tswana.

One of the most prominent Bantu people referred to in Alan Paton's *Cry, the Beloved Country* are the Zulus, Reverend Kumalo's ethnic group, which fiercely resisted the Afrikaners in Natal. Despite their defeat at Ncome River (Blood River), they later returned to the province and soon outnumbered the Afrikaners. The latter then drove them back into the area south of the River Matamuna.

EARLY EUROPEAN SETTLEMENT

The Portuguese were the first Europeans to make contact with the South African population. The Portuguese explorer Bartholomeu Dias navigated around the Cape of Good Hope, which he called the Cape of Storms, in 1487. The Portuguese king, delighted to discover that it was possible to sail around the African continent, changed the initial name to the Cape of Good Hope. The Cape of Good Hope was, in the early days, economically insignificant to Portugal, which was more interested in the treasures of India; the Cape had, furthermore, gained a terrible reputation in 1510 when the Portuguese viceroy De Almeida and his companions, who had challenged and robbed the Khoikhoi on their way to India, were killed upon their return. Despite this horrible reputation, the visits increased in the seventeenth century; when Portugal's power weakened, the Dutch took over their sea routes, and Andrew Shillinge and Humphrey Fitzherbert, both officers of the English West India Company, finally annexed the Cape territory on behalf of King James I, without legal permission, in 1620. According to Alfred Tokollo Moleah, at first, the Cape was solely used for the replenishing of water and as a "post-office stone" (so named because fleets left letters under stones). The Dutch had no intention of settling in South Africa, because both they and the English conducted their business through chartered companies, but then, in 1600, the British created the English East India Company; in 1602, the Dutch founded the Dutch East India Companies; and the French amalgamated their small companies in 1664. Of the three, the Dutch East India Company was financially and structurally the strongest because it had a powerful central committee. In 1651, the English East India Company took possession of the island of St. Helena, the Portuguese took Mozambique, and the French took Madagascar as their half-way stations (107).

The Dutch East India Company created a calling station in 1652 when Jan van Riebeeck occupied Table Bay. It maintained a small group of Dutch agents at this location who secured fresh water, cultivated fresh vegetables for the crew to prevent scurvy, and traded with the local natives for meat. Within a few years, this victualing station proved to be incapable of meeting all the needs of the company, so the Company's previous employees were allotted land for individual farms. Some of the employees also rejected the regulations of the company and migrated beyond the boundaries of the settlement. By 1677, to obtain land for Company farming and cattle as well as settler lands, the Company extended beyond the Cape peninsula. After a bitter war with France, the Dutch East India Company desired to increase the number of farms, but due to low immigration to the colony, it did not have the necessary manpower. It was compelled to bring to the Cape orphaned girls to fulfill the needs of the overwhelmingly male white population. In 1688, French and Belgian Huguenots (Calvinist Protestants) who had taken refuge in Holland also joined the mainly Dutch-speaking German and Dutch settlers; they were quickly assimilated.

By the end of the century, there were thousands of white settlers and a similar number of slaves from Madagascar, Angola, East Africa, Ceylon, India, Indonesia, and Malaya. Cargoes of slaves from Angola and the Gulf of Guinea were brought to the Cape, but the slaves were difficult to keep in captivity. The majority of the slaves were male, and, since there were virtually no white women in the colony, miscegenation involving white people, local Hottentots, Indonesians, Malagasy, and slaves resulted in the creation in the Cape

Province of a mixed race known as the "Cape Coloreds," part slave and part free. These Cape Coloreds adopted Western culture and religion, except for the Malays, who remained Islamic.

From this racial colored group emerged a racial group referred to as the Bastards, Orlams, or Griqua; they, according to J. D. Omer-Cooper, consisted of Coloreds, Koisans, and free blacks who owned property. The Coloreds were at first assimilated by the white community and had the responsibility of supervising other servants. Their masters also usually trusted them and, at times, treated them as members of the family. About 1750, they lived in Khamiesberg, but, as the settlers needed further land, around 1780, they were pushed further into the territory to the Middle Valley of the Orange. In 1802, missionaries established the London Missionary Society in the area; it was under their influence that they began to call themselves Griqua (31).

The arrival of Europeans resulted in the decimation of the Khoisan. The conflict grew out of disputes over land and livestock possession. The West India Company needed more livestock than the Khoikhoi were willing to sell. When the Company failed to persuade them to give up their livestock, the Europeans used force. The settlers also took advantage of the Khoikhoi practice of raiding each other's cattle by allying themselves with certain clans and attacking others. Deemed undesirable, the San retreated to the Kalahari Desert, whereas the Khoikhoi were systematically physically decimated and assimilated. While some historians contend, according to Susan Newton-King, that the confrontation between the Koisans and the European settlers was gradual because the Europeans relied on the assistance and the cattle of the former to survive, economic greed and racial ideologies certainly contributed to their decimation (38–44).

There were two major wars between the Dutch and the Khokhoi. The first was in 1659, when the Khoikhoi attacked the Dutch and made them retreat to their fort. The second Dutch-Khoikhoi war, which forced the Khokhoi into servitude, occurred between 1673 and 1677. The European settlers raided the Chochoqua and, with their Khoikhoi allies, appropriated their cattle. As arable land become rare, the Dutch moved into the interior of the land. They were so much on the move that they became known as *Voortrekkers,* which means "pulling" (a wagon). The Khoisan resistance continued to weaken the Dutch, who had to fight not only the Khoikhoi but also the more resilient Xhosa. The latter eventually drove them out of Zuurveild and took possession of their land and cattle. During this troubled period of conflict, the European settlers, later identified as Boers and still later as Afrikaners, became the dominant group despite their defeats, so they marginalized and considered other groups inferior.

BOER REPUBLICS

From the onset of South Africa's colonization, the Dutch and the Germans made up the majority of the settlers. The Dutch, the Germans, the French, and other Western groups were quickly absorbed into the increasingly amalgamated Afrikaner community. According to Davenport and Saunders, the British gradually gained control of the Cape Colony. In 1795, a British force successfully landed at False Bay after the French had invaded the Netherlands, or the Batavian Republic. This British invasion was conceived with the complicity of the Netherlands' House of Orange, which opposed the French. The British administration, established under Earl Macartney, persistently strove to secure the Dutch settlers' continuing support and loyalty for the House of Orange.

In February 1803, the British withdrew and handed the Cape back to the Batavian Republic, or the Netherlands, as the country was called at the time. The Batavians, unlike the British, came to the Cape permanently, as heirs of the Dutch East India Company. They were tolerant rulers; they made Dutch the official language and transformed the Company's administrative board into a regular government instrument. However, because of their tolerant views toward creeds and their secularization of education, they alienated the conservative Cape Colony population.

The British returned, a second time and for good, in 1806, after Napoleon resumed hostilities in 1805 when the Treaty of Amiens, which handed the Cape to the Batavians (the former United Netherlands) fell into abeyance. They landed at Blomberg, on Table Bay. They did not get legal possession of the Cape Colony until April 1815, when the Netherlands officially transferred the colony to Britain. This time the British came to stay, and Earl Caledon reinstated an autocracy even more stringent than that of the East India Company. The British Parliament passed a law abolishing slavery in their empire in 1834, with abolition to be followed by four years of apprenticeship, and introduced circuit courts. Unfortunately, the emancipation of slaves in the Cape Colony did not automatically result in racial equality and African ownership of land. The British also began to move into the interior and subsequently created commercial centers. Even though some intermarriage between Afrikaners and British took place, the British, unlike the French Huguenots, retained their distinct cultural identity.

Land remained a major issue between the government and white settlers during this period. Missionary lobbying for natives, aggravated the tension between the British government and the settlers. While the colonists requested equality, fraternity, and liberty for themselves, they viewed Africans as subhuman. As God's chosen race and people, they considered themselves above menial work, which they considered appropriate for Africans. The London

Missionary Society, the Roman Catholic Church, the Church Missionary Society, and the German Moravian Brethren believed that these principles extended to nonwhites. The Dutch Reformed Church, in contrast, fostered and disseminated ideologies of white superiority. The three main factors leading to this conflict were disputes related to ideological positions on the nature and fate of the natives, native education policies, and minority rights. Dr. John Philip, considered one of the most revolutionary missionaries, earned the hatred and ire of the Afrikaners for influencing the implementation of Ordinance 50, which repealed the law requiring Hottentots to carrying passes and requiring that children born during an 8-year tenure serve their master for 10 years. Philip and Andries Stokenstrom also endeavored to influence the annexation policies of Queen Adelaide Province and attempted to introduce a treaty system in their dealings with Xhosa chiefs.

The Great Trek

Desiring to escape from British rule, some Cape Boers, or Afrikaners, fortified by their Calvinist religion, decided to relocate to the interior where they could govern themselves. Although trekking was inherent to Afrikaner migratory life because of the settlers' need for territorial expansion and pastoral farming, the Great Trek was unique in its permanency, the nature of its organization, and the number of people involved. The major factor that caused the Great Trek, according to Piet Retief's manifesto, was the "turbulent and dishonest conduct of vagrants who are allowed to infest the country in every part" (qtd. in Moleah 144). Motivated by their racial prejudice, their fear of British slavery and land reforms, and the possibility of losing their Dutch cultural heritage and language, the *Voortrekkers,* or *trekboers* (pioneers), as they were called, began leaving the Cape toward the end of 1835.

Three Boer reconnaissance trek parties were organized in 1834. According to Alfred Tokollo Moleah, the group that went north to present-day Botswana and into Namibia brought back unfavorable news, whereas the group that went north across the Orange and Vaal Rivers "enthusiastically reported of well-watered and fertile lands" (143). The most exciting report came from the third group, which had gone to present-day Natal. The first groups to undertake the Great Trek did not leave until 1834.

The first Voortrek was led by Louis Trigardt (also spelled Trichart) and the second by Janse van Rensburg in May 1835. These two parties eventually united and formed a single group. Later, after a quarrel, they eventually separated, only to be reunited once again when Jan Pretorius, Trigardt's second-in-command, left and was later rescued when his followers died of fever. The Trigardt and Rensburg voortrek was ultimately nearly eliminated by the Africans and fever.

Before Trigardt's party had crossed the Vaal River, two larger contingents, led by Andries Hendirk Potgieter and Sarel Cilliers (three Kruger families and, most importantly, the future president of the South Africa Republic were among these trekkers), set forth in 1836. The two parties converged, went further than Trigardt had, and were subsequently joined later by another contingent led by Gerrit Maritz, who had come to their rescue. Potgieter was eventually elected commandant of both treks and chairman of the *Krygsraad* (Council of War) and Maritz voorsitter (President) of the *Volksraad* and Court. Maritz was jealous of Potgieter's power, so a quarrel ensued over the distribution of loot from a campaign and Maritz's inability to install Erasmus Smit as the official predickant (Walker 113–32). The two leaders eventually separated. The last party, led by Piet Retief, did not leave the Cape until February 1837. These Afrikaners moved into the interior of the land and dispossessed Africans, especially the Zulus and the Ndebele, of their lands. Because the *Voortrekkers* threatened their independence, the Zulus fiercely resisted their invasion, almost wiped them out, and killed Piet Retief and his companions after negotiations failed. Maritz also died before the settlers obtained relief before Andries Pretorius, who had been called upon to lead the voortrekkers after the death of Retief, arrived to give succor to them. The trekkers massacred more than 3,000 Zulus during the Battle of Blood River (Ncome) and obtained a large part of the Natal territory from the Zulu chief Dingane, who was subsequently eliminated by some of his own people. His successor, Mpande, submitted to the authority of the Afrikaners, who asserted their dominance in the area. A major result of the Great Trek was the *Voortrekkers*' expansion of European racialist ideas into the interior and beyond.

REPUBLIC OF NATALIA, 1839–1843

Following their victory over the Zulu, the *Voortrekkers* established the first Boer state, the Republic of Natalia, bordered by the black Umfolonsi, the Drakensberg, and the Umzumvubu. These *Voortrekkers* who went north of the Vaal desired the most to be free of the British. In order to establish a viable state, Hendrick Potgieter negotiated to furnish Portuguese and Dutch traders with ammunition and other goods in exchange for animal skins and ivory. These Afrikaner settlers, the *Potchefstroom,* began to refer to their territory as the South African Republic. They attempted to subdue the Tswana, and, when they resisted, the settlers blamed the missionaries and traders. They also attacked the Kwena, the Rolong, and the Mulopa.

These Voortrekkers were very suspicious of unrestrained authority, so they created a state governed on democratic principles and with no executive independent of the chair of the *Volksraad* (People's Council), a body of 24 men. This *Volksraad* took on the appearance of a federation when Natalia incorporated Highveld communities into the *Volksraad.* Pretorius worked for amalgamation, so when he visited the Mooi River settlement (where Potchefstroom was constructed), he created an *Adjunkt Raad* (consisting of *Volksraad* members). When Natalia surrendered to the British in 1842, Potchefstroom succeeded in 1843 and formed a new republic in 1844. But it lost its importance when Potgieter decided to move to Andries Ohrigstad, where he aspired to create independent business centers. He soon alienated his followers, however, when he established a military government. He eventually moved to a new settlement, Soutpansberg. Andries Pretorius returned from British-controlled Natal to lead the Afrikaner resistance to Harry Smith's (the British High Commissioner for the Affairs of the Interior) annexation of Trans-Orangia in 1848. During this resistance, Hendrick Potgieter's influence waned while that of Pretorius increased within the Voortrekker community (Davenport 80–84).

Potchefstroom and Southpansberg unified in a *Volksraad* presided over by four representatives—Pretorius (Mooi River and Magaliesberg), Potgieter (Soutpansberger), W. F. Joubert (Lyndensburg, the capital of Ohrigstad), and J. A. Enslen (Marico). These four officials were subjected to the United Volksraad, yet Pretorius negotiated the Convention of Sand River (which entitled Voortrekkers to possess African lands) without its support. Following this achievement, Pretorius became increasingly popular and began to act more like a head of state. The Republic of Natalia came quickly to an end when the British annexed it to the Cape Colony, in 1845.

ORANGE FREE STATE

Upset by the annexation of the Republic of Natalia, numerous Afrikaners joined other trekkers and relocated in the region between the Orange and the Vaal Rivers. The British government attempted to curb their independence by annexing the territory, but its efforts were made futile by Afrikaner resistance. However, because controlling this movement required massive financial outlays, the British decided to leave the Afrikaners alone and, after the Sand River Convention of 1852, granted them the right to govern themselves beginning in 1854.

Unlike Natalia, the Orange Free State constitution, modeled on the American and the European constitutions, made provisions for a president. This state was virtually controlled and populated by white farmers after the elimination of the Griqua (people of mixed African and European ancestry) and the purchasing of land from the Rolong. Although other non-Afrikaner whites were admitted to the state, they were a minority. The British, in their desire to protect their commerce, objected to the admission of Indian traders in the 1880s, and the *Volksraad* (People's Council) prohibited the admission of Indians to the state in 1890. If Indians had many difficulties winning acceptance in this state, Africans, who constituted the majority, did not fair better, for they were denied land ownership, even though they were the rightful owners.

THE TRANSVAAL

The British decision to cease interfering in Afrikaner affairs resulted in the creation of the South African Republic (Transvaal). This state, like the Free State, had its moments of conflict. But, unlike in the Free State, where the conflict was political, in the Transvaal it was primarily of a religious nature. The *Nederdutse Gereformeerde Kerek* (NGK) of the Cape had refrained from supporting the Great Trek, but it nonetheless built churches at Potchefstrom, Rustenburg, Lyndenburg, and Schoemansdal between 1842 and 1852. When Pretorius became president of the state, the *Volksraad* (parliamentary) community suspended him and designated J. H. Grobler as president. When Grobler resigned, Stephanus Schoeman replaced him. Once again, because of Pretorius's follower Paul Kruger's standing within the community, Schoeman was censored, and W. C. Janse van Rensburg was elected acting president. Because of the opposition from Schoeman's supporters, a civil war ensued. Van Rensburg was elected president, while Pretorius was given a military position. When Schoeman once again attempted to regain power, Pretorius emerged as a victor and remained in power for seven years. He later won other elections in 1888, 1893, and 1898. His presidency was marked by wars with African states and religious conflicts. The South African Republic, or the Transvaal, was finally annexed by the British in 1877. Unhappy with the annexation, the Afrikaners appealed to Britain to grant them their independence, but they were able only to win permission for the Transvaal to become a bilingual country. Discontent, they rebelled and defeated the British in 1881 during the Battle of Majuba Hills. But this victory was short lived, for the British and the Afrikaners continued to fight until August 1881, when war ended with the Pretoria Convention, which granted the Afrikaner republics limited internal self-government but gave the British control over their foreign affairs and oversight of their internal policies toward Africans. This convention, far from dispelling Afrikaner resentment, simply inflamed it further, since the

Afrikaners resented being subjects of the British. Subsequently, T. F. Burgers became president of the Transvaal. He was elevated, in Afrikaners' imagination, to epic status because he opposed British rule. Unfortunately, Burgers, who eventually went into exile, lost this status when his government was defeated during the Anglo-Boer war of 1902. This era saw the rise of modern Afrikaner nationalism, a reaction to British nineteenth-century imperialist policies, which galvanized the Afrikaner community because it offered, according to G.H.L. Le May, "common victims to mourn, common injuries upon which to brood, a common cause in the restoration of republicanism and, in the tragic figure of Kruger, dead in exile, a martyr around whom myths could be woven" (213).

BRITISH COLONIES

The British occupied the Cape with the complicity of the Netherlands. Their occupation was brief, though, because, with the Peace of Amiens, they transferred the territory to Batavia (the Netherlands, as the country was known at the time). The Batavians assumed control of the Cape, previously under the leadership of the Dutch East India Company. The rule of the Batavian was also short lived, since the Cape was once again invaded by the British, in 1806. The Dutch lost the colony because of their weakness after numerous European wars, commercial rivalry from the French and the English, and the corruption and ill management of the Dutch East India Company. The increasing discontent of the colonists, who believed that they were not being effectively protected against Africans, culminated in a rebellion.

When the British first occupied the Cape, in 1795, their main goal was to ensure that the Colony did not become a French possession because of the French expansion under Napoleon into Holland and the possible disintegration of the Dutch East India Company. Great Britain was not interested in the Cape per se, but, because of its strategic geographical position, halfway between western Europe and India, Britain wanted to keep it from falling under French control. This British administration was not revolutionary; it worked primarily to win the colonists' loyalty to the Dutch House of Orange. It also did not menace the existing order even though British citizens held the higher-level administrative positions. By 1803, the Batavian Republic retained the British, albeit in low, subordinate positions, introduced more humane policies toward African peoples, and reformed the judicial system.

In May 1803, England resumed war with France, and the battle continued until 1815. In fear of losing its colonial territory in India, Britain captured the Cape in 1806, but the Colony did not officially become a British possession until 1815, when its transfer was made part of the peace settlement reached at the Congress of Vienna following the defeat of Napoleon. This British administration was not as tolerant as the Batavian government; apart from the introduction of circuit courts, the administration remained primarily Boer. The Cape Burgher Senate continued to function as the town council, and the general economy worsened. But there were some improvements, such as in education, the postal system, and health facilities (although there were not any major improvements during this period). The British administration also attempted to introduce a new currency and set limits on government expenses. The Dutch Reformed Church had a lot of freedom during this period, since government officials no longer attended the meetings of the Synod; the Roman Catholic Church was extended privileges equal to those enjoyed by all the other denominations; and the press gained more freedom of expression. English criminal law also replaced the old Roman-Dutch criminal law during this period. In 1833, English, to the discontent of the Boers, who eventually set off on the Great Trek, was proclaimed the official language of the colony. Once they became a conquered people, the Boers ceased to have political power. They sought an administration that was representative, but their petitions were rejected, although some minor concessions were made in the creation of the Advisory Council, with two Afrikaner-nominated seats. Finally, in 1834, an Executive Council was established in the Cape Colony, but it did not have much power, since the governor had discretionary authority and the king had the last word.

During this period, there continued to be clashes between the colonists and the African population. The Afrikaners at the frontier of the Cape Colony were continuously driving Africans from their lands. Of all the Africans, the Xhosa challenged the colonists the most, to the extent that they defeated them and became de facto owners of the land between the Fish and the Sunday Rivers. In 1812, the British government extended its territory by creating the district of Zuurveld (later called Albany), hoping it would be a buffer zone between the Colony and the Xhosa. After the Napoleonic wars, the government, in 1815, enticed British residents who were suffering from unemployment and misery at home to immigrate to the Cape. They were given free passage as long as they had more than 10 people in their party, and free land. This political immigration movement brought in British farmers. Up to this point, the British had done mainly administrative work, so this new class of British settler broke the Afrikaner monopoly of farming. The Albany settlement did not, however, eliminate the existing clashes between the colonists and the Xhosa, since the issue of land remained unresolved.

One of the most determining historical conflicts was the Kaffir war of 1834. This war centered on cattle thefts by both Xhosa and Boers. Moreover, the Boers were bent on appropriating the lands of the Xhosa. This war had devastating consequences, since many Afrikaners died and lost their property; through Governor Benjamin D'Urban's leadership and with the assistance of Afrikaners, the Xhosa were also decimated, deprived of their land, and forced out of the territory. D'Urban, at the end of the war and to the satisfaction of the Afrikaners, annexed the territory, which was renamed the Province of Queen Adelaide; some Xhosas were graciously allowed to return because the Zulus and the other people who lived in the territory to which they had fled did not accept them, either. But they could live on the land only on the condition that they did not settle south of the Kei (where the land was reserved for Europeans), submitted to European authority, became British subjects, and abided by British laws. But the British government reversed D'Urban's annexation, to the dismay of the colonists. Neither did it endorse the annexation of the District of Natal, which had been given to Allen Gardiner in his treaties with the chiefs of the Zulu, Dingane, and the Xhosa chief Moshoeshoe.

The Boers who headed southeast to the area between the Caledon and the Orange—the area of the Griqua, the Rolong, the Tlokwa, the Taung, and the Sotho—settled permanently in the area without King Moshoeshoe's permission. In 1843, the Cape governor made a treaty with King Moshoeshoe. The treaty was, unfortunately, inefficient in maintaining peace despite the presence of the British Henry Wardman, who was placed at Bloemfontein. In 1848, the Cape governor Sir Harry Smith annexed the territory and called it "The Orange River Sovereignty." This move, seen by the Boers as part of the British effort to curtail Boer independence, resulted in Pretorius's rebellion, which was quashed by the British. The British subsequently attempted to limit the power of the Sotho by creating the Warden Line of 1848, which established the boundary between the Sotho kingdom and the Boer territory. Giving less land to the Sotho than had been recognized by the Napier Treaty of 1843, the Warden Line aggravated matters. The Sotho felt betrayed, so they carried out raids against British properties. To humble and lessen the power of the Sotho, the British waged two wars, in 1851 and in 1852, but these were unsuccessful because the British failed to defeat the Sotho. The Boers subsequently gained their independence from the British in 1854 at the Bloemfontein Convention when the British handed over the territory to the Afrikaners, who renamed it the Orange Free State. Increasing dissension within the Afrikaner group soon created factions, resulting in the creation of three splinter republics: Lydenburg, Soutpansberg, and Utrecht. By 1857, there were five Afrikaner states—the Orange Free State, the South African Republic, Lyndenburg, Soutpansberg, and Utrecht—and three British colonies—The Cape Colony, Natal, and British Kaffraria.

When Britain adopted a more expansionist policy, the result was greater unification among the Afrikaners. Likewise, the British contemplated unifying their colonies into a federation. The Cape governor, George Grey, even recommended that the Orange Free State be considered a member of the federation. But the Afrikaners disregarded the authority of the British government, so the project never successfully materialized. However, the British were able to annex Basutoland and Griqualand West, to the dissatisfaction of the Boers. Following the discovery of diamonds in Griqualand West, it became a British territory, in 1880. Moreover, Germany's increasing scramble for land compelled the British to annex Bechuanaland to the Cape Colony and to make the northern part, currently Botswana, its protectorate. Later, in order to ensure that the Transvaal was under British control, especially since it was rich in minerals, Cecil Rhodes planned an invasion of the territory under the leadership of Dr. Leander Starr Jameson. Unfortunately, this invasion was unsuccessful because non-Afrikaners did not rebel as anticipated. Jameson was arrested, and British/Afrikaner relationships worsened. The Transvaal and the Orange Free State, on the other hand, became even more united, as they both had suffered British aggression. Paul Kruger's popularity rose; Britain lost its standing; and Germany became an implicit ally of the Afrikaners. The animosity fostered by this invasion, above all, laid the groundwork for the Anglo-Boer War of 1899–1902.

The failed invasion of the Transvaal generated animosity between the British and the Afrikaners, who were each suspicious of the other's motives. The British believed in their superiority and their right to rule others, including Afrikaners; therefore, they exaggerated anti-British sentiments among Afrikaners when the latter adamantly defended their land and autonomy. After Kruger's third election to the presidency, in 1883, it was evident that Sir Alfred Milner, the governor of the Cape Colony, was seeking all means possible to wage war against the Transvaal. Under pretense of speaking for and protecting the *Uitlander* (outsider or foreigner) underdogs, Milner fortified his army near the Transvaal border. The war began when Kruger's request that the troops be removed was not heeded. Even though the Boer republics were better prepared than the British, they were soon weakened. The British settlers obtained assistance from their English metropolis, or British government, and its colony, India. After numerous losses, they finally defeated the Afrikaners at Bloemfontein. But this was not the end of the war because the Afrikaners waged a guerrilla against the British. Outnumbered, famished, diseased, and fighting the British Empire without an ally, when they had initially believed that Germany would side with them, the Afrikaners finally capitulated but remained united and strong. The struggle finally concluded with the Peace of Vereeniging; the Afrikaners were compensated for their losses, were promised local autonomy, and ultimately became British citizens. The British, on the other hand, ceased to advocate human rights, thus eliminating one of the major ideological differences that was a source of contention between the two European parties.

Changes moving the country toward unification gradually took place. Louis Botha and Jan Christians Smuts created, in the Transvaal, a political party called the *Het Volk Party* (the People's Party), in 1905. It advocated reconciliation and upheld the provisions of the Vereeniging treaty. J. H. Hofmeyr, in the Cape Colony, also transformed an all-Afrikaner party into a more inclusive party, the South African Party. Moreover, Sir Alfred Milner agreed to grant Transvaal a representative government in 1906 and self-government by the more liberal British government in 1907. The Orange River Colony was given similar concessions the following year, and Botha was elected prime minister and Smuts his deputy. The desire to consolidate South Africa emanated not from a political meeting but from an economic conference on intercolonial railways; the participants believed that it was important to remove impediments to economic growth. At the National Convention of 1908, the two Afrikaner and British groups adopted bilingualism, agreed to have one legislative authority under the British government, and changed the name of the Orange River Colony to the Orange Free State. The constitution of a united South Africa, disenfranchising non-Europeans, was drafted at this conference and was finally approved after the British government amended it, on May 31, 1910. The Union of South Africa, headed by Prime Minister General Botha, was thus based on the autonomous-dominion model of Canada and Australia. Both Afrikaner and British colonists looked forward to a bright future, but the new Union of South Africa symbolized, for South African people of color, British capitulation to Afrikaner racial ideals.

THE UNION OF SOUTH AFRICA (1910–1948)

The British conquest and the nature of British rule, including applications of aspects of the Enlightenment, contributed to the emergence of Afrikaner nationalism. British actions during the Anglo-Boer wars (termed the South African wars by Afrikaners) and their eventual victory reinforced the Afrikaners' cosmology. The major sources of contention between Afrikaners and the British colonists focused essentially on cultural survival and power. Since both groups considered themselves superior and destined to rule, clashes inevitably ensued. At the time of unification, although the Afrikaners were unified and had created Afrikaner states, there was an imbalance of power, given that the British dominated the civil service, transportation, industry, and the railways. Moreover, the English language was dominant, whereas Afrikaans and its cultural productions were considered inferior. The Afrikaner community thus sought to make its culture and language prominent. In their efforts to promote Afrikaner culture, two movements arose: the radical movement headed by James Barry Munnik Hertzog and the more moderate movement led by Louis Botha and Jan Christian Smuts. Hertzog believed in Afrikaner hegemony and the superiority of Afrikaner language and culture. According to him, Afrikaners were capable of directing the country alone and should therefore avoid all collaboration with the British. Botha and Smuts, while moderates, concurred with Hertzog's hegemonic theory, so they also promoted Afrikaans and encouraged the patronization of Afrikaner schools. And since mental oppression is the best way to subject a people, they encouraged and promoted the publication of Afrikaner literature and discouraged the consumption of English literature and all its cultural by products.

The Boers were prominent in South African politics and dominated the government. At the formation of the Union of South Africa, the Afrikaner Botha was prime minister, and other Afrikaners, such as Smuts and Hertzog, were also in the government. Conversely, the British were in the opposition, with the English-speaking Unionist Party, led by Dr. Leander Starr Jameson. In 1912, after a major conflict between Hertzog and Botha and Smuts, the former was dismissed from the government. Hertzog remained, however, at the forefront of South African politics as the president of the Nationalist Party, formed in 1913. This party was very popular with the Afrikaner electorate, so, even though it lost the 1920 election, it ultimately won in 1924 because it had opposed South Africa's involvement in the First World War. This war was unpopular because it depleted state funds even though South African interests were not at stake. Once Hertzog's earlier republican concerns were put to rest with the independence of South Africa from Britain subsequent to the Imperial Conferences of 1926 and 1930, he abandoned his radical positions, only to be replaced by Dr. Daniel Malan. In 1934, Smut's South African Party and Hertzog's Nationalist Party merged to form a powerful party, the United South African Nationalist Party. The discontented members of Smuts's party who disapproved of the merger, which they considered a movement towards radicalism, formed a new party, the Dominion Party; Malan also created the radical Afrikaner party called the "Purified" Nationalists. In 1948, the Nationalists and other Afrikaner parties won the election, and in 1951 the Nationalist Party and all other Afrikaner parties merged to become the Nationalist Party (NP).

Despite the existence of all these various parties, party policies were very similar, for they all advocated and upheld white privilege. Malan's party fervently believed that nonwhites should be maintained in a position of inferiority and that rigid structures should be established to ensure the separation of races and white economic prosperity. The United Party advocated white hegemony, apartheid, and Bantustans but failed to clearly articulate its policies. Conversely, the liberal and moderate political parties—the Progressive Party (1959) and the Liberal Party (1953)—believed in human rights and equality, but their memberships were weak because "even many whites who frowned at the extremism of new legislation felt it was necessary to maintain law and order" (Furlong 385). After the Second World War, South African nationalism increased, and republican ideals became central to South African politics. The country finally became a republic when the South African constitution was changed in April 1961. Nonetheless, because of its racialist policies, it was forced to leave the British Commonwealth the same year, after its membership was suspended and it was faced with expulsion because of pressure from new, post–World War II Commonwealth members in Africa and Asia.

THE OPPOSITION: ANC AND PAC

From the early days of European settlement in Southern Africa, African natives had not passively accepted the discriminatory and oppressive laws imposed by Europeans that dehumanized them, according to Pierre L. van den Berghe; on the contrary, they manifested their resistance in numerous ways. They resisted Afrikaner incursions before and during the Great Trek. The Zulu revolt over a poll tax in Natal was the last major African act of warfare against the colonists. From that moment, African resistance shifted from warfare to political struggles.

African activism, however, began as a class opposition before it transformed into African nationalism. African nationalism should be understood differently from Afrikaner nationalism, which entails a common language and culture. African nationalism and the subsequent resistance movements were, according to Monica Wilson and Leonard Thompson, the result of the routine subjection of Africans and of the Afrikaners' nationalist determination to dominate Africans completely.

The early forms of African resistance included raids, cattle rustling, and spiritual mass movement. Prophets and messiahs promised to rid the land of Europeans and to restore the Golden Age of pre-European settlements, as in the case of the Zionist sect clashes and the Zulu cow killings of the 1850s when the Zulus refused to leave their sacred location. And when the Union of South Africa was formed and Africans were excluded from the constitution, Africans from all over South Africa who had been educated in Britain and in the United States met at Bloemfontein in 1912 and created the South African Native National Congress (SANNC), which became, in 1923, the

African National Congress (ANC). The Congress elected Reverend John L. Dube as president, the Zulu lawyer Pixley Ka I Seme as treasurer, and the first African South African writer, Sol Plaatje, as general secretary. According to Shillington, this Congress "opened and concluded with the first public singing of *Nkosi Sikelel' lAfrika* ("God Bless Africa") composed by the Xhosa poet Enoch Sontonga," a song, as evinced in Alan Paton's *Cry, the Beloved Country,* that calls for African unity. As the young demonstrator claims, "we do not work for men, that we work for the land and the people. We do not even work for money" (268). Trade unions also played an important role between 1919 and 1929. The Industrial and Commercial Workers' Union (ICU), led by Clements Kadalie, was founded in 1919 when Africans in search of jobs were thrown off their land and relocated in crowded urban areas. The literary John Kumalo, in *Cry, the Beloved Country,* making fiery rhetorical speeches but failing to act, embodies this trade movement. The South African Communist Party (SACP), created in 1921, also made a major impact on trade union activism.

The South African Native Congress, with Dr. Alfred Xuma as its first president, was created in January 1912, at Bloemfontein, with the aims of politically unifying the various tribes, defending blacks' human rights and right to justice, educating blacks politically, and fighting for their political representation (Esterhuyse 10). Some analysts contend that this Congress was ineffective during the period 1920–1936 because it relied on rhetoric to liberate Africans and believed in a nonracial South Africa for all South Africans. But Wilson and Thompson reject this theory of inefficiency because it assumes a naiveté and an inability among Africans to realistically assess political situations. From 1937 to 1938 after the Second World War, when the African National Congress sought to initiate more collaboration with other non-African organizations, such as that of Coloreds and Indians, a younger generation of ANC members became disenchanted with the party's pacifist approach and called for a more militant one. This call resulted, in 1943, in the formation of the ANC Youth League (ANCYL), an adjunct of the Congress.

This Youth League called for a more engaged approach, better education for blacks, an end to segregation, and greater participation of African people in the South African economy. It refused to define the oppression of Africans in terms of class when it was in fact racial. The party was against the oppression of all nonwhites and was willing to collaborate with other oppressed groups on common issues, but it believed that "the only force which could achieve freedom was that of African nationalism organized in a national liberation movement led by Africans themselves" (Wilson and Thompson 459). In 1949, its program of action was adopted by the Congress, and its leaders,

Nelson Mandela, Oliver Tambo, and Walter Sisulu, became influential board members of the ANC. The organization became more threatening and militant in its approach to European South Africa, so, despite its relative weakness and its nonviolent philosophy, the government harassed party members and took numerous measures to control the movements of its leaders. Later, other organizations, such as the Natal Indian Congress (NIC), the South African Communist Party (SACP), the European Congress of Democrats (COD), and the South African Coloured People's Organization (SACPO), joined forces with the African National Congress (ANC), led by Chief Albert Luthuli. Under the African National Congress and its allies' leadership, the Congress of the People adopted, in 1955, the Freedom Charter, demanding universal democracy, since South Africa belonged to all, the "restoration of 'human rights,' the nationalization of mines and industries, and a redistribution of all land" (Were 187).

Some members of the ANC were unhappy with this charter, which they considered to be the product of multiracial organizations, white liberals, and communist Indian manipulation. According to them, it diverted the African National Congress from its initial objectives and diluted its African nationalism. The party splintered in two. The succeeding party created, in 1959, the rival Pan-African Congress (PAC), led by Robert Mongaliso Sobukwe. It advocated African majority rule and was committed to pan-Africanism. The Pan-African Congress's organization, in 1960, of peaceful demonstrations against the requirement that blacks carry passes, initially conceived by the ANC, resulted in the massacres at Sharpeville. Subsequently, both parties were banned when the ANC's successful call for a day of mourning showed the European South Africans the power that black Africans could wield. The parties went underground and into exile, and the party became a militarized resistance. "Nelson Mandela organized in 1961 the ANC armed wing, the *Umkhonto we Sizwe* (Spear of the Nation or MK), but Mandela's capture, along with other ANC and PAC leaders, and the Rivonia trial forced all active resistance underground by 1964" (Furlong 387). The leaders of PAC and ANC—Chief Albert Luthuli, Robert Sobukwe, Nelson Rolihlahla Mandela—were arrested and incarcerated. Winnie Mandela, the spouse of Mandela, was also arrested in 1969, released in 1970, and put under house arrest. Prime Minister Hendrik Frensch Verwoerd was assassinated in 1966 and replaced by B. J. Vorster, a former minister in the Verwoerd government who introduced indefinite detention without trial law. During this period, pass laws were reinforced, and political prisoners mysteriously disappeared (Furlong 388).

But, in the 1970s, things changed as blacks became more and more defiant. South Africa was subjected to international bans, embargoes, and guerrilla wars in South African–occupied Mozambique and Angola. The student "Black Consciousness" movement, led by Steve Biko, who was murdered in 1977, emerged during this period. During protests against mandatory education in Afrikaans, "the language of oppression," as many as 1,000 children in the black township of Soweto were killed. During this time, factory workers also organized illegal strikes (Furlong 388). A political crisis ensued when the United Party collapsed and the majority of its members joined the Progressive Federal party (PFP), which became the opposition party (Furlong 389). In response to a government proposal that a tricameral legislature including whites, coloreds, and Indians be established, the resistance movement created the United Democratic Front in 1983. In 1990, Mandela was released, the ANC was again made legal, and clashes occurred between the ANC and Gatsha Mangosuthu Buthelezi's Inkatha Party. The ANC played an important role in South African politics during this period when the country moved from confrontations to talks, which eventually led to the election of Mandela as the president of South Africa, on May 10, 1994. During this final phase of the struggle, there were three opposition movements: ANC and its ally the SACP, the former UDF, and the militant trade unionists. The second group included the unionists—PAC and the Azanian People's Organization, among many others, and the ethnically based subnationalist groups such as Inkatha. Despite their ideological differences, all these organizations were dedicated to the dismantling of apartheid.

APARTHEID 1948–1994

Since its genesis, South African history has been marked by colonialists' will to power and economic hegemony, appropriation of African lands, and the disenfranchisement of Africans and other non-European people. The South African problem, according to Were, is racial since all Southern African politics and conflicts have been founded, despite cultural differences among the European colonialists, on racial relationships, or what he refers to as "'racial segregation,' 'separate development' and 'racial discrimination'" (166). Afrikaner South Africans sought to be at the center of their country's politics, economics, and culture, so they have been impelled, throughout centuries, to question, as Julia Kristeva states in her discussion of master-slave relationships, to what degree they are masters of and are at home in their countries and are in control of their future. Suspicious of the foreigner, she writes, the new "'master' develops 'regressive and protective rage' and wonders if (s)he should create an exclusive world and 'expel' the intruder, or at least, keep him in 'his' place. The 'master than changes into a slave hounding his conqueror. For the foreigner perceived as an invader reveals a buried passion within those who are entrenched: the passion to kill the *other,* who had first been feared or despised, then promoted from the ranks of dregs to the status of powerful prosecutor against whom a 'we' solidifies in order to take revenge" (20).

Dr. D. F. Malan, according to Patrick Furlong, came to power in 1948 with the slogan of "apartheid." Although he participated in the establishment of a segregated South Africa, he was still moderate. He was later replaced by the more radical J. G. Strijdom, who advocated *Baasskap* (white boss-ship). "The apartheid regime," he writes, "had a very simple aim: to make South Africa safe for a small, relatively poor people new to the city and incapable without state assistance of surviving either English guile and business experience or black competition on an open labor market. The mechanisms no longer seemed enough. A planned economy, a rigged political system, and a rigidly segregated society provided the desired recipe" (385).

The belligerent British and Dutch Europeans who both feared and fought each other for power and to retain their cultural identities solidified into a "we" when it came to the protection of white interests in ensuring that Africans and all other colored minorities were marginalized and disenfranchised, not just in everyday practice but through legislative acts. As early as 1913, the Land Act was implemented to control native movement. According to this Act, which reinforces racial residential segregation, natives were to live in their allocated spaces, the reserves, except when they worked for a European. This act resulted in mass removals of Indians and Coloreds. The 1923 Native Urban Acts, on the other hand, controlled the number of Africans who could live in urban areas. This act also recommended that Africans who were living in small areas be granted land, so the South African Native Trust, charged with the mission of purchasing land for the Africans, was established; at the time, 87 percent of the land belonged to Europeans, who constituted only 20 percent of the South African population.

To ensure that the ideology of different racial development was mapped geographically, the government created Bantu homelands, otherwise called Bantustans, in response to international criticism of apartheid and in conformity with the growing African nationalism throughout the African continent and calls for self-government. The H. F. Verwoerd government seemingly sought, under the slogan of "Separate Development," to empower Africans to govern themselves in their homelands, but in reality the purpose of these Bantustans was to make Africans foreigners on their own land and dependent on white leadership within an African Commonwealth. Transkei became the first self-governed homeland, and others followed soon after. However, these hometowns were never viable (Furlong 387).

The 1950 Group Acts, on the other hand, further segregated residential areas along racial lines and classified the population as Colored, African, or white. It made racially coded identity cards compulsory and included, for the first time, women and Coloreds in the pass laws (Furlong 385). Besides having to endure residential restrictions, Africans were also restricted professionally. The 1911 Mines and Works Acts limited the nature of the jobs they could obtain. Skilled labor was the province of whites only. The government banned interracial unions, and in 1937, it outright prohibited Africans from belonging to a registered trade union. (This act was later slightly relaxed by the Native Labor Acts, which allowed Africans to create their own unions.)

Africans were not only barred from owning land and denied equal employment; they were also politically disenfranchised. Coloreds could vote in the Cape Colony in 1936, but the Representation of Natives Act removed them from the common roll and created a separate African roll. Africans, unfortunately, could be represented only by whites. Although Africans were given a semblance of power through the advisory Native Representative Council, the recommendations of this organ were generally ignored. The Bantu Authorities Act was replaced by 1951. To contain African activists and liberal Europeans, the Suppression of Communism Act, permitting the blacklisting of citizens and allowing media censorship, was introduced, and civil rights were further limited through the Public Safety Act and the Criminal Law Amendment.

If residential segregation was a major concern for the Afrikaner community, social segregation was even more important. Hence, interracial marriage was prohibited through the Prohibition of Mixed Marriages Act. This act was further extended, according to Gideon S. Were, under the Immorality (Amendment) Act. The restriction "was extended to physical love between white and non-white men and women, referring to it as 'irregular carnal intercourse'" (172). This act was not new but only legalized earlier practices. The law had existed in the Cape Colony, where it was introduced in the nineteenth century by the British, who later repealed it. But Afrikaners maintained this law in their colony and, in 1910, at the formation of the Union. These restrictions were again repealed in 1952, but the government introduced even more constricting pass laws, which limited the mobility of Africans.

The education of Africans was tailored to meet the ideological needs of the European community. The education of Africans, according to Were, quoting Dr. Verwoerd, "was to 'train and teach people in accordance with their opportunities in life'" (174). Referring to the *Oxford History of South Africa,* Were claims that the Bantu Education Act of 1949 "recommended that Afrikaans and English be taught from the very beginning but 'in such a way that the Bantu child will be able to find his way in European communities; to follow oral or written instructions; and to carry on a simple conversation with Europeans about his work and other subjects of common interest'" (174). Higher education was prohibited for Africans for fear that they would become more aware of their condition. Education reinforced Africans' inferiority, limited their professional competitiveness, fostered parochialism, and encouraged ethnicity. Modeled on South African racial ideologies, the Extension of University Education Act of 1959 extended educational apartheid, which was formalized for public schools in the 1905 Cape School Board Act, through the creation of African, Colored, and Asian universities. Because of the fear that uneducated European South Africans would compete with Africans for skilled jobs, the white educational system was reformed and emphasis was placed on farming and industry technology. The Apprenticeship Act of 1922, which stipulated that one had to have eight years of schooling to be employed in an industry, further protected white employment and ensured that skilled labor remained exclusively the province of whites.

Increasing internal and external pressures compelled the South African government to review its policies. To resolve the racial problem in South Africa, the more liberal branch of the Nationalist Party (NP), decided, in the best interest of the country, to elevate Africans to junior partners in an NP-dominated state. The election of P. W. Botha, in 1978, after the scandal over Botha's misuse of government funds had led to his ouster, brought even more changes. He created numerous investigative commissions, legalized African and nonracial trade unions, integrated many public amenities, and tacitly allowed Africans to own property. "By 1985," writes Furlong, "even the old 'sacred cows,' the laws against interracial sex or marriage, had been repealed. The abolition of the pass laws followed in 1986" (389). Botha worked to make the homelands truly independent and to integrate Indians and Coloreds into the government, but with no success, since they and the Africans, excluded from even token participation in the government, refused to participate. The nonwhite boycott of the 1984 elections resulted in the creation of the United Democratic Front (UDF). Botha also attempted to eliminate some discriminatory employment laws but these attempts also failed. The coups in the homelands made his insurgency politics ineffective. White death squads terrorized the townships, and white opposition to military conscription rose. Botha's strategy to divide the black community failed, since the blacks were not corruptible as he had assumed; instead, they became more vocal. In 1989, he was finally forced out of power following a stroke and was succeeded by F. W. de Klerk.

In 1990, de Klerk reinstated the ANC, the PAC, and the SACP. He freed Nelson Mandela and supported the creation of a new constitution that would grant political rights to all South Africans, with special clauses protecting the rights of white minorities. The ANC-Communist alliance accepted the new propositions. But Mangusuto Buthelezi's Inkatha movement and the African state Bophuthatswana were not supportive of this move. De Klerk repealed the Separate Amenities Act, the 1913 Lands Act, and the Population Registration Act and opened the membership in the NP to Coloreds and Indians. These actions were not favorably received by the white community, so white-instigated black-on-black violence increased in the townships and between Inkatha, backed by the government, and the ANC. The increasing violence in the townships eventually led to an interracial conference. The talks did not result in immediate action because of differences in ideology; the ANC wanted immediate majority rule, whereas NP desired a protracted transition, with the party playing a major role. Ultimately, after much violence, the incorporation of Bophuthatswana, the last homeland, into South Africa, and the agreement by Buthelezi and Afrikaner generals to participate in the elections, Mandela became president of South Africa and formed a government of National Unity. The beginnings of this new government were not without their difficulties. There were massive unemployment, strikes, a slow return of capital, and fear among whites that they would lose their position of privilege (Furlong 399). Apartheid was finally vanquished, and the Truth and Reconciliation Commission (TRC) "offered a compelling alternative to the spectacle of show trials of those accused of atrocities under the old regime" (400). Finally, in 1999, Mandela retired and was succeeded by his deputy, Thabo Mbeki. Yet, much remains to be done as South Africa traces its path toward unity, equal rights, and prosperity, since Africans continue to be discriminated against in landownership, racism remains resilient despite some changes, whites continue to control the country's economy, and AIDS has become a major plague and political issue.

This historical survey provides a background to Alan Paton's *Cry, the Beloved Country.* In order to understand the period described in the novel, the 1940s,one needs to understand the factors and events that created the fictional present. While Alan Paton could only surmise what the future of South Africa might be, the future is now the present, so the mystery raised at the end of the novel has been unraveled.

FROM W.H.I. BLEEK, *THE NATAL DIARIES OF DR. W.H.I. BLEEK 1855–1856*

(TRANS. O. H. SPOHR. CAPE TOWN: PUBLISHED FOR THE FRIENDS OF THE SOUTH AFRICAN LIBRARY BY A. A. BALKEMA, 1965: 21–24)

This excerpt, from the German linguist who researched San language and folklore, provides understanding of the scholarly discussion on the nature and origins of the indigenous people of Southern Africa, as well as the ethnological assumptions that undergird the assumptions.

Early in October 1855, it became known that Sir George Grey in his capacity as High Commissioner of South Africa, would visit Natal soon.

We can safely assume that when Bleek heard of the imminent arrival of Sir George he suspended his fieldwork in the mountains of Natal and returned to Pieter-Maritzburg. By that time Bleek had already become acquainted with the published parts of the 'Record' and a recent pamphlet by Donald Moodie; 'A Voice from the Kahlamba. [57] Moodie was anxious to resume the publication and possibly the reprinting of the **'**Record**'.** Bleek was still a budding African explorer. They joined forces in producing a pamphlet: 'Cape History and Science**'.** [55]

Bleek's letter in support of Moodie's plea is by far the greater part of the pamphlet. It is at the same time the first contribution by Bleek printed in South Africa.

The parts contained in Mr. Moodie's tiny pamphlet are reprinted here in full (Moodie's underlining has been printed bold):

Extract from a Letter (3rd Nov., 1855) from W.H.J. Bleak, Esq, P.D., to D. Moodie, Compiler of the Cape Records.

> "But, however this may be, nobody will deny that the Hottentots are a most curious and interesting nation, and have accordingly always attracted attention to the journals of the travellers from whom our information is derived.
>
> But all that can be gathered from this source is very inferior indeed, both in its amount, and in its intrinsic value, to what may be collected from the Cape Records. * * *
>
> Consisting as they do, of words written at the time and on the spot, they cannot but contain such a mass of reliable detail, as no mere traveller, or private individual, could have procured.
>
> I can, therefore, conceive no undertaking better calculated to give a thorough insight into South African ethnography, than the publication of these Records. * * * And I cannot but consider it a great loss to the history of this colony, and to that of its inhabitants, that circumstances obliged you to discontinue your work.

The object was, indeed, rather historical and political than ethnological or scientific. Yet I beg to assure you, that **I never met with a book that appeared to me of so much value for imparting an accurate knowledge of the ethnography of Southern Africa, and none so rich in facts. . . .**

To what account they may be turned in this respect, may be seen from the two chapters of 'South African Annals,' which you have lately issued.

Your 'Voice from the Kahlamba' elucidates the origin of a people, whom a mistaken theory, suggested by philanthropic zeal, had represented as the product of European oppression, within the last two centuries.

You have clearly shown how unfounded has been this supposition; and how satisfactorily these authentic documents set forth that the Bushmen already existed at, and before the very beginning of the Cape settlement, and long before any oppression could have begun there.

The manner in which you have proved this fact needs, I think, no further and it seems almost superfluous to say, that I believe that whatever new evidence can be gathered on the subject, will only tend to set your statements in fuller light.

As regards my proper department, the philological branch, I can assure you that, without being at all aware of the conclusion to which your researches led, the scanty information I was able to collect (from the vocabularies of Lichtenstein and others) concerning the Bushman language, had already impressed me with the same view of the case.

All the other Hottentot dialects—such as those of the Namaquas, Korannas, and others, are very much alike, whereas the Bushman tongue is so distinct from them, that we cannot even consider it as perfectly proved that both belong to the same family of languages. * * *

There can now be no doubt whatever, that the existence of the Bushmen dates long before European civilization began its work at the Cape. This fact alone accounts for the wide dispersion of these children of the desert, whom we find not only along the inhospitable western coast. (I believe as far north as the 19th degree of south latitude), but also throughout the Kaligari, and beyond the lake Ngami.

Dr Livingstone, who penetrated into the far interior, beyond the 10th degree of south latitude, is said to have met them, scattered the whole way, so far north.

There are many curious questions connected with this tribe (or rather with these tribes), and their peculiarities well deserve the particular attention of ethnological enquirers.

A very interesting account of them is given by the Rev. Robert Moffat, In his 'Missionary Labours and Scenes in South Africa', and his testimony with regard to the Origin of the Bushmen quite coincides with what is proved in your 'Voice from the Kahlamba'.

He says (p.7)—'That the Bushmen are the people from whom the Hottentot tribes have descended, is irreconcileable with existing facts; that they are a distinct race is still further from probability; and that **they are plundered**

Hottentots, is, in my humble opinion, a preposterous notion, resulting from limited information on the subject.

'If this were to be admitted, then we must also admit that the Hottentots, in being deprived of their cattle, and becoming Bushmen, were deprived of their language also; for it is well known, from the earliest records that can be obtained, on the subject of their language (which has, in addition to the **click** of the Hottentots, a croaking in the throat), **that they never understood each other without interpreters'.** * * *

That the Bushmen never possessed domestic cattle (always excepting the two kinds—"a dog and a louse," specified by Van der Walt) is asserted by the oldest records, as well as by almost all the travellers, missionaries, and colonists.

At page 63, Mr Moffat gives their own tradition on the subject, and, as his account shows the **conservative** character of these people in full, I shall quote it. 'I know' (says Mr M.) 'an individual who was struck with the difficulty which the Bushwomen had in rearing their infants, after the term of suckling, from the entire absence of any thing in the shape of mill or grain. Dried meat, or ixia bulbs, is hard fare for a babe. He tried to persuade them to purchase goats with ostrich feathers, or the skins of game procured in the chase. At this proposal they laughed inordinately, **asking him if ever their forefathers kept cattle? intimating that they were not intended to keep, but to eat, as their progenitors had always done.'**

It would occupy too great space in this letter to quote from Mr M. more interesting particulars illustrative of the ethnography of the Bushmen; nor have I been able to find time to compare them with the accounts of other missionaries and travellers, and particularly with all the very valuable details contained in the 'Records'.

I must add, that fully as I agree with the arguments by which you have proved your case in your little book, I cannot fall in with one of your statements. I do not believe that European ethnologists, generally, place much reliance upon the testimony of certain excited parties; or that they ever, to any extent, favored the opinion that the Bushmen, through European oppression, had descended from the pastoral to the hunting state.

Still, from the great ignorance that prevails in Europe generally, as to African geography and history, we should not be surprised when we meet the grossest misrepresentations in ordinary writers, when those most justly eminent-have fallen into the gravest errors.

For instance, take the following sentences:

> 'We shall not be very much surprised by the fact, that the idiom of the degraded Bushmen (whom Linneus identified with the ourang-outang) cruelly hunted down by the Hottentots and Kafirs, can be traced to a corrupt Hottentot language; and that the Hottentot language itself, is only a degraded dialect of the noble language of Sechuana, and other branches of the Kafir tribes, the oppressors of the Hottentots.'

And again:
'The language of the Bushmen, as before mentioned, is a degraded Hottentot language, and their language is probably only a depravation of the noble Kafir tongue.'

It will be clear to any one, who knows but a little of the nature of the Kafir and Hottentot languages, that these positions are utterly wrong. Yet this was written by a man who has done, I may say, more than any other living man for African discoveries and researches, who is himself an eminent scholar, in different branches of literature, and who, in addition to a warm interest in all philological and ethnological studies, possessed certainly the best opportunities for acquiring every kind of information on such topics.

That Chevalier Bunsen—whose name I cannot pronounce without feelings of the deepest respect and gratitude—should have fallen into such a mistake, speaks sufficiently of the confused ideas generally entertained (see note 12)."

FROM FERDINAND KRAUSS, *TRAVEL/CAPE TO ZULULAND; OBSERVATIONS BY A COLLECTOR AND A NATURALIST, 1830–40*

(ED. O. H. SPOHR. CAPE TOWN: PUBLISHED FOR THE FRIENDS OF THE SOUTH AFRICAN LIBRARY BY A. A. BALKEMA, 1973: 71–72)

This excerpt provides insight into European dispossession of chiefs' power alluded to by John Kumalo in *Cry, the Beloved Country* and into the ways the natives were subjugated and robbed of their land and cattle.

Towards the evening of October 25th, the waggon arrived with the rest of the members of the commission; three other Afrikaaners had joined them. The wagon outspanned near Mpanda's kraal and Landdrost Roos and van Breda immediately went to Mpanda's hut to greet him. He received them in a friendly manner although they felt that his welcome was not as hearty as at the time of his visit to the Congella camp. They therefore refrained from entering into negotiations that same evening, especially as it was already rather late.

The evening was even more sultry than the day; the wind was burning hot, and when night came we had a terrible thunderstorm with heavy rain, which lasted the whole night. We protected ourselves under our tent as well as possible, and each slept with a loaded gun beside him.

The next morning we prepared everything for the reception of Mpanda: in front of the hut the tri-coloured flag, red, white and blue, but distinct from the French or Dutch flag, was hoisted. After we had taken up our places without arms, Mpanda was called to the tent. As interpreter we had a young Kaffir, who had been with Veldcornet Jan Meyer for a long time and spoke Dutch and Zulu fluently.

After Mpanda had arrived and sat down on his chair, which a servant had carried after him, Landdrost Roos presented him with a blue flowered coat and a scimitar as gifts with which he immediately adorned himself.

Roes then questioned him on these main points: whether he wanted to be and remain an ally and friend of the Afrikaaners in Natal; submit to their laws; not start any war with another nation without the consent of the Afrikaaners; cease killing his own people without thorough investigation and sufficient grounds; whether he was prepared to compensate the Boers with cattle, horses, etc stolen by his brother Dingaan. Further whether he would leave his new present dwelling place between the Umdloti and Umvoti rivers, where he had come after the defeat of his brother Dingaan and return to the Tugela river, etc.

Mpanda accepted all points. He was then told to call his three best friends and chiefs, and to ask them: whether they recognised Mpanda as their king, would obey him, and stand by him unto death.

Furthermore they were told that they had to vouch for Mpanda's life and that they had to prevent all fights over robbery of women and cattle. They affirmed everything, which satisfied Mpanda greatly.

After an hour's conference Mpanda returned to his hut, promising that he would celebrate the day with festive dances, and he gathered 4000 Kaffirs in a circle about 200 feet from our tent. After we had waited an hour for Mpanda's return, there was a commotion outside, and we learned to our surprise that they were busy battering and killing one of the three indunas who had been in our tent, and whom they thought was a friend of Dingaan's and a spy. I immediately hurried out and was just in time to see that they had smashed his skull.

We were very upset by this incident. Landdrost Roos immediately called the king, who arrived somewhat embarrassed. He asked whether he knew about this murder; he denied this, but soon afterwards he betrayed himself by telling us that he had given the order to kill him three days before.

This was rather inconsistent with his action of a few hours before, when he had called the same man into our *camp* as his friend. This put us on our guard, and we realised how little one could depend on the word of a Kaffir. Roos enquired from Mpanda, how he could allow a murder to happen in the presence of our commission, which had come specifically on a peaceful mission. Mpanda's excuse was that it had not been his will. It seemed, however, that the rival group of this chief had taken the occasion of our presence to carry out the murder, because this induna still had some supporters.

Meanwhile all the Kaffirs had sat down in a tight semi-circle around our tent and Mpanda addressed them, walking up and down between them with great dignity. Raising his voice he warned them not to murder any more in future, and said that this was to be the last murder. He reproached them for having done this in our presence and said that they had disgraced him. Some Zulu kept on rising and tried to prove that this chief had deserved his fate as he had treated them badly. Mpanda listened quietly to their speeches but replied frequently. Mpanda showed a dignified and imperious attitude in front of his people, and his speeches, warnings and commands did not fail to influence his audience. Nevertheless there was no servility towards the king everyone could have his say, and spoke with a loud voice, clearly and convincingly.

To end their debate and to avoid the possibility of further unpleasant situations, Roos told Mpanda that he would like to see his people happy now and that they should dance. On a given sign the Zulu lumped with raised sticks, shrill whistles and dull humming some hundred yards backwards and rushed back to the tent again, where they arranged themselves in a half circle. The dance started with a monotonous sing-song and stamping of their feet to an exact rhythm; at the same time they raised their sticks, making a quick forward and backward movement of their shoulders.

The stamping of the 4000 Zulu was so terrific that the ground trembled. From time to time they rested, and people glorifying the ruler took over. These were usually clever young men, who praised the king, his good character, his large cattleherds, the large number of his followers and the greatness of his country etc while jumping and gesticulating along the rows of the other Kaffirs, who applauded by gestures, screams and waving their hands and sticks. After the dance was finished, another similar one started in which they continuously repeated the word 'congo'. Finally the women joined the dance. During this dance Mpanda sat on his chair in the middle of the semicircle and the members of the commission took their stand around him. At Mpanda's request we fired a salute with our guns at the beginning of the dance; the Zulu, however, were not frightened in the least and did not bat an eyelid. Towards evening it started to rain, and the Zulu went home to their different kraals, from where they had been called.

The next morning Roos had another conference with Mpanda, which dealt mainly with the cattle Mpanda had presented to him and the others. They did not want to accept the cattle as their own but wanted it to be distributed among the Boers as a sort of national claim. This was quite impossible to explain to Mpanda; he felt offended because he felt they did not want to accept his present.

This and other reasons made Roos terminate the conference, and as we thought it not advisable to remain any longer in his kraal, we immediately set off on our return journey and arrived safely at the Congella Camp on October 28th.

ANC YOUTH LEAGUE MANIFESTO—1944

(Online posting at <http://www.africawithin.com/mandela/ancyl_manifesto.htm>)

The ANC Youth League Manifesto is also an important document in that it changed the nature and the methods of the ANC struggle for freedom. It sought change within the organization and advocated initiatives and actions conceived from the perspective of the people. This political vision is encapsulated in *Cry, the Beloved Country* through the demonstrator's *Nkosi Sikelel' IAfrika.*

The Manifesto was issued by the Provisional Committee of the ANC Youth League in March 1944. Nelson Mandela was a founder member of the Youth League and participated in the drafting of this manifesto.

Preamble

WHEREAS Africanism must be promoted i.e. Africans must struggle for development, progress and national liberation so as to occupy their rightful and honourable place among nations of the world;

AND WHEREAS African Youth must be united, consolidated, trained and disciplined because from their ranks future leaders will be recruited;

AND WHEREAS a resolution was passed by the conference of the African National Congress held in Bloemfontein in 1943, authorising the founding and establishment of the Congress Youth League;

WE therefore assume the responsibility of laying the foundations of the said Youth League.

Statement of Policy

South Africa has a complex problem. Stated briefly it is: The contact of the White race with the Black has resulted in the emergence of a set of conflicting living conditions and outlooks on life which seriously hamper South Africa's progress to nationhood.

The White race, possessing superior military strength and at present having superior organising skill has arrogated to itself the ownership of the land and invested itself with authority and the right to regard South Africa as a White man's country. This has meant that the African, who owned the land before the advent of the Whites, has been deprived of all security which may guarantee him an independent pursuit of destiny or ensure his leading a free and unhampered life. He has been defeated in the field of battle but refuses to accept this as meaning that he must be oppressed, just to enable the White man to further dominate him.

The African regards Civilisation as the common heritage of all Mankind and claims as full a right to make his contribution to its advancement and to live free as any White South African: further, he claims the right to all sources and agencies to enjoy rights and fulfill duties which will place him on a footing of equality with every other South African racial group.

The majority of White men regard it as the destiny of the White race to dominate the man of colour. The harshness of their domination, however, is rousing in the African feelings of hatred of everything that bars his way to full and free citizenship and these feelings can no longer be suppressed.

In South Africa, the conflict has emerged as one of race on the one side and one of ideals on the other. The White man regards the Universe as a gigantic machine hurtling through time and space to its final destruction: individuals in it are but tiny organisms with private lives that lead to private deaths: personal power, success and fame are the absolute measures of values; the things to live for. This outlook on life divides the Universe into a host of individual little entities which cannot help being in constant conflict thereby hastening the approach of the hour of their final destruction.

The African, on his side, regards the Universe as one composite whole; an organic entity, progressively driving towards greater harmony and unity whose individual parts exist merely as interdependent aspects of one whole realising their fullest life in the corporate life where communal contentment is the absolute measure of values. His philosophy of life strives towards unity and aggregation; towards greater social responsibility.

These divergences are not simplified by the fact that the two major races are on two different planes of achievement in the Civilisation of the West. This is taken advantage of to 'civilise' the African with a view to making him a perpetual minor. This obstruction of his progress is disguised as letting him 'develop along his own lines'. He is, however, suspicious of any 'lines' of development imposed on him from above and elects to develop along what the Natives' Representative Council[1] recently called the 'lines of his own choosing'.

In practice these divergences and conflicts work to the disadvantage of the African. South Africa's two million Whites are highly organised and are bound together by firm ties. They view South African problems through the perspective of Race destiny; that is the belief that the White race is the destined ruler and leader of the world for all time. This has made it imperative for the African to view his problems and those of his country through the perspective of Race. Viewing problems from the angle of Race destiny, the White man acts as one group in relations between Black and White. Small minorities view South African problems through the perspective of Human destiny. These number among their ranks the few Whites who value Man as Man and as above Colour. Yet these are so few that their influence on national policies is but little felt.

The advantages on the side of the Whites enable two million White men to control and dominate with ease eight million Africans and to own 87 per cent of the land while the Africans scrape a meagre existence on the remaining 13 per cent. The White man means to hold to these gains at all costs and to consolidate his position, has segregated the African in the State, the Church, in Industry, Commerce etc., in all these relegating him to an inferior position where, it is believed, the African will never menace White domination.

Trusteeship

To mislead the world and make it believe that the White man in South Africa is helping the African on the road to civilised life, the White man has arrogated to himself the title and role of Trustee for the African people.

The effects of Trusteeship alone have made the African realise that Trusteeship has meant, as it still means, the consolidation by the White man of his position at the expense of the African people, so that by the time national awakening opens the eyes of the African people to the bluff they live under, White domination should be secure and unassailable.

A hurried glance at legislation passed by the Trustees for the African during the last forty years shows what a bluff Trusteeship is. The very Act of Union[2] itself established as a legal right the claim of the White man to dominate the man of colour. It did not recognise the African as a citizen of the then newly formed Union; it regarded him as a beggar at the gate.

This was followed by the 1913 Land Act which deprived the African of Land and Land Security and in that way incapacitated him for that assertion of his will to be free which might otherwise have been inspired by assured security and fixed tenure. The Act drove him into urban areas where he soon made his way to skilled trades etc. But the Trustees had not brought him to urban areas to civilise him by opening to him avenues to skilled work. They had brought him so that he might be a cheap and nearby reserve of unskilled labour. This was finally established by the Colour Bar Act[3] which shuts Africans from skilled trades etc., thereby blocked their way to Civilisation via these channels.

In 1923 the Trustees passed the Urban Areas Act and this measure as amended warned Africans clearly that they were bidding farewell to freedom.

This Act imposed forms of control on the Africans which would have stirred into revolt any other section of the population. But because the Africans were not organised they yielded to more oppression and allowed themselves to be 'controlled' from birth to the grave. This control had the effect of forcing Africans to remain impotent under unhealthy urban conditions which were set up to add their due to the ruining of the African's resistance to disease. The legalised slums, politely called Native Locations, were one aspect of these conditions.

But the Trustees were not satisfied with the emasculation of an entire community. In the 1927 Native Administration Act,[4] they established the White race as the Supreme Chief of the African people. The conquest of the African was complete.

As the African accepted none of these measures to 'civilise' him without a struggle, the Trustees had always been worried by his prospects as long as the Cape Franchise remained. With little compunction, in 1936 the last door to citizenship was slammed in the face of the African by the Natives Representation Act which gave us three White men to represent eight million Africans in a house of 150 representing two million Whites. At the same time a Land Act was passed to ensure that if the 1913 Land Act had left any openings for the African, then the Natives Land and Trust Act would seal them in the name of 'humanity and Modern Civilisation'.

The 1937 Native Laws Amendment Act closed up any other loophole through which the African could have forced his way to full citizenship. Today, Trusteeship has made every African a criminal still out of prison. For all this we had to thank the philosophy of Trusteeship.

While Trustees have been very vocal in their solicitations for the African their deeds have shown clearly that talk of Trusteeship is an eyewash for the Civilised world and an empty platitude to soothe Africans into believing that after all oppression is a pleasant experience under Christian democratic rule. Trusteeship mentality is doing one thing and that very successfully, to drive the African steadily to extermination. Low wages, bad housing, inadequate health facilities, 'Native education', mass exploitation, unfixed security on land and halfhearted measures to improve the African's living conditions are all instruments and tools with which the path to African extermination is being paved.

But Africans rejects the theory that because he is non-White and because he is a conquered race, he must be exterminated. He demands the right to be a free citizen in the South African democracy; the right to an unhampered pursuit of his national destiny and the freedom to make his legitimate contribution to human advancement.

For the last two hundred years he has striven to adapt himself to changing conditions, and has made every exertion to discover and derive the maximum benefits from the claims of the White man that they are his Trustees. Instead of meeting with encouragement commensurate with his eagerness and goodwill, he has been saddled with a load of oppression dating from the unprovoked wars of the last century and now containing such choice discriminating legislation as the 1913 Land Act, and such benefits of Trusteeship as official harshness which recently attempted to hang an African under the very roof of the very State Department established to protect him and guide him on his way to civilisation, just because he could not answer questions as quickly as the impatience of the Pass Office Trustees wanted.

In this very war[5] South Africa is fighting against oppression and for Freedom; a war in which she has committed herself to the principle of freedom for all. In spite of this, however, it would be the highest folly to believe that after the war South Africa will treat the Africans as citizens with the right to live free. South African blood—of Whites and Africans alike—has been shed to free the White peoples of Europe while Africans within the Union remain in bondage.

For his loyalty to the cause of human freedom and for his sacrifices in life, cash and kind, he has been promised a 'Suspense Account'—another way of telling him that, in spite of all he has done for his country in its hour of darkest need, for him there will be no freedom from fear and want.

Loss of Faith in Trusteeship

These conditions have made the African lose all faith in all talk of Trusteeship. HE NOW ELECTS TO DETERMINE HIS FUTURE BY HIS OWN EFFORTS. He has realised that to trust to the mere good grace of the White man will not free him, as no nation can free an oppressed group other than that group itself.

Self-determination is the philosophy of life which will save him from the disaster he clearly sees on his way—disaster to which Discrimination, Segregation, Pass Laws and Trusteeship are all ruthlessly and inevitably driving him.

The African is aware of the magnitude of the task before him, but has learnt that promises, no matter from what high source, are merely palliatives intended to drum him into yielding to more oppression. He has made up his mind to sweat for his freedom; determine his destiny himself and THROUGH HIS AFRICAN NATIONAL CONGRESS IS BUILDING A STRONG NATIONAL UNITY FRONT WHICH WILL BE HIS SUREST GUARANTEE OF VICTORY OVER OPPRESSION.

The African National Congress

The African National Congress is the symbol and embodiment of the African's will to present a united national front against all forms of oppression, but this has not enabled the movement to advance the national cause in a manner demanded by prevailing conditions. And this, in turn, has drawn on it criticisms in recent times which cannot be ignored if Congress is to fulfill its mission in Africa.

The critics of Congress attribute the inability of Congress in the last twenty years to advance the national cause in a manner commensurate with the demands of the times, to weaknesses in its organisation and constitution, to its erratic policy of yielding to oppression, regarding itself as a body of gentlemen with clean hands, and to failing to see the problems of the African through the proper perspective.

Those critics further allege that in that period Congress declined and became an organisation of the privileged few—some Professionals, Small Traders, a sprinkling of Intellectuals and Conservatives of all grades. This, it is said, imparted to the Congress character taints of reactionism and conservatism which made Congress a movement out of actual touch with the needs of the rank and file of our people.

It is further contended by the critics of Congress that the privileged few who constituted the most vocal elements in Congress strongly resented any curtailment of what they considered their rights and, since the popularisation of the Congress character would have jeopardised or brought about the withdrawal of those rights by the Authorities, Congress was forced to play the dual role of being unconscious police to check the assertion of the popular will on the one hand and, on the other, of constantly warning the authorities that further curtailment of the privileges of the few would compel them, the privileged few, to yield to pressure from the avalanche of popular opinion which was tired of appeasing the Authorities while life became more intolerable.

These privileged few, so the critics of Congress maintain, are not an efficiently organised bloc. Their thinking itself lacks the national bias and this has made Congress a loose association of people who merely react negatively to given conditions, able neither to assert the national will nor to resist it openly. In this connection, Congress is accused of being partly suspicious of progressive thought and action, though it is itself unable to express correctly the views of the mass of the people.

Finally, the critics say that because the privileged few who direct Congress are poorly organised and have no marked following, Congress cannot openly defy popular wishes; hence to maintain its precarious existence, it is compelled to be very vocal against legislation that has harsh effects on the African underdog while it gives no positive lead nor has any constructive programme to enforce the repeal of all oppressive legislation.

Challenge to Youth

Some of these criticisms are founded on fact, it is true, but it does not advance the national cause if people concentrate on these while little or no effort is made to build Congress from within. It is admitted that in the process of our political development, our leadership made certain blunders. It was inevitable that this should have been the case, encompassed as the African people were and still are with forces inimical to their progress. But it does no good to stop at being noisy in condemning African leaders who went before us. Defects in the organisation of the people against oppression cannot be cured by mouthing criticisms and not putting our heads together to build what has been damaged and to find a way out of the present suffering.

Both the oppression and the causes that give rise to the criticisms of Congress cannot be allowed to go on indefinitely. Soon the point must be reached when African Youth, which has lived through oppression from the cradle to the present, calls a halt to it all. That point, happily, is now reached—as witness some of the clear-cut national demands by Youth at the Bloemfontein conference and the formation of Youth movements and political parties. All this is proof that Youth wants action and is in sympathy with the rank and file of our oppressed people. It is all a challenge to Youth to join in force in the national fight against oppression.

In response to the demands of the times African Youth is LAYING ITS SERVICES AT THE DISPOSAL OF THE NATIONAL LIBERATION MOVEMENT, THE AFRICAN NATIONAL CONGRESS, IN THE FIRM BELIEF, KNOWLEDGE AND CONVICTION THAT THE CAUSE OF AFRICA MUST AND WILL TRIUMPH.

Congress Youth League

The formation of the African National Congress Youth League is an answer and assurance to the critics of the national movement that African Youth will not allow the struggles and sacrifices of their fathers to have been in vain. Our fathers fought so that we, better equipped when our time came, should start and continue from where they stopped.

The formation of this League is an attempt on the part of Youth to impart to Congress a truly national character. It is also a protest against the lack of discipline and the absence of a clearly-defined goal in the movement as a whole.

The Congress Youth League must be the brains-trust and power-station of the spirit of African nationalism; the spirit of African self-determination; the spirit that is so discernible in the thinking of our Youth. It must be an organisation where young African men and women will meet and exchange ideas in an atmosphere pervaded by a common hatred of oppression.

At this power-station the league will be a co-ordinating agency for all youthful forces employed in rousing popular political consciousness and fighting oppression and reaction. It will educate the people politically by concentrating its energies on the African homefront to make all sections of our people Congress minded and nation-conscious. . . .

The Congress Progressive Group will stand for certain clear-cut national ideals within Congress; it will stand for specialisation within the national movement, to reinforce the latter's representative character and to consolidate the national unity front; it will keep a vigilant eye on all un-national tendencies on the national unity front and in Congress policies.

We must be honest enough to realise that neither Congress nor the African people can make progress as one amorphous mass. At a certain stage we must cultivate specialised political attitudes. Failure to recognise this will wreck Congress and encourage revolts from it until it ceases to be a force in national politics.

By recognising this fact, Youth does not confess sympathy with those who revolted against the national movement. These failed to realise that the formation of parties out of Congress was a serious weakening of the national unity front. They recognised the fact that Congress is a national liberation movement but were not sufficiently experienced politically to form their party within the national fold and to develop opposition from within, while strengthening the national unity front. . . .

THE IDEAL OF NATIONAL UNITY MUST BE THE GUIDING IDEAL OF EVERY YOUNG AFRICAN'S LIFE

Our Creed

a. We believe in the divine destiny of nations.

b. The goal of all our struggles is Africanism and our motto is 'AFRICA'S CAUSE MUST TRIUMPH'.

c. We believe that the national liberation of Africans will be achieved by Africans themselves. We reject foreign leadership of Africa.

d. We may borrow useful ideologies from foreign ideologies, but we reject the wholesale importation of foreign ideologies into Africa.

e. We believe that leadership must be the personification and symbol of popular aspirations and ideals.

f. We believe that practical leadership must be given to capable men, whatever their status in society.

g. We believe in the scientific approach to all African problems.

h. We combat moral disintegration among Africans by maintaining and upholding high ethical standards ourselves.

i. We believe in the unity of all Africans from the Mediterranean Sea in the North to the Indian and Atlantic oceans in the South—and that Africans must speak with one voice. . . .

NKOSI SIKELEL' IAFRIKA

(Online posting at <http://www.polity.org.za/html/misc/nkosi.html?rebookmark = 1#hist>)

Nkosi Sikelel' IAfrika is sung by the demonstrator in *Cry, the Beloved Country.* This young man is an embodiment of the politicized revolutionary youths of 1940s South Africa; he expresses the desires of Africans for justice and equity. This song, about the suffering of Africans in Johannesburg, was composed by Enoch Sontonga in 1897, and Samuel E. Mqhayi added more stanzas in 1927. It was sung at concerts and at political rallies as an act of defiance. It became one of two South African anthems until it was combined with *Die Stem* (Call of South Africa), in 1996.

Classic Xhosa Version

The first verse and chorus of this version are the original words composed by Sontonga in 1897. The remaining verses were added in 1927 by Samuel E [sic] Mqhayi.

Nkosi, sikelel' iAfrika;
Malupakam'upondo lwayo;

Yiva imitandazo yetu
Usisikelele.
Chorus
Yihla Moya, Yihla Moya,
Yihla Moya Oyingcwele
Sikelela iNkosi zetu;
Zimkumbule umDali wazo;
Zimoyike zezimhlouele,
Azisikelele.
Sikelel' amadol' esizwe,
Sikelela kwa nomlisela
Ulitwal'ilizwe ngomonde,
Uwusikilele.
Sikelel'amakosikazi;
Nawo onk'amanenekazi;
Pakamisa wonk'umtinjana
Uwusikilele.
Sikelela abafundisi
Bemvaba zonke zelilizwe;
Ubatwese ngoMoya Wako
Ubasikelele.
Sikelel'ulimo nemfuyo;
Gxota zonk'indlala nezifo;
Zalisa ilizwe ngempilo
Ulisikelele
Sikelel'amalinga etu
Awomanyana nokuzaka,
Awemfundo nemvisiswano
Uwasikelele.
Nkosi Sikelel' iAfrika;
Cima bonk' ubugwenxa bayo
Nezigqito, nezono zayo
Uyisikelele.

God Bless Africa

Original Lovedale English Translation

Lord, bless Africa;
May her horn rise high up;
Hear Thou our prayers And bless us.
Chorus
Descend, O Spirit,
Descend, O Holy Spirit.

Bless our chiefs
May they remember their Creator.
Fear Him and revere Him,
That He may bless them.
Bless the public men,
Bless also the youth
That they may carry the land with patience
and that Thou mayst bless them.
Bless the wives
And also all young women;
Lift up all the young girls
And bless them.
Bless the ministers
of all the churches of this land;
Endue them with Thy Spirit
And bless them.
Bless agriculture and stock raising
Banish all famine and diseases;
Fill the land with good health
And bless it.
Bless our efforts
of union and self-uplift,
Of education and mutual understanding
And bless them.
Lord, bless Africa
Blot out all its wickedness
And its transgressions and sins,
And bless it.

THE FREEDOM CHARTER

(Online posting at <http://www.anc.org.za/ancdocs/history/charter.html>)

The Freedom Charter is an important document in South African history, since it advocates universal freedom for all in a decolonized South Africa. South Africa was granted independence in 1910 by Great Britain, but it continued to be a colony, since this independence was granted to only a minority of people. This document incorporates the desire for freedom, equity, and justice sought by all South Africans as expressed through the manifesto of the ANC Youth group, the miners' strike of 1946, and the African Claims and Bills of Rights of 1945.

Adopted at the Congress of the People, Kliptown, South Africa, on 26 June 1955

WE, THE PEOPLE OF SOUTH AFRICA, DECLARE FOR ALL OUR COUNTRY AND THE WORLD TO KNOW:

that South Africa belongs to all who live in it, black and white, and that no government can justly claim authority unless it is based on the will of all the people:

that our people have been robbed of their birthright to land, liberty and peace by a form of government founded on injustice and inequality; that our country will never be prosperous or free until all our people live in brotherhood, enjoying equal rights and opportunities; that only a democratic state, based on the will of all the people, can secure to all their birthright without distinction of colour, race, sex or belief;

And therefore, we the people of South Africa, black and white together—equals, countrymen and brothers—adopt this Freedom Charter. And we pledge ourselves to strive together, sparing neither strength nor courage, until the democratic changes set out here have been won.

The People Shall Govern!

Every man and woman shall have the right to vote for and to stand as a candidate for all bodies which make laws;

All people shall be entitled to take part in the administration of the country;

The rights of the people shall be the same, regardless of race, colour or sex;

All bodies of minority rule, advisory boards, councils and authorities shall be replaced by democratic organs of self-government.

All National Groups Shall Have Equal Rights!

There shall be equal status in the bodies of state, in the courts and in the schools for all national groups and races;

All people shall have equal right to use their own languages, and to develop their own folk culture and customs;

All national groups shall be protected by law against insults to their race and national pride;

The preaching and practice of national, race or colour discrimination and contempt shall be a punishable crime;

All apartheid laws and practices shall be set aside.

The People Shall Share in the Country's Wealth!

The national wealth of our country, the heritage of all South Africans, shall be restored to the people;

The mineral wealth beneath the soil, the Banks and monopoly industry shall be transferred to the ownership of the people as a whole;

All other industry and trade shall be controlled to assist the well-being of the people;

All people shall have equal rights to trade where they choose, to manufacture and to enter all trades, crafts and professions.

The Land Shall be Shared Among Those Who Work IT!

Restrictions of land ownership on a racial basis shall be ended and all the land redivided amongst those who work it, to banish famine and land hunger;

The state shall help the peasants with implements, seed, tractors and dams to save the soil and assist the tillers;

Freedom of movement shall be guaranteed to all who work on the land;

All shall have the right to occupy land wherever they choose;

People shall not be robbed of their cattle, and forced labour and farm prisons shall be abolished.

All Shall be Equal Before the Law!

No one shall be imprisoned, deported or restricted without a fair trial;

No one shall be condemned by the order of any Government official;

The courts shall be representative of all the people;

Imprisonment shall be only for serious crimes against the people, and shall aim at re-education, not vengeance;

The police force and army shall be open to all on an equal basis and shall be the helpers and protectors of the people;

All laws which discriminate on grounds of race, colour or belief shall be repealed.

All Shall Enjoy Equal Human Rights!

The law shall guarantee to all their right to speak, to organize, to meet together, to publish, to preach, to worship and to educate their children;

The privacy of the house from police raids shall be protected by law;

All shall be free to travel without restriction from countryside to town, from province to province, and from South Africa to abroad.

Pass Laws, permits, and all other laws restricting these freedoms shall be abolished.

There Shall be Work and Security!

All who work shall be free to form trade unions, to elect their officers and to make wage agreements with their employers;

The state shall recognize the right and duty of all to work, and to draw full unemployment benefits:

Men and women of all races shall receive equal pay for equal work;

There shall be a forty-hour working week, a national minimum wage, paid annual leave, and sick leave for all workers, and maternity leave on full pay for all working mothers;

Miners, domestic workers, farm workers, and civil servants shall have the same rights as all others who work;

Child labour, compound labour, the tot system and contract labour shall be abolished.

The Doors of Learning and of Culture Shall be Opened!

The government shall discover, develop and encourage national talent for the enhancement of our cultural life:

All the cultural treasures of mankind shall be open to all, by free exchange of books, ideas and contacts with other lands;

The aim of education shall be to teach the youth to love their people and their culture, to honour human brotherhood, liberty and peace;

Education shall be free, compulsory, universal and equal for all children;

Higher education and technical training shall be opened to all by means of state allowances and scholarships awarded on the basis of merit;

Adult illiteracy shall be ended by a mass state education plan;

Teachers shall have all the rights of other citizens;

The colour bar in cultural life, in sport, and in education shall be abolished.

There Shall be Houses, Security and Comfort!

All people shall have the right to live where they choose, to be decently housed, and to bring up their families in comfort; and security;

Unused housing space to be made available to the people;

Rent and prices shall be lowered, food plentiful and no one shall go hungry;

A preventive health scheme shall be run by the state;

Free medical care and hospitalisation shall be provided for all, with special care for mothers and young children;

Slums shall be demolished, and new suburbs built where all have transport, roads, lighting, playing fields, creches and social centres;

The aged, the orphans, the disabled and the sick shall be cared for by the state;

Rest, leisure and recreation shall be the right of all;

Fenced locations and ghettoes shall be abolished, and laws which break up families shall be repealed.

There Shall be Peace and Friendship!

South Africa shall be a fully independent state, which respects the rights and sovereignty of nations;

South Africa shall strive to maintain world peace and the settlement of all international disputes by negotiation—not war;

Peace and friendship amongst all our people shall be secured by upholding the equal rights, opportunities and status of all;

The people of the protectorates Basutoland, Bechuanaland and Swaziland shall be free to decide for themselves their own future;

The rights of all the peoples of Africa to independence and self-government shall be recognized, and shall be the basis of close cooperation.

Let all who love their people and their country now say, as we say here:

'THESE FREEDOMS WE WILL FIGHT FOR, SIDE BY SIDE, THROUGHOUT OUR LIVES, UNTIL WE HAVE WON OUR LIBERTY.'

TOPICS FOR ORAL OR WRITTEN EXPLORATION

1. After reading the historical background to *Cry, the Beloved Country,* to what extent does Alan Paton's *Cry, the Beloved Country* convey the historical consciousness of the South African experience?

2. In what ways is the history of South Africa similar to and different from that of the United States?

3. Do Reverend Stephen Kumalo's personality and his interactions with James Jarvis reflect the paternalism of the early settlers?

4. Which factors, according to you, contributed to the creation of apartheid, and which main factor created racial and class divisions in South Africa?

5. Are African consciousness and African resistance similar to Afrikaner nationalism and resistance?

6. Imagine you are a Khoisan who remained in Cape Colony when your family fled to Botswana. You fall ill, and a fellow Koisan decides, right before the Afrikaners' Great Trek, to fellow in their footsteps. Write, from the point of view of the ailing Koisan, a letter detailing the situation of the Khoisans living in the Cape to his clan members.

7. On the basis of the South African historical background you have read, do you believe that Reverend Stephen Kumalo's son, Absalom, will have a fair trail?

8. Historically, Afrikaners seem to be the source of racism and apartheid in South Africa. Do you believe the British are ideologically any different from the Afrikaners?

9. Describe the pre-1994 sociopolitical conditions of Africans in South Africa and research that of the other nonwhites.

10. History presents the South African situation as one of perpetual conflict. Were there, historically and in *Cry, the Beloved Country,* European groups or individuals who sought to establish justice and equality? How committed to change were they, according to the historical documents you have read?

NOTES

1. An African advisory board established in 1936 to replace the limited voting rights for Africans in the Cape Province. It had no powers and dissolved itself in 1946 after one of its members had described it as a "toy telephone" (quoted in H. J. and R. E. Simons, *Class and Colour in South Africa 1850–1950*).

2. In 1910, following the Anglo-Boer War of 1899–1902, the whites of the four territories—Cape and Natal (formerly British) and Transvaal and Orange Free State (formerly Boer)—joined together to form the Union of South Africa under the British Crown. Only in the Cape did some blacks retain a qualified franchise: it was later withdrawn.

3. The Mines and Works Act of 1926.

4. This Act made the Governor-General (representing the British Crown) "Supreme Chief" over all African areas, which were thenceforth ruled by proclamation. When South Africa became a Republic in 1961, this power passed to the State President.

5. The Second World War 1939–45, in which the Union of South Africa fought with the Allies against Nazi Germany and Fascist Italy.

SUGGESTIONS FOR FURTHER READING

Esterhuyse, Willie, and Philip Nel, eds. *The ANC and Its Leaders.* Cape Town: Talfelberg, 1990.

Furlong, Patrick, J. "South Africa." In *Understanding Contemporary Africa.* Ed. April A. Gordon and Donald L. Gordon. Boulder and London: Lynne Rienner, 2001.

Hein, Marais. *South Africa: Limits to Change: The Political Economy of Transition.* London: Zed Books, 2001.

Omer-Cooper, J. D. *History of Southern Africa.* Portsmouth, NH: Heinemann, 1987.

Paton, Alan. *South African Tragedy.* New York: Charles Scribner's & Sons, 1965.

Shillington, Kevin. *History of Southern Africa.* Essex, England: Longman, 1987.

Thompson, Leonard. *A History of South Africa.* New Haven: Yale University Press, 2001.

Were, Gideon, S. *A History of South Africa.* New York: African Publishing Company, 1974.

WORKS CITED

Alexander, Peter. *Alan Paton.* Oxford: Oxford University Press, 1994.

Clingman, Stephen. "Literature and History in South Africa." In *History from South Africa. Alternative Visions and Practices.* Ed. Joshua Brown et al. Philadelphia: Temple University Press, 1991: 105–118.

Collins, Harold R. "Cry, the Beloved Country and the Broken Tribe." *College English* 14, no. 7 (1953): 379–385.

Davenport, H.R.T, and Christopher Saunders. *South Africa.* 5th edition. New York: St. Martin's Press, 2000.

Furlong, Patrick, J. "South Africa." In *Understanding Contemporary Africa.* Ed. April A. Gordon and Donald L. Gordon. Boulder and London: Lynne Rienner, 2001.

Gannett, Lewis. Introduction to *Cry, the Beloved Country,* by Alan Paton. New York: Collier Books, 1948; rpt. 1986: xi–xix.

Gibbons, Reginald, et al. *Writers from South Africa.* Evanston, IL: TriQuarterly Series on Criticism and Culture, no. 2, 1982.

Kristeva, Julia. *Strangers to Ourselves.* Trans. Leon S. Roudiez. New York: Columbia University Press, 1991.

Le May, G.H.L. *British Supremacy in South Africa 1899–1907.* Oxford: Clarendon Press, 1965.

Moleah, Alfred Tokollo. *South Africa.* Wilmington, DE: Disa Press, 1993.

Newton-King, Susan. *Masters and Servants on the Cape Eastern Frontier.* Cambridge: Cambridge University Press, 1999.

Omer-Cooper, J. D. *History of Southern Africa.* Portsmouth, NH: Heinemann, 1987.

Paton, Alan. *Cry, the Beloved Country.* New York: Collier Books: New York, 1948, rpt. 1986.

———. *Towards the Mountain.* New York: Charles Scribner's Sons, 1977.

Shillington, Kevin. *History of Southern Africa.* Essex, England: Longman, 1987.

Shostak, Marjorie. *Nisa.* New York: Vintage Books, 1983.

Simons, Jack, and Ray Simons. *Class and Color in South Africa 1850–1950.* London: Southern Africa, 1983.

Walker, Eric Anderson. 1934. *The Great Trek.* London: Adam and Charles Black, 1965.

Were, Gideon, S. A *History of South Africa.* New York: African Publishing Company, 1974.

Wilson, Monica, and Leonard Thompson, eds. *The Oxford History of South Africa.* New York and Oxford: Oxford University Press, 1971.

3

The Land and People of South Africa

Alan Paton's *Cry, the Beloved Country* makes numerous references to rivers and locations within the Natal province and Johannesburg, and other cities. It also makes references to the multiethnic and multinational nature of the country, encompassing several racial groups. The South Africa of *Cry, the Beloved Country* is inhabited by Britons, Afrikaners, and Africans, subdivided into Xhosa, Zulu, and so on. In addition to these groups, South Africa is also home to Hindus, Indonesians, and other Asians. The novel deals only with interactions between whites and Africans, but Paton ensures that the Indian and Colored presence is acknowledged in the introduction. Paton's *The Land and People of South Africa,* taking the reader on a journey through South Africa, best presents the landscape, the social and political events that shaped the nation and the race relationships that inform the novel.

Cry, the Beloved Country is set in a segregated society in the process of laying the groundwork for apartheid; it is a society that separates and classifies its population racially into whites (British and Afrikaner); Coloreds (people of mixed races, such as the Cape Coloreds), Indians, Asians, and Africans. These populations are also hierarchical, with whites, considered superior to the groups, at the top and Africans at the bottom. The 1974 publication *Multi-National Development in South Africa: The Reality,* from the State Department of Pretoria, explains the nature of this racial hierarchy in terms of evolutionary development and civilization; accordingly, one polarity is formed by the small Bushmen minorities living in the central desert regions of the subcontinent and the other polarity represents whites, considered to be the most socioeconomically advanced (14). The Hottentots, in this hierarchical system, are on the lowest rung of the social ladder. Yet, these racial castes, according to Pierre L. van den Berghe, are not clearly demarcated but are arbitrary, since some Cape Coloreds could pass for white and some whites were contaminated by blackness; it was not, however, easy to move from one group to another.

The Republic of South Africa, generally referred to as South Africa, became a self-governing state when it became the Union of South Africa on May 31, 1910; it acquired its sovereignty on May 1, 1934, and left the British Commonwealth on May 31, 1961, to become the Republic of South Africa, or RSA. Nelson Mandela was elected president on April 27, 1994, under the country's new constitution; the nation is currently led by Thambo Mbeki.

South Africa is located at the southern tip of Africa and covers 1,227,200 square kilometers; it is almost twice the size of Texas. It shares its borders with the totally landlocked Botswana and Swaziland, Lesotho (which it completely surrounds), Mozambique, Namibia, and Zimbabwe. Its coastlines also border both the Atlantic Ocean, on the west, and the Indian Ocean, on the east. It has extraterritorial holdings—Robben Island, Dassen Island, and Bird Island, in the Atlantic Ocean, and Price Edward Island and Marion Island, southeast of Cape Town in the Indian Ocean. It is also separated by rivers from its neighboring countries: the Orange River separates it from Namibia, the Limpopo River from Zimbabwe and southeastern Botswana, and the Molopo River from Botswana. Despite all its rivers, South Africa suffers chronic and severe water problems and has had to resort to artificial lakes to provide water for farming irrigation.

South Africa is a country rich in gold, chromium, antimony, coal, iron, ore, talc, titanium, antimony, manganese, nickel, phosphates, tin, uranium, gem diamonds, platinum, copper, vanadium, salt, and natural gas. It has a variety of climates: Mediterranean conditions in the far southeast, a desert climate in the northwest, and a subtropical climate in the northeast. It has two seasons, dry and sunny winters (April–October) and summer raining season (November–March), like most sub-Saharan African countries. The northern area is different from the other regions, though, because it rains there all year round.

South Africa has a population of about 44,187,637 people, according to 2006 estimates, and has more than 10 official languages, among which are IsiZulu, isiXhosa, Afrikaans, English, Sepedi, Setswana, xitsonga, Siswati, TshiVenda (Lu Venda), and IsIndebele. The population is 80 percent Christian; traditional religion remains strong in the rural area; Asian and Hindu beliefs are also practiced;

and Islam is progressively growing. This population is generally divided into four groups: (1) whites—Afrikaners and English-speaking Europeans, (2) Coloreds—Cape Coloreds, Griquas, and Malays, (3) Asians—predominantly Indians from northern (Hindi and Gujarathi) and southern India (Tamil and Telugu Indians, Indonesians, and Malays), and (4) Africans—Zulu, Xhosa, Tswana, North Sotho, South Sotho, Shagaan, Nbelele, Venda, and other African groups. Although race is the defining criterion for an individual's or group's status, there are also subdivisions within these various racial divisions.

Europeans originally came from numerous western European countries but especially the Netherlands, Britain, Germany, and France. The descendants of the earliest Dutch settlers, as well as integrated German and French Huguenot settlers, are known as Boers (farmers), because most Dutch were into farming, or Afrikaners (people of Africa). After the early European settlement, there continued to be a flow of new European immigrants. The majority of Europeans, during the 1936–1946 period covered in Paton's *Cry, the Beloved Country,* have been urban people ever since the discovery of diamonds at Kimberly, in 1870, and the Rand goldfields, in 1871. The two dominant languages—Afrikaans and English—have both been adapted to the African context and experience, since Afrikaans is considered a distinct Indo-European language and English has acquired a distinctive vocabulary, having borrowed words from other languages. Despite the presence of immigrants from other European countries, British administrative and political structures dominate. Even though Europeans constitute a single group, they constitute three different social categories: Afrikaner, English-speaking (including all Europeans), and Jewish. Not race, according to Paton, but culture, language, and law are the determining factors in placing an individual into the appropriate white division (24); however, status and political power also play major roles. Afrikaners were the least educated and the poorest of the three groups; state subsidies ultimately eliminated the poor-white phenomenon. According to Pierre van den Berghe, Jews were considered different from Europeans but were linguistically assimilated into English-speaking Europeans. Even though they were more educated than Afrikaners, they were excluded from political and civic service, except in Natal and the larger municipalities of Eastern Cape and the Transvaal. These localities tended to minimize class consciousness because the majority of whites belonged to the bourgeoisie.

Coloreds were more color-conscious than whites and were stratified almost like the European community. Class was more of an issue among them, since the majority of Coloreds were proletarian unskilled or semiskilled workers. Malays were slightly better off than other Coloreds. Among Coloreds, there was an upper and a lower middle class, consisting of artisans and petty clerks, and a small upper class consisting mainly of professionals, businessmen, and schoolteachers. They had more difficulties identifying with Africans, whom they considered inferior.

Indians, on the other hand, came to South Africa to fill a labor shortage on sugar cane plantations. Between 1860 and 1913, approximately 150,000 Asians came to South Africa either as indentured servants with the option to return home or to settle down permanently or as free passengers interested in commercial ventures in this new country (Whittington 13). The vast majority of the Asian population lived mainly in Natal for this reason. The working conditions for these indentured servants were harsh and restrictive and very close to those of slaves. They, like the Coloreds, were given some privileges, even though they were repressed, disenfranchised, and subject to relocation. Indians had more social status than Coloreds, even though they both occupied a middle position between Africans and Europeans. Of all the groups, Indians were the most disunited because they were divided along religious and linguistic lines. These divisions were not racially hierarchical but were based on socioeconomic and religious criteria. The most significant division was the religious rift between Hindus and Muslims. There were also other cultural divisions, such as that between northern and southern Indians. Position was also based on one's immigration status, whether one arrived as an indentured slave or as a passenger.

Africans are also not a homogeneous group, since they consist of numerous subgroups. They are divided according to linguistic subdivisions—Nguni, Sotho, Tswana, Venda, and Shanagaan-Tsonga. The four groups are also generally divided into nine other groups—Sotho Swana, North Sotho, South Sotho, Vhavenda, Shagana-Tsonga, Nguni, Zulu, and Ndebele. Paul Maylam, in *A History of the African People of South Africa,* recommends caution, however, in using these classifications. According to him,

> The rigid classification and demarcation of ethnic groups has been a major obsession of successive white governments in South Africa. . . . Race, physical type, language, and culture represent the most convenient means of labeling. However, the common tendency in southern Africa is for at least one of these criteria to overlap between "different" societies so that it becomes virtually impossible to use all the major criteria at the same time to define nearly differing, self-contained entities. Reification is another dangerous consequence of classification, because in the process southern African societies become not only mutually exclusive ethnic entities, but also static, timeless units. (20)

Indeed, Desmond Tutu states, in *The Words of Desmond Tutu,*

> Apartheid is upheld by a phalanx of iniquitous laws, such as the Population Registration Act, which decrees that all South Africans must be classified ethnically, and

> duly registered according to these race categories. Many times in the same family one child has been classified white whilst another with a slightly darker hue has been classified colored, with all the horrible consequences for the latter of being shut out from membership of a greatly privileged caste. There have, has a result, been several child suicides. This is too a high a price to pay for racial purity. (63)

In the twentieth century, claims Maylam, the vast majority of Africans were classified into two groups: Nguni and Sotho (there are doubts about the authenticity of the term "Nguni," which, according to an analyst, is a 1930s academic appropriation used during the retribalization of Africans). The latter can be divided into a northern group—the Zulu and the Swazi—and a Southern group—the Xhosa, the Thembu, the Mfengu, the Mpondo, and the Mpondmise. Sotho, according to him, is another generic term that is used to designate a large group of people who share similar linguistic and cultural characteristics. The Sotho can be divided into three main groups—the Western Sotho, or Tswana, the northern Sotho, consisting of the Pedi and the Lobedu, and the Southern Sotho, or Basotho. Despite these different terminologies, both groups speak Bantu languages and are cultivators, herders, and hunters who live in patrilineal societies ruled by chiefs. Despite these similarities, their languages are linguistically different, and, while the Nguni, primordially a pastoral people, live in dispersed settlements, the Sothos tend to be more concentrated (20-21).

During the time in which *Cry, the Beloved Country* is set, Africans, unlike Coloreds who strove for whiteness, aspired to become Westernized, since social status was increasingly defined in terms of education, profession, clothing, Christianity, and moral respectability. Of all the racial groups, they were the most oppressed and the most economically and socially restricted. Excerpts from both Peter Abrahams's *Return to Goli* and Ezekiel Mphahlele's "Nationalism" provide great insights into the status of the different populations of racialized South Africa during apartheid. These excerpts demonstrate the importance of racial identities in the Union of South Africa and the threat that South African Indians posed for Europeans. They also focus on the Coloreds as a deracinated people and the extent of South African blacks' acculturation. "Examination of Mr. Kathrada" focuses on the Indian plight that brought South Africa to the attention of the world, as Alan Paton affirms in the introduction of the second author note of the second edition of *Cry, the Beloved Country.* The article "How to Be a South African," by Humphrey Tyler, from the *Mail and Guardian,* on the other hand, shows how racial definitions are perceived by Europeans in a minority position and explores the need to create inclusive and egalitarian identities.

FROM EZEKIEL MPHAHLELE'S, "NATIONALISM"

MPHAHLELE, EZEKIEL. "NATIONALISM." IN *THE AFRICAN IMAGE.* NEW YORK: FREDERICK A. PRAEGER, 1962: 68–70

The Mphahlele excerpt from "Nationalism" appropriately illustrates the power relationships that undergird South African relationships and explain why Africans are rightly the center of Alan Paton's preoccupation, since they are the most oppressed and on the bottom rung of the social and economic ladder.

Having been born into the dark side of a segregated existence, I've never been encouraged to think anything except that I'm black. For three hundred years this has been drummed into our heads; first by cannon fire, then by acts of parliament, proclamations and regulations. Our minds have been so conditioned that a number of our responses have become reflex: everywhere, instinctively, we look around for separate entrances, exits, reception counters, bank tellers, separate public lavatories, train coaches, platforms, hospitals. Instinctively, we make sure that wherever we are, we have permits in the form of passes to stay in a particular location, to work or look for work in a particular town, to leave a particular town, to leave a white man's farm, to look for work in a district. And these permits have definite time limits. Our minds have been so conditioned that, whether we like it or not, we have come to rate our qualifications lower, in terms of wages and salaries than the whites do who possess exactly the same qualifications.

Always we have been thwarted as a group—as blacks. The Coloured people[1] were brought up on the idea that they were an appendage of the white man. They were more or less treated as such. They did not carry passes or permits; they were not harassed by police raids; they could look for work or live anywhere they chose and were on the common voters' roll in the Cape Province; they received higher wages than us in all fields of occupation; they had better opportunities for a university education, although they did not make much use of them, being, like whites, sheltered already; they lived in separate townships. They still enjoy these privileges, apart from their removal from the voters' roll.

But since 1948, when the Nationalist Party came into power, it has been gradually but sharply brought home to the Coloureds that they are a separate racial group, not white, not black, not Indian. They can now only vote for white senators to represent them. They are also being reclassified. Overnight, some find themselves reclassified as 'natives'. This new identification brings with it passes, lower wages, change of residence, humiliation and contempt from their fellow-Coloureds.

The Indians have been treated like Coloureds for the most part, except that, in freehold areas, the Indians live separate, and they have never had the vote, direct or indirect. Indian communities are now being moved out of towns and cities, where the merchants had acquired property, to live in segregated areas. Here they are expected to trade among themselves. Their cultural exclusiveness would defy anybody who dared regard them as an appendage.

During my early life in Pretoria we in our locations were physically close to the Indians. We were as interdependent as trader and customer can be expected to be. Being sticklers for tradition, they didn't make it easy for us to know them beyond the shop counter or the jingle of coin on it. But it was a very happy relationship. The Coloured folk in a nearby location were a very easy lot to live with, too. Their men came to us to drink, and our men went to them for liquor brews that their own women didn't have. As boys we met Coloured boys at the market to carry vegetables and fruits for the white people.

When I went to live in Johannesburg I found the Indian wholesale merchant class, whose businesses depended on whites rather than on blacks, too full of themselves, even hostile to Africans. The retailers, who served Africans mostly, were much more human. Even the curly-haired boys from merchant families, very much to the disgust of their parents, fraternized with Coloured girls. Between the two of them, they released enough arrogance to make sour the lives of Africans who found themselves thrown in their midst.

For instance, there are two Indian-owned cinemas in Johannesburg—the Lyric and the Majestic. For a long time Africans have been going to these houses and made to sit in front, near the screen. The back rows were for Indians and Coloured, and it didn't matter how much the African could afford to pay. I remember the burning hurt I felt on the two occasions I went to each of these cinemas. Then I stopped going there altogether. So did a number of other Africans. Those who continued to go must have done so simply because it was part of a huge segregation machine: they were so used to the noise it made that they had ceased to be startled by it. Only when it stopped, perhaps, would they become aware that they had been outraged.

A good few Indian fruiterers who were right in the centre of Johannesburg never made the 'mistake' of serving a black man, or even another Indian, before a white customer, no matter who had come first.

In Natal, because of a longer period of contact between Indians and Africans, there should have been a closer association between them than in any other province. But in fact the rift has been the widest. The 1948 brutal riots between Indians and Africans showed this. The tribalism of the English in Natal had, since the days of Shepstone, been driving into the heads of the Zulus a sense of superiority over the other African tribes—a feeling which they, the English, could not justify by their treatment of the blacks as a child race. They resented the Indian's increasing economic power earned by sheer industry. And so it was easy for them to project this resentment into the blacks. The English openly incited the Africans against the Indians in those riots.

Thus the white man, the Indian, and the Coloured, each in his peculiar compensatory response—often a neurotic one—has through the years driven the Africans into a defensive position. It made him very colour-conscious. In 1912, when the African National Congress was formed in South Africa, it was a national response to the challenge which the Act of Union constituted: the whites had ganged up against us. Once and for all it was made clear that the black man was to occupy an inferior place in the eyes of the law, in the legislature and in the social and economic life of the country. Every time an African became a doctor, a lawyer, a university graduate, he was made a symbol of *African* achievement by us. He had fought for every inch he gained. The more it became difficult for the black man to stay in primary school for more than six years (he was not allowed to begin until he was seven) the more spectacular it looked when batches of graduates came out of university.

The last war did a lot to jolt the youth. They saw men limping back from the war, broken and shell-shattered. They were coming back to serfdom. White ex-soldiers were receiving special concessions to complete their university education.

FROM PETER ABRAHAM'S, *RETURN TO GOLI*

(LONDON: FABER AND FABER, 1953: 4, 42, 82, AND 83)

Peter Abrahams's *Return to Goli* provides insight into the multinational composition of South Africa, the place of each group, and the complexity of South African identities.

Everywhere else in the world the word 'coloured' generally means a non-white person. In the United States the blackest American Negro is as coloured as Walter White with his very fair skin, his blonde hair and his blue eyes. In London the blackest West African is a coloured man. In the Union the word is turned into a proper noun and given a special significance so that only half-castes are known as Coloureds. The half-castes regard being called 'half-castes' insulting. From time to time they have tried to call themselves 'Eurafricans', but the word has never gained much currency, so they have remained as 'Coloureds'. Officially they are called 'Cape Coloureds' because the early mixture between the first arrivals from Europe and the Africans took place in the Cape and the Coloured community came into existence there. . . .

The dark people of the Union are known variously, depending on which group is talking about them, as Africans, Natives, Blacks, or kaffirs. The word 'African' explains itself. If, however, it were used with its general meaning instead of with its highly specialist South African meaning, then the Coloureds, the Indians and the descendants of the Voortrekkers would also be called Africans. But by Coloureds, Indians and the sons and daughters of the trekkers alike this would be regarded as insulting. The descendants of the trekkers do, however, call themselves *Afrikaners.* This makes nonsense of words and the meaning of words unless we invest them with a special *mystique,* which is what the descendants of the trekkers do. The same thing has happened with the word 'Native'. Coloured Indian and Afrikaner all claim, and with justice, that South Africa is as much their home as it is the home of the 'African'. An Englishman whose home is in England would not object to being called a native of England, nor would a Frenchman to being called a native of France nor an American to being a native of his country. In the Union, while Coloureds, Indians and whites insist that they were born there and belong there, they would not be called natives of South Africa. Instead, they give the word a capital 'N' and apply it only to the so-called 'pure-blooded blacks'. And the whites, though they and their ancestors have been born in South Africa for generations back, insist on calling themselves 'Europeans', thus making nonsense of that word as well. The people of Australia, New Zealand and Canada are Australians, New Zealanders and Canadians—only the whites of the plural societies are not Africans but 'Europeans'.

But on to the next word. 'Bantu' is an African word which in its literal sense simply means 'people'. Logically, therefore, all those who live in the plural societies of South, Central and East Africa, all those who have become native to those lands, are the peoples of those lands, the 'Bantu', the natives, the Africans, be they white or brown or black.

But if this were to be the case, if all these words were to be given their proper meaning, then so much of the pseudo-moral justification for the policies of the plural societies would fall away. If the whites were not ‘Europeans’ defending ‘European culture and civilisation’, if they were not ‘European guardians of the Western way of life’, but a small minority with all power in their hands holding sway over a large majority . . .

Over the years the Indians proved themselves the most hard-working, sober and quiet section of the South African non-Whites. Soon, a very small band of them began to prosper. They set up trading stores and other businesses and held their own in open competition with the Whites. Compete with ‘Whites! God, no! The ‘coolies’ are a menace. Something had to be done about the new threat. Whites suddenly found that Indians stank. God-fearing, Christian, civilised Europeans hurled curses at the ‘curry arses’. The cry of an ‘Indian menace’ was in full swing.

The Transvaal was the first to act. It denied Indians all citizen rights in 1885. Six years later the Orange Free State banned Indians completely. Those who were already in the Free State were expelled. Ten years after the Transvaal had made the first move Natal turned on the Indians she had been so anxious to bring into the country. Natal imposed a £3 tax on each Indian at the end of his period as an indentured labourer. Next it withdrew the Indian vote. Next, in 1897, it outlawed marriage between Indian and White. Soon there was total prohibition of all immigration from Asia. In 1924 the Indians were deprived of their municipal vote in Natal. . . .

Ghandi fought the South African Government in a series of dramatic struggles from 1911 onwards. Then he went over to India to lead a nation to its freedom. Today the leaders of that free nation that Gandhi fathered are among the most sane and humane of the world’s statesmen. Today that free nation has taken the cause of the Indians of South Africa on to the floor of the United Nations. . . .

One of the most popular and most successful South African lies is the picture of 365,000 Indians all rolling in dubiously acquired wealth, buying up White residential areas and turning them into slums, exploiting Blacks, and cooking up horrible plots for turning South Africa, and indeed the whole of the African east coast, into a colony of India.

The truth is the complete opposite of this Hollywoodish picture of ‘oriental villainy’.

Less than 5 per cent of the total Indian population are successful merchants and businessmen. Some members of this small minority have made vast fortunes. Like most rich businessmen, they have tried to invest their money wisely. Real estate is an obviously good investment. So some acquired land and property. But while this would have been considered wise and good business if a White man had done it, it became a dangerously challenging act when done by an Indian.

HUMPHREY TYLER, “HOW TO BE A SOUTH AFRICAN”

(Online posting at *Mail and Guardian* Online, January 13, 2006, at <http://www.mg.co.zalprintPage.aspx?area=/insight/insight_comment_and_analysis/&art. 04/28/2006>)

This article addresses the fears and the identity issues that confront the minority Europeans once they have lost their hegemonic position within South Africa and the need, as *Cry, the Beloved Country* asserts, for there to be justice for all, for all racial categories to be eliminated, and for all citizens of the country to be defined as South Africans.

13 January 2006 12:00

The mind boggles at the sometimes extraordinary advice South Africa's so-called whites are being given about how to make it in the New South Africa. There have been caring suggestions even from a highly paid senior academic (well, he is employed at a university) from KwaZulu-Natal. He recommends, for example, that whites should learn to dance like Johnny Clegg, the entertainer, and come to relish delicacies like walkie-talkies—the feet and heads of dead chickens.

More recently, the *Mall & Guardian* also devoted space to the perceived problem of how whites can become Africans so that they could then get along fine with blacks and live here happily.

Some of this is actually absolute nonsense, of course, and it suffers from a serious lack of definition.

For a start, physiologically there is as much chance of a white becoming an African as there is of a hyena changing into a hound dog (or Elvis Presley). So it is a mental thing, something cultural that we are supposed to be talking about. Well, right on and straight away, many people will applaud the Pan Africanist Congress's Themba Godi's recent M&G quote ("How to be a white African," December 14, 2005) from Mangaliso Sobukwe, the PAC founder, that "there is only one race to which we all belong—the human race". Hooray. And more cheers when Themba Godi reminds his readers that the PAC has refused to identify people in terms of colour "since its inception". (So different from the racist bile put out by some of the congress's later leaders, one must say.)

But then things go off the rails, and "indigenous people" and "Africans" crop up, and "whites", and we start to particularise and then generalise—like "everyone in Africa should become an African, identify with Africa . . . and respect and embrace its values and norms".

Sounds really great but, ahem: Just which values and norms?

Are we talking Tutsis and Hutus here, for example, and genocide?

So, apart from Clegg and some bits of chicken, what are we really talking about when we want whites, or any others, to become "African"?

In fact, it is some idealistic but unrealistic notion for South Africa that is not concrete enough to have practical application.

Is there another way to go?

It comes back to particulars and to definition.

South Africa has nearly always had problems with definitions. I was born to be an "English-speaking white South African" and I found this weird creature impossible to define. I concluded I was merely South African.

Many Afrikaners, especially at the height of Afrikaner Nationalist domination, regarded themselves as simply—Afrikaners. Maybe some conceded they might be

"South Africans" also, as a remote second, but many were certain that the only real South African had to be Afrikaans. English-speakers hardly came into the picture. Blacks didn't come into it at all. Nor Jews. Nor lots of others who had every right.

And even today there are Zulus who are just Zulus. They live in KwaZulu-Natal and they have a king and that is that.

But we can get somewhere constructive very quickly if, instead of talking about whites becoming "Africans", we talk about their acknowledging that already they are not just whites at all but actually a very separate breed: South Africans. Then get Zulus to do the same, and all the rest of us, and then get everybody thinking about what that could mean. And, of course, the responsibilities this entails.

Whatever our colour, being South African is stamped on us somewhere.

It is like the American writer, James Baldwin, a negro, who exiled himself from the United States to Paris to avoid racist humiliation. He found to his astonishment in those strange surroundings that he couldn't escape his Americanness.

"I proved to my astonishment that I was as American as a Texas GI," he wrote.

It would cost a lot to ship us all to Europe so we could find out we are South Africans, but we can start at home.

As a start, we need to acknowledge, then get to relish, our indelible common South Africanness, and build on it, admit our interdependence and to stick up, individually and collectively, for the values we can contribute, values that built this country (and sometimes maybe nearly destroyed it) and which our common society desperately needs. It needs ramrods up its spine. Blacks are right to assert themselves right now. It is a twist of history. Go for it. But whites (and others) are doing nobody a favour if they fail to assert their own values and importance and rights as well.

They are stupid when they go belly up to some perceived "black domination", when they try to "be black" or just chuck up their hands and "let the blacks get on with it". That is the worst kind of racism—the arrogance of low expectations.

This is a great African country. But no one group now can keep South Africa going all by itself. Good luck to Clegg with his dancing. He is part of us anyway. But I am not so sure about the dead chickens' feet.

Humphrey Tyler is the author of Life in the Time of Sharpeville. *He was a* Drum *staffer and edited the magazine for a while and was editorial director of the* World *(now the* Sowetan*).*

EXAMINATION BY MR. KATHRADA

(Online posting at <http://www.anc.org.za/ancdocs/history/congress/molvi-16.html>)

The comments of Mr. Kathrada provide insight into the experience of other non-Western populations living in South Africa that are not discussed in Paton's *Cry, the Beloved Country.* This information is vital since the first author note does not refer to them, their fate being less dire than that of blacks.

However, since their fate following the Tenure and Indian Representation Act of 1946 brought them into the international limelight, Paton felt obligated to include them in his second author note.

June 21, 1960

You are a detainee in terms of the Emergency Regulations promulgated under the Public Safety Act?—That is so, my Lord, I was arrested on the 30th March of this year. . . .

Are you physically fit to give evidence in this case?—My Lord, as we are kept, we are rather in difficulty for the simple reason that I am suffering from cold, that is a common disease which affects me, and more particularly now that we are confined to the cell. It is very cold, we have to sleep on a cement floor, and my body is definitely aching. I am over fifty. The lighting conditions too in the cell are not bright, very dull, one cannot read much, and apart from that there is some provision made for the accused, where they call it a library where we could read and so on, but that cell is even colder, so I could not stay there for more than an hour, and that is one of my difficulties. So under those circumstances, if I give evidence only in the mornings, I think that would give me some relief.

Mr. Justice Rumpff:

Are you seated at the moment? You may be seated.

Mr. Kathrada:

You were born in Johannesburg on the 5th of December 1908?—Yes, My Lord.

You attended the Government Indian School in Johannesburg?—Yes, My Lord, I attended the Government Indian School where I studied up to Standard Four.

Did you attend any other school in the afternoon?—Yes, in the afternoon I attended the Urdu School, and in the evenings the Gujarati school.

When did you go to India?—In the year 1924 I left for India.

What did you go to India for?—I went there to study and I went to a place called Deoband where the Muslim University is situated, and I attended that University as a student.

In what language did you study at the Deoband University?—I studied in Persian and Arabic, and it was through the medium of Urdu, our main language.

Did you study the Koran and the *Hadis* then?—Yes, I studied the Koran and the *Hadis* then, that is, the study of Prophet Mohammed and some Islamic laws.

Did you then qualify as a theologian and a teacher according to the tenets of Islam?—That is correct.

Did you also study Muslim law?—Yes.

When did you qualify?—In 1930. . . .

When did you return to South Africa?—In 1931.

I understand that during your youth and student days certain factors had a profound influence on your political viewpoint?—That is so.

Would you say that these factors determined your approach and outlook when you became politically active in later years?—That is correct.

The next law that I want to deal with briefly is Law No. 15 of 1898, which I believe was repealed and re-enacted in 1908?—That is so. It is commonly known as the Gold Law.

Briefly describe how this law affected Indians in regard to ownership of land in proclaimed areas and occupation of land in proclaimed areas?—Insofar as ownership of land is concerned, they were debarred from occupying in the proclaimed areas for the purposes of residence, but they were allowed to trade in proclaimed areas.

In regard to immigration, I want to refer you to the 1902 Transvaal Ordinance. What was the effect on Indian immigration into the Transvaal?—Immediately after the cessation of war, [2 The South African War of 1899–1902] an Ordinance was passed which was generally known as Peace Preservation Ordinance, which checked on the people who came to the Colony. Before the war Indians were quite entitled to enter into the Colony, but since this Ordinance of 1902, they would only be allowed provided they would prove that they had been in the Transvaal before, and therefore no new immigration was allowed—rather no newcomers were allowed to enter into the Transvaal.

Do I understand that prior to 1902 there were no such restrictions?—No.

Was there a further law dealing with immigration in 1913?—Yes, Immigration Regulation Act of 1913.

What was its effect?—According to that Act no new Indian immigrant could enter into the Union from that date. . . .

Did this Act impose restrictions on the movement of Indians between the provinces?—That is correct, that was also one of the provisions, that the resident of one province cannot enter into the other province freely.

What formalities do you have to comply with in order to visit another province? By you I mean Indians?—They apply to the Immigration Office for a permit and if he gets a permit, he would be entitled to enter into another province. If an Indian has entered into another province on a permit he cannot reside there for more than three months a year. . . .

What effect did the Township Act of 1908 have on the Indians' right to trade?—The Township Act . . . meant that any township which would carry a clause debarring the Non-Europeans to occupy lands or premises . . . the non-European people, would not be able to occupy land or premises in these townships.

Prior to 1919 were there any restrictions in regard to the formation and operation of Indian companies?—No, there was no restriction in forming Indian companies before 1919, and there is no restriction now to form an Indian company.

Were there restrictions promulgated in 1919 to prevent Indian companies from operating in certain fields?—The Asiatic private companies were not entitled to hold fixed properties since 1919.

Under the Mines and Works Act, is the position of Indians in skilled trades affected in any way?—Yes, they were debarred from becoming skilled workers.

Was the position of Indian ownership of shares in private companies dealt with by the legislature in 1932?—Yes, the Asiatic Land Tenure Act of 1932. Under this Act any Asiatic private company was not entitled to hold any fixed property at all, whereas in 1919 any company, even a private company holding fixed property, if the Asiatics had a few shares in that or the minority shareholding, that was permissible, but from 1932 no private company was entitled to own fixed property.

Coming to nominees, was the position of nominees also dealt with by the legislature in 1932?—Yes. The position of nominee holding was such that in the year 1888 an Indian firm in Klerksdorp purchased a property from public auction, and when the papers were sent to Pretoria to register a transfer, it was then informed by the registrar that Indians cannot be registered holder of such property . . . since then the practice of holding properties by Europeans on behalf of Indians started, and that practice grew and remained as such until 1932. Although there was a lot of risk attached to that, the Indian people preferred that way, because there was consent of the government to holding properties in that manner. In 1932 nominee holdings were totally stopped.

Now coming to 1939, what steps were taken by the legislature in regard to the occupation of land by Indians?—In 1939 an Act called Asiatic Land and Trading Act was introduced. . . . By virtue of that Act the position of the Indians in the Transvaal in relation to business, trading and residence, was pegged; that means they were only able to occupy those premises which were already in occupation by members of the Indian community on that date. This Act was an interim measure for two years.

Prior to 1939 were there any such restrictions outside the townships and the gold proclaimed areas?—No, Indians could take up legally any occupation on any land or premises anywhere in the Transvaal, with of course those two exceptions.

Was this Asiatic Land Act followed by the Pegging Act of 1943?—Yes, that is correct.

Did the Pegging Act apply only to the Transvaal?—No, it applied to Natal as well.

Were there any restrictions in Natal prior to that date?—Not of occupation only, but in regard to the ownership of properties too, there were no restrictions whatsoever.

Were these two measures then consolidated in an Act of Parliament in 1946?—Yes, the Asiatic Land Tenure and Indian Representation Act was passed in 1946, whereby no further occupation and ownership of the Indians were allowed, that they did not occupy on that date. But this Act recognised one principle, and that was of the trade, that there was no restriction on the trading, for the purpose of trading, as it was ever since 1885, as far as the Transvaal is concerned, since the Indians came into the Transvaal. . . .

When did the Indians first arrive in Natal?—Indians first came to Natal in 1860. The first batch came in 1860 as a result of very lengthy negotiations which went on between the Natal Government and the British Government on the one hand and the Indian government on the other hand, and after some years of negotiations eventually an agreement was reached whereby the Indians were brought—rather the indentured labourers were brought to Natal.

This followed the abolition of slavery?—Yes.

Did these indentured labourers come on any fixed contract?—Yes. They came on a fixed contract to work at a certain wage, I think about ten shillings a month, for a period of three years, which was afterwards increased to five years.

Were there any conditions attached to the agreement as to what would happen to the labourers after their term of indenture expired?—Yes, on expiration of their contract, if they wished to go to India, they would be given a free passage back, and in case they stay in this country, they would stay as free citizens under the common law of the government at the time.

I believe that at about this time also another type of Indian came into Natal, known as free immigrants?—Yes, there was no legal restriction attached to any Indians coming into Natal, and therefore quite a number of people who were domiciled in Mauritius or carrying on trade there, they came here. And quite a number of Indian traders followed from India, from various provinces, particularly from the Western part of India.

What was the predominant form of Indian immigration at this time?—Indentured.

Were the indentured Indians allowed to farm after their period of indenture had expired?—After a while, after a few years this flow of indentured labourers slackened, and as a result of that the Natal Government again made representation to India, and in 1874 a Bill was passed by the Natal Government giving more facilities to these indentured labourers if they did not wish to return to India. If they wished to stay in this country, they would be given a plot of land to farm on, given for free.

How long did this position continue?—It remained so till 1891.

What happened then?—In 1891 the facilities were taken away, and instead if the indentured labourer wished to remain in this country, he was subjected to a poll tax of 3 [pounds] to be paid annually by him. [3 The 3 tax was introduced by the Indian Immigration Amendment Act of Natal in 1895.]

Was the immigration of Indians into Natal ever restricted?—Yes, in 1897, some restrictions came into operation. [4 Under the Immigration Restriciton Act of 1897.]

What was the position with regard to the Parliamentary franchise in Natal prior to 1896?—Indians were entitled to a franchise right in Natal up to 1894. In that year the franchise was taken away by an Act of Parliament. [5 Natal enacted a law in 1894 to deprive Asiatics of Parliamentary franchise, but Royal assent for the law was denied after protests by the Indian community.] In 1896, Natal enacted another law with the same effect, but without specific mention of "Asiatics", and it received assent.

Mr. Justice Bekker

Were all Indians entitled?—Yes.

Indentured labourers?—Those would become free, immediately their contract is over, my Lord, and entitled to franchise rights.

Free immigrants?—Free immigrants were entitled to franchise rights.

As a matter of interest, how big were these plots of land which were given to them?—A few acres of land, which would be sufficient for the upkeep of that family.

Mr. Kathrada

Could you tell us what the provisions were with regard to the Municipal franchise before and after 1924?—The Indians were entitled to Municipal franchise up to 1924, and in that year they were deprived of that franchise as well.

What effect did the 1946 Asiatic Land Tenure Act have on Indian ownership and occupation of land in Natal?—This was the first time in history that Indians were debarred from occupation and ownership of land in Natal. . . .

Is it correct that the Group Areas Act for the first time exposed the Indian community to the dangers of having their land confiscated?—Yes, that is so. Powers were given under the Act that if any land is held illegally perhaps or it becomes illegal at any time . . . then the land may be confiscated. This is the first time confiscation of the properties really began.

How has the South African Indian Congress regarded the wide powers which the Minister of the Interior has under the Group Areas Act?—The Indians believed that these wide powers in the hands of the Minister was something like dictatorial powers, which affect the Indian community in practically every aspect of their lives, and this is the first time in the history of South Africa that Indians were subjected to be ruled by proclamation.

What in the opinion of the South African Indian Congress was the real intention and policy of this Act?—This Act, the Indian people mean, was to exterminate the Indian community and to repatriate them if possible from this country.

Was this view of the SAIC strengthened by the reports of any government committee?—Yes. The Joint Committee on the Land Tenure was established by the Minister of the Interior, and the findings were published just before this Act was enacted in Parliament, and there was the sort of reason given in the report. . . .

> "'After the effect of the Group Areas Act had been felt, Indians will only be too pleased to get out of South Africa', said Mr. W. A. Maree at a report back meeting held in the Town Hall."

Next I want to quote from the Manifesto of the Nationalist Party in 1948.

> "The Party holds the view that Indians are a foreign and outlandish element which is unassimilable. They can never become part of the country and they must therefore be treated as an immigrant community." (From the *Programme and Principles of the Nationalist Party*)

Does the South African Indian Congress accept these statements as having been made by the Minister concerned and by the Nationalist Party?—Yes. . . .

Are you aware of a statement made by the former Chairman of the Group Areas Board, Mr. de Vos Huge, who is at present a Judge in the Supreme Court, about the Indians and the Group Areas Act?—Yes, where he refers to the fact that the Indians—something to the effect that they are undesirable and they are robbers.

If I put this sentence to you, would you be able to recognise it? "Indians were a band of robbers who won't part with their ill-gotten gains, unless forced to do so." Is that what you are referring to?—Yes.

TOPICS FOR ORAL OR WRITTEN EXPLORATION

1. To what extent are the people of South Africa defined racially and culturally? Is this racial mosaic illustrated in *Cry, the Beloved Country?* And, given the history of South Africa, will race and culture be effaced from South African identities?

2. According to "Examination by Mr. Kathrada," what has been the experience of other nonwhite groups in South Africa?

3. Explain why nonwhite groups did not rally for a common cause in segregated South Africa? What form of colonization, according to Mphahlele, best divides this nation?

4. What is a native, and why is being a native an issue in South Africa?

NOTE

1. Those of mixed parentage—black and white, speaking mostly Afrikaans as their mother tongue.

SUGGESTIONS FOR FURTHER READING

Paton, Alan. *The Land and People of South Africa.* Philadelphia and New York: J. B. Lippincott, 1955.

Paton, Jonathan. *The Land and People of South Africa.* New York: HarperCollins, 1990.

State Department of Information Pretoria. *Multi-National Development in South Africa: The Reality.* Pretoria: State Department of Information, 1974.

Whittington, G. W. *Land and People of South Africa.* London: Hicks Smith & Sons Ltd., 1974.

WORKS CITED

Abrahams, Peter. *Return to Goli.* London: Faber and Faber, 1953. "Examination of Mr. Kathrada" is online at http://www.anc.org.za/ancdocs/history/misc/molvi-16.html.

Maylam, Paul. *A History of the African People of South Africa: From the Early Iron Age to the 1970s.* New York: St. Martin's Press, 1986.

Mphahlele, Ezekiel. *The African Image.* New York: Frederick A. Praeger, 1962.

Paton, Alan. *Cry, the Beloved Country.* New York: Collier Books, 1986.

Paton, Jonathan. *The Land and People of South Africa.* New York: HarperCollins, 1990.

State Department of Information Pretoria. *Multi-National Development in South Africa: The Reality.* Pretoria: State Department of Information, 1974.

Tutu, Desmond. *The Words of Desmond Tutu.* Ed. Naomi Tutu. London: Spire, 1989.

Tyler, Humphrey. "How to Be a South African." *Mail and Guardian Online,* April 29, 2006. Online at www.mg.co.za/articlePage.asp?articleid=261253&area=/insight/insight_commen.

Van den Berghe, Pierre L., ed. "Race Attitudes in Durban, South Africa." *Africa. Social Problems and Conflict.* San Francisco: Chandler, 1965: 248–266.

Whittington, G. W. *Land and People of South Africa.* London: Hicks Smith & Sons Ltd., 1974.

4

The Roots of Apartheid

Alan Paton's *Cry, the Beloved Country* opens with Lewis Gannett's Introduction, which quotes at length Alan Paton's speech presented on October 1949 in New York at the Book and Author Luncheon. In this introduction, Paton presents the historical background to his novel, detailing the development of South Africa and the factors that engendered apartheid. In his speech, he proposes three factors: colonial domination, differences of opinion between the British and Afrikaners on the treatment of Africans, and Afrikaners' fear of losing their cultural and linguistic identity. After all, as he writes in *Towards the Mountain,* he has "grown up in a strange society where race and its concomitant emotions of fear, hate, tolerance, love, contempt shape [their] thoughts and actions from cradle to grave" (20).

Paton's historical overview, quoted by Gannett, narrating the becoming of South Africa from a Western historical perspective, contends that Afrikaners developed segregationist positions because of their need to survive. At the onset of European settlement, the Bushmen and the Hottentots, he claims, were not a match for the powerful European settlers, so they quickly "melted away" (xv). However, as they moved further into the interior, "the black men were numerous and savage and determined; the history of this encounter is one of terror and violence. The black people became truly a part of the white man's mind" (xvi). Because of the imminent danger of being expunged by blacks, "the Afrikaner attitude toward black men hardened. The safety and survival of the small band of white people were seen as dependent on the rigid separation of white and black. It became the law that the relationship between white and black was to be that between master and servant; and it became the iron law that between white men and black women, between black men and white women, there was to be no other relationship but this" (xvi).

Afrikaners and Britons had different economic interests and racial ideologies. This, and the British will to dominate the Afrikaners, entrenched their desire for independence and fostered their nationalism. British liberalism and entrepreneurship, which pursued Afrikaners even when they fled into the interior during the Great Trek, intensified the Afrikaners' fear of being engulfed. Afrikaner nationalism, therefore, was behind the creation of "cultural societies for the protection of [Afrikaner] customs, history and language" (xvii). And, with the increasing encroachment of Africans on urban areas in South Africa, white South Africans, Paton contends, "voted in favor of a party that advocated stern control and separation of the races as the 'only solution' of South Africa's ever more complicated and difficult problems" (xviii).

Paton's lecture highlights the three roots of apartheid; it presents the African tragedy solely from a European perspective; and, even as it highlights the horror of this historical trauma, it diminishes Western responsibility through the use of words such as "melting" (entailing nonviolence) and "savage" (reinforcing colonial ethnocentric perceptions) when describing Africans. It also fails to examine all the historical and cultural factors that engendered apartheid. The novel, on the other hand, well depicts the sordid existence of Africans in segregated South Africa, both in rural and urban settings. Yet, it is evident from the humble characterization of Reverend Stephen Kumalo, from the titles "umnumzana" (sir) and "inkosana" (little master) that Reverend Kumalo uses to address James Jarvis and his grandson, respectively, and from the bipolarized and racialized description of the landscape that the paternalism of the colonial era remains strong. Indeed, the novel begins with the juxtaposition of the lush land of James Jarvis and the sterility of Ndotsheni without providing the most significant explanation for the disparity, one that goes well beyond the agricultural technique and ignorance of the African population. Moreover, Jarvis's laudable conversion does not reach to support for racial equality but only leads him to call for the amelioration of the living conditions of the people of Ndotsheni. His conversion does not jeopardize his position of privilege within this hierarchical racial relationship. Indeed, when John Harris invites James Jarvis to leave John Kumalo's rally, Jarvis is incapable of accepting the possibility that Europeans might lose their privileged position. While he acknowledges that the historical forces of change are in motion and that he does care for such things, John Harris observes that he is too old to face this reality (187). Jarvis's paternalism is, perhaps, a reflection of Alan Paton's own liberalism, since, as he states in his autobiography, he was a strong pronationalist in 1938, and it was not until December 16, 1938, that he became an antinationalist after attending the centennial celebration of the Great Trek. "With Malan's brand of exclusive nationalism, and particularly with his race theories," he writes, "I wished to have nothing to do. I went back to Diepkloof and said to Dorrie, 'I'm taking off this beard, and I shall never wear another'" (308). And as a liberal, he belonged to the kind, he writes in *Towards the Mountain,* that "cling[s] to the irrational idea that one could maintain white supremacy and yet be just" (240).

So what is apartheid? It is an Afrikaans word meaning separateness and is used to refer to the South African political ideology of separate development. It advocated the separate development of specific racial groups: Africans, Coloreds, Asians, Afrikaners, and English-speaking Europeans. This political policy, according to UNESCO, advocated (1) the legalization of segregation practices through the extension and consolidation of racial separation legislation; (2) Afrikaner control of South African social life and economics; (3) white supremacy; (4) government and economic control of racial segregation through language, culture, race, and education; and (5) restrictions on the development of African nationalism by the indirect control of traditional chiefs (3).

There are two scholarly positions on the origins of South African: that of the idealists and that of the materialists. The idealists contend that it is the Christian/heathen dichotomy that led to the South African racial divide in the eighteenth century, whereas the materialists claim that racism began in the nineteenth century with the rise of capitalism. Idealists assume, on the basis of the interracial marriages that existed during the early days of colonialism, that there was no racism during that time. This assertion is far from the truth; according to Paul Maylam, precolonial society was perhaps tolerant, but racism already existed since European expansionism fostered racist dogma.

The term "racism," referring to racial and cultural differences, was coined in 1508, but the concept of the Other (the stranger or the individual different from oneself) was also constructed in the fifteen century, although the Other had existed since biblical times. The Dutch, according to Leonard Guelk, brought their prejudice to the Cape even before they encountered Africans. Analysts contend that a racial order existed before the industrial era, as evinced in the writings of Jan van Riebeeck. The initial objectives of the Dutch when they arrived at the Cape were to control the production of the natives and to trade with them; as a result, they had a permissive policy in their dealings with the natives.

But, as the Company shifted to a colony settlement and established a class hierarchy among the population–employees, burghers (farmers) slaves, and

Khoisans (the status of the latter varied in accordance with their Christianization or slave status). This class stratification was already indirectly racialized, since the first two social categories consisted only of whites, implicitly Christians and assumed to be superior to nonbelievers and slaves. Moreover, they alone could not be enslaved and, unlike Asians and Africans, were given land and political power by the Dutch West India Company.

By the end of the seventeenth century, race had become the major index of humanness or class, and the Calvinist religion, stricter than the Catholic Church, with its beliefs in divine election, reinforced this rigid racial stratification. The idea of predestination, which is not specific to South Africa, manifested itself elsewhere in the world in terms of a group's prosperity, but in South Africa it took the form of skin color, or race. As God's elects, Europeans were superior to Africans, who were associated with heathenism and evil and thus to be dominated. The complicity of the church in the establishment of segregation and apartheid is illustrated in *Cry, the Beloved Country* when John Kumalo claims that the "Church too is like the chief. You must do so and so and so. You are not free to have an experience. A man must be faithful and meek and obedient, and he must obey the laws, whatever the laws may be. It is true that the Church speaks with a fine voice, and that the Bishops speak against the laws" (36). The Christian dilemma, is once again well articulated in Arthur Jarvis's manuscript when he ponders the nature of South African Christianity, which upholds brotherhood yet advocates the oppression of blacks. "And we are therefore compelled, in order to preserve our belief that we are Christian, to ascribe to Almighty God, Creator of Heaven and Earth, our own human intentions, and to say that because he created white and black, He gives the Divine to any human action that is designed to keep black men from advancement. We go so far as to credit Almighty God with having created black men to hew wood and draw water for white men" (154).

Apartheid as corroborated by Courtney Jung, in *Then I Was Black,* was also morally supported and justified by the exclusive and race-based biblical interpretation of the Calvinist Dutch Reformed Church (DRC). The Church's indifference to the fate of Africans is exposed in *Cry, the Beloved Country* through the discrimination within the Church, which John Kumalo decries when he tells his brother, Reverend Kumalo, and Reverend Msimangu, "The Bishop says it is wrong, . . . but he lives in a big house, and his white priests get four, five, six times what you get, my brother" (37). Despite all the sordid events taking place around them, the Anglican clergy talk about black crime and other insignificant issues but do not suggest any solution or action for the more pressing problems of oppression and injustice. No wonder the Dutch Reformed Church was referred to, according to Allister Sparks, as the

"National Party at Prayer" because it was heavily involved in the formulation of apartheid ideology, even if it did not initiate the policies. The Church, he writes, "replaced the sense of guilt with a sense of mission, teaching not only that apartheid is not sinful but that it is in accordance with the laws of God. To implement it is therefore a sacred task which the Afrikaner people have been specifically 'called' to perform" (153).

This racial separation ultimately led to apartheid, which, according to T.R.H. Davenport and Christopher Saunders, Peter F. Alexander, and other scholars, was the result of early segregationist policies and Broederbond, a political mafia of the 1930s that fought for the "vertical" separation of races. This racialist Afrikaner ideology was reinforced by capitalism; Oliver Fox states, in *Caste, Class, and Race* (1948), that apartheid was not "an abstract, natural immemorial feeling of mutual antipathy between groups, but rather a practical exploitative relationship" (27). Apartheid was an instrument of exploitation and a means of protecting white privilege as *Cry, the Beloved Country* so well illustrates. The European community doubts that Africans have the ability to organize a strike, says the narrator of *Cry, the Beloved Country,* because "the thought of so fantastic a thing is terrifying, and white people realize how dependent they are on the labour of the black people" (189).

The fear of assimilation, religion, and economics are at the foundation of South African segregation, but they are not necessarily the only elements that were instrumental in the rise of apartheid. The Great Trek was also an important moment in Afrikaner identity formation since it was associated with the rebirth of Afrikaner identity. The nineteenth century produced Afrikaner intellectuals, and the twentieth-century economic context of poor-whiteism produced an Afrikaner intelligentsia, which had the mission of redeeming the *volk* (folk) and which formulated the ideology of apartheid. The increasing migration of Africans to urban centers also shifted Afrikaners' fear of being assimilated by the British to fear of the ever-increasing black population. Fear that bastardization, as Geoff Cronjé contends, would "contaminate the blood-purity of Afrikanerdom's posterity, destroying its natural identity and submerging it in a single, unidentified 'mishmash' race" (148) was at its strongest.

Apart from the fear of losing one's identity, a seminal force that Alan Paton does not foreground in *Cry, the Beloved Country* is the impact of Hitler's Nazism. Afrikaners had an emotional tie to Germany since they had a related language and a common ancestry. A lot of South African intellectuals had also studied in Germany and had been influenced by Hitler and German philosophers. Their prejudices were echoed by this leading German nation, an adversary of England, from which they wished to be liberated. The main ideas, the religious concept that Afrikaners are God's chosen people and the political and religious idea that the *volk* were given their attributes at creation, are the foundation of apartheid. The fusion of these two religious and ethnic concepts led to the idea that Boers were not simply God's chosen people but people with a mission to preserve their cultural identity and that of other nations. Hence, apartheid was not just a political program but very much a religious ideology. Unlike American segregation, apartheid, according to Sparks, was a "radical, programmatic restructuring of a country, of a socially intermixed society becoming daily integrated economically, dividing it into separate living areas, separate towns, separate economies, separate living areas, separate towns, separate economies, separate 'nations,' total separation," according to Geoff Cronjé (qtd. in Sparks 149–150).

The Broederbond (Band of Brothers) controlled Afrikaner cultural life through the Federation of Afrikaner Cultural Unions and other educational and funeral institutions. It created an investment company, universities, a burial society, and the Rapportyres (a type of Lions Club). It had great political influence because it served as a filter for political actions and ideas, making it the think tank of the government. The Broederbond conceived the political apartheid concept of radical racial division. It paid lip service to Africans in contending that apartheid was a means of providing blacks with "responsible guardianship," but it was a racist ideology in nature, since it construed blacks as spiritually, morally, and intellectually inferior. Apartheid was an ideology that ensured white hegemony, protected whites economically from African competition, and buttressed assumptions of nonwhites' racial inferiority.

Nadine Gordimer, the author of *July's People* and one of South Africa's foremost radical European writers, well defines the nature, the motives, and the social, political, and economic impact of apartheid on the lives of South Africans. Apartheid, according to her, is a virus that is not limited to the Afrikaner community but infects all whites. Peter Abrahams's *The Path of Thunder* connects Lanny's oppression to precolonial days of European, Bantu, and Khoisan land battles. Excerpts from Sarah Gertrude's *God's Stepchildren* and *The King of Bastards,* dealing with issues of miscegenation, embody the race consciousness of early settlers that informs Paton's characters' perception of Africans. Likewise, Nadine Gordimer's *July's People* illustrates how Arthur Jarvis failed to learn about South Africa.

NADINE GORDIMER, "APARTHEID," FROM *MODERN AND CLASSICAL ESSAYS: TWELVE MASTERS*

(ED. PAUL MARX. MOUNTAIN VIEW, CA: MAYFIELD, 1996: 107)

Nadine Gordiner's "Apartheid" gives the reader a good understanding of how the apartheid political system privileged whites and oppressed nonwhites.

1959

Men are not born brothers; they have to discover each other, and it is this discovery that apartheid seeks to prevent . . . What is apartheid?

It depends who's answering. If you ask a member of the South African government, he will tell you that it is separate and parallel development of white and black—that is the official, legal definition. If you ask an ordinary white man who supports the policy, he will tell you that it is the means of keeping South Africa white. If you ask a black man, he may give you any one of a dozen answers, arising out of whatever aspect of apartheid he has been brought up short against that day, for to him it is neither an ideological concept nor a policy, but a context in which his whole life, learning, working, loving, is rigidly enclosed.

He could give you a list of the laws that restrict him from aspiring to most of the aims of any civilized person, or enjoying the pleasures that every white person takes for granted. But it is unlikely that he will. What may be on his mind at the moment is the problem of how to save his child from the watered-down "Bantu Education" which is now standard in schools for black children—inferior schooling based on a reduced syllabus that insists the black child cannot attain the same standard of education as the white child, and places emphasis on practical and menial skills. Or perhaps you've merely caught him on the morning after he's spent a night in the police cells because he was out after curfew hours without a piece of paper hearing a white man's signature permitting him to be so. Perhaps (if he's a man who cares for such things) he's feeling resentful because there's a concert in town he would not be permitted to attend, or (if he's that kind of man, and who isn't?) he's irked at having to pay a black-market price for the bottle of brandy he is debarred from buying legitimately. That's apartheid, to him. All these things, big and little, and many more.

If you want to know how Africans—black men—live in South Africa, you will get in return for your curiosity an exposition of apartheid in action, for in all of a black man's life—all his life—rejection by the white man has the last word. With this word of rejection apartheid began, long before it hardened into laws and legislation, long before it became a theory of racial selectiveness and the policy of a government. The Afrikaner Nationalists (an Afrikaner is a white person of Dutch descent whose mother tongue is Afrikaans: a Nationalist is a member or supporter of the National Party, at present in power did not invent it, they merely developed it, and the impulse of Cain from which they worked lives in many white South Africans today, English-speaking as well as Afrikaner.

Shall I forget that when I was a child I was taught that I must never use a cup from which our black servant had drunk?

DESMOND TUTU, "APARTHEID," FROM *THE WORDS OF DESMOND TUTU*

(ED. NAOMI TUTU. SPIRE: LONDON, 1989: 41)

This excerpt clearly articulates the relationship among slums, misery, and apartheid. It provides background to Paton's slums.

It won't do to tinker with this system. It cannot be reformed. It must be dismantled. It must be destroyed so that a new South Africa can rise.

"Apartheid has decreed the politics of exclusion. Seventy-three percent of the population is excluded from any meaningful participation in the political decision-making process of the land of their birth. . . . Blacks are expected to exercise their political ambitions in unviable, poverty-stricken, arid, Bantustan homelands, ghettoes of misery, inexhaustible reservoirs of cheap black labor, Bantustans into which South Africa is being balkanized. Blacks are systematically being stripped of their South African citizenship and being turned into aliens in the land of their birth. This is apartheid's Final Solution, just as Nazism had its Final Solution for the Jews in Hitler's Aryan madness."

"Detention without trial is an abrogation of the rule of law; it is a subverting of justice. It is to punish someone and to punish him severely without the inconvenience of having to prove his guilt in an open court. It is a very handy device greatly beloved of totalitarian, repressive governments."

"THE BIRTH OF THE BOND," A TRANSLATION FROM A DUTCH PAMPHLET, ISSUED IN 1882, TITLED "DE TRANSVAALSE OORLOG GRAHAMSTON"

(GRAHAMSTON, CAPE OF GOOD HOPE: JOSIAH SLATER, "JOURNAL & PUBLISHING WORKS," 1900: 18, 19, 20, 21, 23)

Alan Paton's *Cry, the Beloved Country* delineates the tensions between Afrikaners and English-speaking Europeans. Both groups have developed stereotypes about the other. This document provides insight into the causes and the reasoning behind these ethnic and political divides. Moreover, the Broederbond in the 1940s saw apartheid as a total separation of races: educational, political, economic, and cultural.

Chapter II.

Form an Afrikander Bond.

This is another matter which we must now carry through. Now or never. We have seen how necessary it is that the Afrikaners should have a general union or body, so as to be able to work together. This was never more necessary than now. Even the *Volksblad,* which formerly was not favourable to such a Bond, and even now objects to its being empowered to watch the Press, finds the establishment of the Bond not only advisable but pressingly needful. It remarks; "All doubt as to the pressing necessity of taking this matter in hand vanishes, now that we see that branches of the London South African Union are being formed at the Cape, so as to give powerful assistance to the English merchants. If there *must* be a conflict between English and Dutch here, then let the Dutch take care that they are ready for it."

The Free State Express of 7th April last publishes the Draft of such a Bond, similar to what we have several times proposed in the *Patriot,* but worked out more in detail by some friends at Bloemfontein. Here follows its constitution

Constitution of the Bond.

The Bond knows no nationality whatever other than simply that of Afrikanders, regarding as such all from whatever origin, who promise under the limits of this Constitution to work for the good and welfare of South Africa.

The object of the Africander Bond is the establishment of a South African Nationality through the cultivation of a true love of this our fatherland.

This object must be attained both by the promotion and defence of the national language ***(volkstaal)*** and by Afrikanders both politically and socially making their power to be felt as a nation. . . .

An Africander Confederation.

All details can further on be discussed and settled. This does not hinder Ward and District Branches from being at once formed, which adopt the fundamental principles of the Bond, and afterwards at meetings of the Provincial and Central Boards the rules can finally be settled, in accordance with the wishes of the lower committees. Such branches have already been formed at Philipstown, Hanover and. Calvinia, and other districts are preparing to form them. Let all do so. The bond must grow up out of the heart of the people: the rules can come after. This is now our time to establish the Bond, while a national consciousness has been awakened through the Transvaal war. . . .

Away with the English Flag.

But so long as the English flag remains here, the Africander Bond must be our Confederation. . . .

Africanders must be on top.

We have seen that our land and people have gained much by the Transvaal war. But if we now in self-complacency relax our efforts, or in dulness [*sic*] of heart sit idle, then the danger is that we shall lose more by the war than we have gained by it. The Jingoes sleep not. They know what they have lost, and are busied day and night to win it back. And. what is more, they will with unexpected violence oppress us Africanders once for all, and so set their foot on our neck, that we shall never be able to lift up our heads again. We have never declared a moral and social war as the result of the Transvaal war, but they have done so. In their spite and rage they have betrayed themselves, and. spoken out their inmost thoughts. "Sprigg must remain in office," they say, "not that his Ministry is so good, but otherwise the Africanders will presently get the upper hand. The Transvaal must first be put down; we must so destroy them that the Africanders shall be in fear for ever. The Africanders are our enemies, they must be subdued, otherwise we English cannot live here," &c., &c.—Thus, let us calculate it is we on top or they on top; they must be under or we under.

Establish the Bond.

What are we to do than? Yes, this is the question which every one ought seriously to ask; and. this is the question which we are how going to answer. We have already set forth more plainly and simply than had heretofore been done, friendship or hostility of the enemy. . . . And while we are more specially dealing with the Republics, we will accordingly give the Boers there one more piece of advice: they must

Sell no Land to Englishmen.

We especially say this to our Transvaal brethren. In any national conflict it is to the advantage of us Africanders that we are the landowners. The great majority of the

English are only birds of passage *(trekvogels)* that go away us soon as they have eaten carrion enough, or there is no more carrion to be got. Our Boers are really the nobility of South Africa. In England they have a very perverted idea of our Boers. They think they are like the English farmers. Among the English the nobles are the landowners, and the "boers" are merely tenants, the slaves in fact of the nobility. Here it is just the reverse. The Boers are the landowners, and the proud little Englishmen are dependent on the Boers. They themselves are now beginning to see it; and therefore will they try to get our ground into their possession. . . .

We Africanders still possess the land of South Africa . . . : do not surrender it. . . . But the English to whom you have once sold land, you will never, never get rid of. We repeat, we mean by English the Jingoes who will sacrifice us and our interests to England. Englishmen that will become Africanders, by accepting our land and nation and language, we are very willing to accept, and that in every way.

From a respected quarter comes the question: "Is it right and Christianlike to abuse all the whole English nation as Soakers, Robbers and Soldiers?" Our reply is: That would be wrong and un-Christian; and therefore we did not do so. We have not said, and shall never say, that the whole English nation consists of those three classes. We said that the Army with which England conquers countries and nations consists of those three classes; and this is quite a different thing. Within its own bounds and limits the English nation has its rights and merits, like any other nation. But our objection is against this threefold army which goes beyond its bounds to invade the rights and freedom of other nations not against the English people, but against this shameful army of conquest we declare war on moral and social grounds, and simply in self-defence; for its object is nothing less than the subjugation of our people and the extinction of our nationality. . . .

War Against the English Language.

This must for all Africanders be another result of the Transvaal war. Now that the war against the English Government is over, the war against the English language must begin, wherever that language has been unlawfully intruded. For English rule was unlawfully forced upon the Transvaal: the Boers have now driven it away with the rifle. But the English language has unjustly intruded itself into our whole country, and is pushing still further in. In our Colonial Parliament and our Courts of Justice the language of the "Reds" *(rooitaal)* reigns unrestrained. This gibberish forces its way vigorously into our schools, churches and houses in the two Republics as well as in this Colony and Natal. We must declare war against it without weapons, and drive away the *rooitaal.* How then? Simply by acknowledging and using our own language, and demanding its rights everywhere, as may be needful. . . .

The Bluffers.

Our Free State friend, who divided the English army of conquest into three regiments, apparently was not well acquainted with the fourth, the most dangerous, the reserve force, which follows the others. Or else we would gladly have known what name he would give to this fourth regiment. We cannot find a suitable name for them, to our mind, but let us call them the Bluffers or wind-makers. The succession then is, (1) Soakers, (2) Robbers, (3) Reds, (4) Bluffers. But what do we mean then by the bluffers? We mean the English and the Anglified schoolmasters, and still more, school- mistresses, who teach our children from early youth

(a) That the English language is the finest and best, whereas it is only a miscellaneous gibberish, without proper grammar or dictionary.

(b) That English history is the most interesting and glorious, whereas it is nothing more than a concatenation of 1ies and misrepresentations.

(c) That they must give the chief place to English geography, whereas all England is nothing more than an island in the North Sea.

(d) That they are educated as soon as they can gabble English whereas they simply make themselves ridiculous by it, in the eyes of every judicious person.

(e) That English books and periodicals are the finest and best to read, though really they are the greatest mass of nonsense (with some exceptions) that you can find anywhere; and finally, in one word,

(f) That it is an honour for everyone to ape the English in everything, and, in fact, to become English, whereas it is the greatest shame and disgrace for any people to belie their own God-given nationality.

This is what we mean by the Bluffers. And why do we call this regiment the most dangerous? Because they work in so unobtrusively, and thus are hard to watch against; because they corrupt our youth, and thereby absolutely take away our whole future; because they flatter natural pride, and thus find the readier access; because they not only oppress our nationality, but totally eradicate it, by making our children English. This so-called English education has done more mischief to our country and nation than we can ever express. Look at our children that have had English education; they are (with few exceptions) Anglicised to a worse degree than the English themselves. . . . We must demand the use of our language *(taal).*

Dutch in the Churches.

4. In our churches especially we must watch that English *(die rooitaal)* does not intrude. . . .

In the Schools.

5. In our Schools, too, we must insist on Dutch for our children. Demand it in Parliament, and if they do not comply, demand it at the elections. The silly saying must be stopped that has misled thousands. "Let your children only learn English, they will learn Dutch of themselves." Nonsense. A child must first learn his own language thoroughly, and then in his own language he can learn other languages and branches of knowledge. . . . By Anglifying the girls, they infect the whole family-life with the English speech. . . .

Disgrace to Speak English.

6. In our conversation we must still more oppose and expel the English. Let English words be dropped out of our speech. Young men must give each other a pinch for using an English word.

PETER ABRAHAMS, "HOME," FROM *THE PATH OF THUNDER*

(CHATHAM, NJ: CHATHAM BOOKSELLER, 1948: 12–14)

Peter Abrahams's "Home" excellently illustrates the colonial forces at the origin of South African racialist ideas, which inform racial relationships during the segregation era in which Alan Paton's *Cry, the Beloved Country* is set and later during the apartheid period.

Coldly the man stared at him, looked him up and down.

"Nice day," Lanny said. "I'm returning home after seven years." The ticket collector stared at him, a cold hostile stare.

And suddenly Lanny remembered. This was not Cape Town. This was the highveld, and on the highveld one did not speak to a white man till he spoke to you. He should have remembered. It was stupid to forget. . . .

He can't intimidate me, Lanny thought. He picked up his cases and passed the man, feeling those eyes on his back as he left the siding. Well, he had made a mistake. . . .

"Do you see what I see?" one of the men asked. The other pursed his lips and looked doubtful:

"I'm not sure. It looks like an ape in a better Sunday suit than I have. But today's not Sunday so I'm not sure."

"Perhaps he wears suits like that every day. . . . Besides, you are wrong, he's too pale to be an ape. That's a city bushy."

The second man rubbed his eyes and looked intently at Lanny. The girl giggled, then broke into laughter.

"Bushy?" asked the second man.

"Yes. In the cities they speak English and call themselves Eurafricans."

"Eurafricans? It's a big word. What does it mean?"

The First man grinned:

"You know. Colored, half-caste, bastard!" He spat out the last word with contempt. . . .

"And that's one of them?"

"Yes."

"He's pretty, isn't he? And look at the beautiful creases in his trousers. I bet you a tailor made that suit for him. And look at his shoes. Did you ever have shoes like that?" . . .

Hey! You! . . .

The man inspected him closely.

"Where you from?" the man shot at him.

"Cape Town."

"What do you want here?"

"I live here." . . .

"What are you?"

"What do you mean?"

"I mean what I say. Have you any fancy titles?" Lanny smiled. "Yes. I have two."

Suddenly the man's hand shot out and cracked across Lanny's mouth. With an effort Lanny controlled the instinctive urge to strike back. The man saw the move and struck again. . . .

"Don't smile at me!" the man hissed.

South Africa, Lanny thought, this is South Africa. And this man in front of him resented him because he was educated and showed independence. . . . This was still the old struggle for conquest. The history of his country. This man in front of him had to dominate him, he was fearful in case he did not. This was the history of South Africa in stark, brutal reality. He saw it clearly suddenly. Not out of books.

Not with kindly lecturers talking and eager or indifferent students making notes. Not these. No.

As he stood there with the morning sun behind him, he saw it all more vividly than he bad ever seen it. South Africa. The landing of Van Rebeck. The feeble resistance of the Bushmen with their poison darts. He could see the surprise on their faces when the blunderbusses spoke and they died. And their retreat from their old playground, the beautiful, rich, food-giving Cape Valley. They had been driven to the valley by the superior Hottentots, and driven from the valley by the coming of the white man. It was easy. They went down easily. They were a weak, feeble crowd who knew only their poison darts. And what are poison darts against blunderbusses? What indeed!

For a while the man's eyes rested on the fountain pen in his pocket.

"Education," the man said bitterly.

And still Lanny saw the battle going on. Zulu impis against white Voortrekkers. The bitterness of that fight. The native fighting for his land. The white man fighting for a foothold and fighting even harder to retain it.

In a few seconds the turbulent history of the country rolled over his head like a huge wave and was gone. He shuddered as the wave passed.

And here I am, Lanny thought, fighting the same battle in the twentieth century. How long would it go on? How much would it change?

SOL PLAATJE, "THE NATIVES' LAND ACT," FROM *NATIVE LIFE IN SOUTH AFRICA*

(Online posting at <http://www.polity.org.za/html/govdocs/legislation/misc/nla1913.html> [No. 27, 1913])

This is one of the most important legislative acts in the history of South Africa in that it legalized African land seizure and racial geographical boundaries, which had been taking place since the days of Jan van Riebeeck. This act explains why the Africans are concentrated in certain areas and why land plays an important role in Alan Paton's *Cry, the Beloved Country.*

Act

TO Make further provision as to the purchase and leasing of Land by Natives and other Persons in the several parts of the Union and for other purposes in connection with the ownership and occupation of Land by Natives and other Persons.

Be it enacted by the King's Most Excellent Majesty, the Senate and the House of Assembly of the Union of South Africa, as follows:—

1. (1) From and after the commencement of this Act, land outside the scheduled native areas shall, until Parliament, acting upon the report of the commission appointed under this Act, shall have made other provision, be subjected to the following provisions, that is to say:—

   Except with the approval of the Governor-General—

   a. a native shall not enter into any agreement or transaction for the purchase, hire, or other acquisition from a person other than a native, of any such land or of any right thereto, interest therein, or servitude thereover; and
   b. a person other than a native shall not enter into any agreement or transaction for the purchase, hire, or other acquisition from a native of any such land or of any right thereto, interest therein, or servitude thereover.

   (2) From and after the commencement of this Act, no person other than a native shall purchase, hire or in any other manner whatever acquire any land in a scheduled native area or enter into any agreement or transaction for the purchase, hire or other acquisition, direct or indirect, of any such land or of any right thereto or interest therein or servitude thereover, except with the approval of the Governor-General. . . .

   (4) Every agreement or any other transaction whatever entered into in contravention of this section shall be null and void *ab initio.*

2. (1) As soon as may be after the commencement of this Act the Governor-General shall appoint a commission whose functions shall be to inquire and report—

   a. what areas should be set apart as areas within which natives shall not be permitted to acquire or hire land or interests in land;
   b. what areas should be set apart as areas within which persons other than natives shall not be permitted to acquire or hire land or interests in land.
   c. The commission shall submit with any such report—

   i. descriptions of the boundaries of any area which it proposes should be so set apart; and
   ii. a map or maps showing every such area. . . .

4. (1) For the purposes of establishing any such area as is described in section *two,* the Governor-General may, out of moneys which Parliament may vote for the purpose, acquire any land or interest in land.

   (2) In default of agreement with the owners of the land or the holders of interests therein the provisions of the law in force in the Province in which such land or interest in land

is situate relating to the expropriation of land for public purposes shall apply and, if in any Province there be no such law, the provisions of Proclamation No. 5 of 1902 of the Transvaal and any amendment thereof shall *mutatis mutandis* apply.

5. (1) Any person who is a party to any attempted purchase, sale, hire or lease, or to any agreement or transaction which is in contravention of this Act or any regulation made thereunder shall be guilty of an offence and liable on conviction to a fine not exceeding one hundred pounds or, in default of payment, to imprisonment with or without hard labour for a period not exceeding six months, and if the act constituting the offence be a continuing one, the offender shall be liable to a further fine not exceeding five pounds for every day which that act continues.

(2) In the event of such an offence being committed by a company, corporation, or other body of persons (not being a firm or partnership), every director, secretary, or manager of such company, corporation, or body who is within the Union shall be liable to prosecution and punishment and, in the event of any such offence being committed by a firm or partnership, every member of the firm or partnership who is within the Union shall be liable to prosecution and punishment.

6. In so far as the occupation by natives of land outside the scheduled native areas may be affected by this Act, the provisions thereof shall be construed as being in addition to and not in substitution for any law in force at the commencement thereof relating to such occupation; but in the event of a conflict between the provisions of this Act and the provisions of any such law, the provisions of this Act shall, save as is specially provided therein, prevail:

Provided that—

a. nothing in any such law or in this Act shall be construed as restricting the number of natives who, as farm labourers, may reside on any farm in the Transvaal;

b. in any proceedings for a contravention of this Act the burden of proving that a native is a farm labourer shall be upon the accused;

c. until Parliament, acting upon the report of the said commission, has made other provision, no native resident on any farm in the Transvaal or Natal shall be liable to penalties or to be removed from such farm under any law, if at the commencement of this Act he or the head of his family is registered for taxation or other purposes in the department of Native Affairs as being resident on such farm, nor shall the owner of any such farm be liable to the penalties imposed by section *five* in respect of the occupation of the land by such native; but nothing herein contained shall affect any right possessed by law by an owner or lessee of a farm to remove any native there from. . . .

(2) Those heads of families, with their families, who are described in article *twenty* of Law No. 4 of 1895 of the Orange Free State shall in the circumstances described in that article be deemed to fall under the provisions of Ordinance No. 7 of 1904 of that Province or of any other law hereafter enacted amending or substituted for that Ordinance.

(3) Whenever in Chapter XXXIV of the Orange Free State Law Book the expressions "lease" and "leasing" are used, those expressions shall be construed as including or referring to an agreement or arrangement whereby a person, in consideration of his being permitted to occupy land, renders or promises to render to any person a share of the produce thereof, or any valuable consideration of any kind whatever other than his own labour or services or the labour or services of any of his family.

8. (1) Nothing in this Act contained shall be construed as,—

   a. preventing the continuation or renewal (until Parliament acting upon the report of the said commission has made other provision) of any agreement or arrangement lawfully entered into and in existence at the commencement of this Act which is a hiring or leasing of land as defined in this Act; or

   b. invalidating or affecting in any manner whatever any agreement or any other transaction for the purchase of land lawfully entered into prior to the commencement of this Act, or as prohibiting any person from purchasing at any sale held by order of a competent court any land which was hypothecated by a mortgage bond passed before the commencement of this Act; or

   c. prohibiting the acquisition at any time of land or interests in land by devolution or succession on death, whether under a will or on intestacy; or

   d. preventing the due registration in the proper deeds office (whenever registration is necessary) of documents giving effect to any such agreement, transaction, devolution or succession as is in this section mentioned; or

   e. prohibiting any person from claiming, acquiring, or holding any such servitude as under Chapter VII, of the Irrigation and Conservation of Waters Act, 1912, he is specially entitled to claim, acquire, or hold; or

   f. in any way altering the law in force at the commencement of this Act relating to the acquisition of rights to minerals, precious or base metals or precious stones; or

   g. applying to land within the limits in which a municipal council, town council, town board, village management board, or health committee or other local authority exercises jurisdiction; or

   h. applying to land held at the commencement of the Act by any society carrying on, with the approval of the Governor-General, educational or missionary work amongst natives; or

   i. prohibiting the acquisition by natives from any person whatever of land or interests in land in any township lawfully established prior to the commencement of this Act, provided it is a condition of the acquisition that no land or interest in land in such township has at any time been or shall in future be, transferred except to a native or coloured person; or

   j. permitting the alienation of land or its diversion from the purposes for which it was set apart if, under section *one hundred and forty-seven* of the South African Act, 1909, or any other law, such land could not be alienated or so diverted except under the authority of an Act of Parliament; or

   k. in any way modifying the provisions of any law whereby mortgages of or charges over land may be created to secure advances out of public moneys for specific purposes mentioned in such law and the interest of such advances, or where under the mortgagee or person having the charge may enter and take possession of the land so mortgaged or charged except that in any sale of such land in accordance with such law the provisions of this Act shall be observed.

(2) Nothing in this Act contained which imposes restrictions upon the acquisition by any person of land or right thereto, interests therein, or servitudes there over, shall be in force in the Province of the Cape of Good Hope, if and for so long as such person would, by such restrictions, be prevented from acquiring or holding a qualification whereunder he

is or may become entitled to be registered as a voter at parliamentary elections in any electoral division in the said Province.

9. The Governor-General may make regulations for preventing the overcrowding of huts and other dwellings in the stadts, native villages and settlements and other places in which natives are congregated in areas not under the jurisdiction of any local authority, the sanitation of such places and for the maintenance of the health of the inhabitants thereof.

10. In this Act, unless inconsistent with the context,—

"scheduled native area" shall mean any area described in the Schedule to this Act;

"native" shall mean any person, male or female, who is a member of an aboriginal race or tribe of Africa; and shall further include any company or other body of persons, corporate or unincorporate, if the persons who have a controlling interest therein are natives;

"interest in land" shall include, in addition to other interest in land, the interest which a mortgagee of, or person having charge over, land acquires under a mortgage bond or charge;

"Minister" shall mean the Minister of Native Affairs;

"farm labourer" shall mean a native who resides on a farm and is *bona fide,* but not necessarily continuously employed by the owner or lessee thereof in domestic service or in farming operations:

Provided that—

a. if such native reside on one farm and is employed on another farm of the same owner or lessee he shall be deemed to have resided, and to have been employed, on one and the same farm;
b. such native shall not be deemed to be *bona fide* employed unless he renders ninety days' service at least in one calendar year on the farm occupied by the owner or lessee or on another farm of the owner or lessee and no rent is paid or valuable consideration of any kind, other than service, is given by him to the owner or lessee in respect of residence on such farm or farms.

A person shall be deemed for the purposes of this Act to hire land if, in consideration of his being permitted to occupy that land or any portion thereof—

a. he pays or promises to pay to any person a rent in money; or
b. he renders or promises to render to any person a share of the produce of that land, or any valuable consideration of any kind whatever other than his own labour or services or the labour or services of his family.

11. This Act may be cited for all purposes as the Natives' Land Act, 1913.

What Is Apartheid?

Very few interviewees were willing to provide their actual identities. Their desire to remain anonymous is a testimony to the politics that undergird racial identities and informs identity politics. The voices of Whites, Blacks, and immigrants and current South Africa provide insight in contemporary identity politics and the nature of apartheid.

Interviews on Apartheid

Interview #1 by a White South African

Answers

1) What does apartheid mean to you?

A most crushing system that has irrevocably damaged people long term in many ways. It was a system that attempted to oppress people in social, political, psychological, legal and economic ways. If it saw a gap it would plug it. Even though there has been long term damage it is also something that the black nation has survived with strength and even humour.

2) How did your racial (Black African, white, Indian or Coloured, etc.) identity shape your everyday experience?

I'm a white so it gave me material privileges and opportunities because others of other races couldn't access them. So there were more for me. It thus burdened me with guilt as I also didn't have the courage to stand up to the state as some other whites did.

3) Describe your educational and social experience under apartheid?

It was privileged although it was also compromised as it existed within a culture of conservatism and skulking prejudices.

4) What is your male or female experience of apartheid?

The insidious conservatism very firmly supported notions of gender domination.

5) Have racial issues and social conditions improved since the demise of apartheid?

Yes of course. But white racism is frustratingly surviving. Black people feel it and the anger of some is further fuelled by their own anger so it has a reciprocal effect.

6) Have you read or seen a film adaptation of Alan Paton's *Cry, the Beloved Country?* What is your reaction to either?

Yes, I saw the film. It was grueling. It was very painful for whites who hated apartheid but didn't have the courage to challenge the state. You felt caught between the horror that such injustice was going on around you and dreadful guilt.

TOPICS FOR ORAL OR WRITTEN EXPLORATION

1. Is apartheid a political policy that was instantaneously initiated, or did it take numerous years to materialize?

2. Research the difference between racist and racialism. Is South Africa the only country that has racialist ideas?

3. Compare the apartheid system to the Jim Crow laws and practices that prevailed in the United States after the Civil War and into the twentieth century. What are the similarities and differences?

4. Research apartheid laws. Imagine that you are fifteen and you have a pen pal in the United States. Write your pen pal a letter explaining how you wish you were living in his country because you cannot see a movie or have a birthday at a certain restaurant.

5. Write a story about a family living under the 1913 Land Act.

6. After reading the Land Act of 1913, would you say that it was written to protect African ownership of land?

SUGGESTIONS FOR FURTHER READING

Beinart, William, and Saul DuBow. *Segregation and Apartheid in Twentieth-Century South Africa.* London and New York: Routledge, 1995.

Giliomee, Hermann, and Lawrence Schlemmer. *From Apartheid to Nation-Building.* Cape Town: Oxford University Press, 1991.

Sparks, Allister. *The Mind of South Africa.* London: Heinemann, 1990: 146–182.

UNESCO Press. *Racism and Apartheid in Southern Africa.* Paris: UNESCO Press, 1974.

WORKS CITED

Abrahams, Peter. *The Path of Thunder.* Chatham, NJ: Chatham Bookseller, 1975.

Alexander, Peter. *Alan Paton.* New York: Oxford University Press, 1994.

Davenport, T.R.H., and Christopher Saunders. *South Africa.* New York: St. Martin's Press, 2000.

Fox, Olivier. *Caste, Class, and Race; A Study in Social Dynamics.* Introduction by Joseph S. Roucek. Garden City, NY: Doubleday, 1948.

Gannett, Lewis. "Introduction" to *Cry, the Beloved Country,* by Alan Paton. New York: Collier Books, 1948: xi-xix.

Gordimer, Nadine. "Apartheid." *Modern and Classical Essayists: Twelve Masters.* Ed. Paul Marx. Mountain View, CA: Mayfield, 1996.

Jung, Courtney. *Then I Was Black.* New Haven: Yale University Press, 2000.

Maylam, Paul. *South Africa's Racial Past.* Aldershot: Ashgate, 2001.

Millin, Gertrude S. *God's Stepchildren.* New York: Boni and Liveright, 1927.

———. *King of the Bastards.* New York: Harper and Brothers, 1949.

Paton, Alan. *Towards the Mountain.* New York: Charles Scribner's Sons, 1977.

Sparks, Allister. *The Mind of South Africa.* London: Heinemann, 1990.

Tutu, Desmond. *The Words of Desmond Tutu.* Ed. Naomi Tutu. London: Spire, 1989.

UNESCO Press. *Racism and Apartheid in Southern Africa.* Paris: UNESCO Press, 1974.

South Africa. Courtesy of the *World Fact Book*.

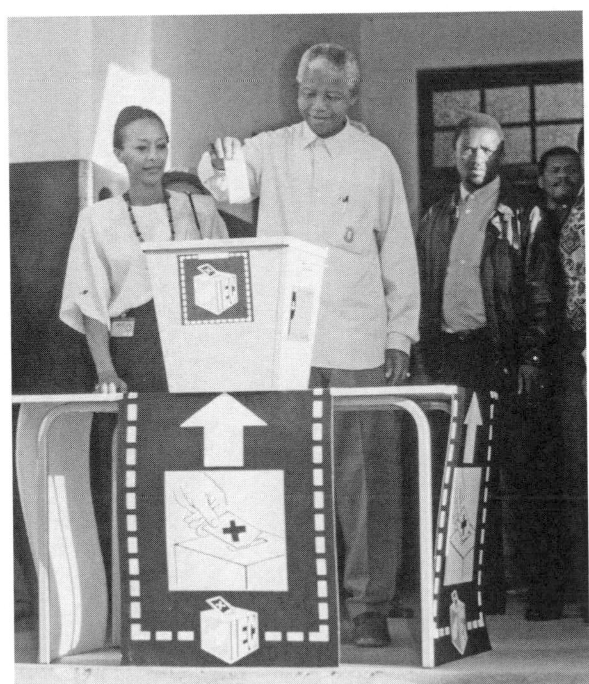

Nelson Mandela, president of the African National Congress (ANC), casting the ballot in his country's first all-race elections. UNITED NATIONS/C/Sattliberger.

A performance by Zulu dancers in traditional dress, carrying spears and shields, was part of the African Union celebration in Durban. UN Photo/Eskinder Debebe.

Young coal miners in South Africa. UNITED NATIONS/P/Mugabane.

Thabo Mbeki, president of the Republic of South Africa, addresses the general debate of the 61st session of the General Assembly, at UN Headquarters in New York. UN Photo/Marco Castro.

Squatters near Cape Town. Many black women risk a precarious existence in such camps in order to be near their menfolk. The men must have permits to work in the "white" areas—actually 87 percent of the country. But their families are considered "superfluous appendages" and are not allowed to live with them: they are supposed to fend for themselves in the remote and neglected areas of the country called "homelands." UN Photo/Marco Castro.

5

History and Work Conditions in the Mines and Workers' Revolts

South African mines are at the center of Alan Paton's *Cry, the Beloved Country.* As the train heads toward Johannesburg, there is a sudden cry when the mines come into sight. Having never seen the mines, Kumalo asks if the "white flat hills are the mines," only to be informed that they are rocks from the mines from which the gold has been extracted. He is curious to know the process involved in mining, and a miner informs him that they go down into the mines to dig out the rocks, and when they are incapable of removing them, Europeans use dynamites to blow them out. Then they clear away the debris and load the trucks, which go up in a cage. The miner explains to Reverend Kumalo, who wishes to know how the cage goes up, that it is wound by a wheel:

> A great iron structure rearing into the air, and a great wheel above it, going so fast that the spokes play tricks with the sight. Great buildings, and steam blowing out of pipes and men hurrying about. A great white hill, and an endless procession of trucks climbing upon it, high up in the air. On the ground, motor-cars, lorries, buses, and one great confusion. (16)

The mines are so central to South Africa's livelihood and economy that the trial of Reverend Kumalo's son, Absalom, who has killed James Jarvis's son, Arthur, is all but forgotten when gold is discovered in Odendaalsrust, in the Orange Free State. There is much excitement but also contention within the European community. Clashes ensue between rich and poor. shareholders and nonshareholders, since the mines, the mainstays of the country's economy, enable farmers to be productive, ensure employment, determine wages, and increase urbanization. Even the Africans, states a sarcastic narrator, "need not starve on the reserves. The men can come to the mines and bigger and better compounds can be built for them, and still more vitamins be put in their food. But we shall have to be careful about that, because some fellow has discovered that labour can be over-vitaminized. This is an example of the Law of Diminishing Returns" (171).

The industry depends on cheap labor to make profits, so African miners are given the bare minimum, which Father Beresford and other supposedly *Kaffirboeties* find unacceptable. Some might assume that only those who profit from their shares in the companies take such a position, yet Sir Oppenheimer, a great man of the mines, is also of the opinion that money was made to serve men and to improve their lives. But since capitalism does not provide for all, John Kumalo, Reverend Kumalo's brother, is the voice of the resistance, which fights for raises for black miners. Aware of the vital importance of African miners to the South African mining business, he warns European mineowners of an impeding strike (strikes are considered a crime under South African law); the strike threat has not been taken seriously by the owners.

But a strike does take place; "the worse trouble was at the Driefontein, where the police were called in to drive the black miners into the mine. There was fighting, and three of the black miners were killed" (189). The annual Synod of the Diocese of Johannesburg takes a position on the matter and calls for the country to acknowledge the African Mine Workers' Union to avoid a national bloodbath. But all this talk, according to the narrator, "supposed that he [the clergyman representing the Synod of the Diocese] meant that the Union should be treated as a responsible body, competent to negotiate with the employers about the conditions of work and pay" (189). But, the fear that mineowners might have to offer increased salaries puts all these calls for action to rest.

Alan Paton's *Cry, the Beloved Country* well delineates the critical importance of the mines in the South Africa of the 1940s. He depicts the mining process and gives the reader insight into his contemporaries' attitudes toward trade unions and African miners in his novel; he also discusses the miners' work conditions in *The Land and People of South Africa.* But there is still much to be learned about the nature of the work African miners performed and the history of trade unions in the country.

It is evident that race plays a primordial role in employment in Alan Paton's *Cry, the Beloved Country* since it determines the job you do, your status, your wages, and your professional aptitudes. According to Sheila T. van der Horst, the greatest occupational gulf in South Africa existed between Europeans and Africans (109). Europeans were managers, engineers, supervisors, and qualified miners; Asians and Coloreds held some of these skilled jobs, but no blacks. Europeans held high-level, skilled positions in all professional fields, except for nursing, teaching, and religion, areas in which each group catered to its own. Africans were hired only for certain types of jobs in mines, since the Mines and Works Acts of 1926 precluded Africans from obtaining certificates of competency that would enable them to do skilled labor. However, they were allowed to use pneumatic drills to drill rocks, and coalminers were allowed to operate coal cutters. Msimangu tells Reverend Kumalo, in *Cry, the Beloved Country,* "It is strange how we move forward in some things, and stand still in others, and go backwards in yet others. Yet in this matter of nurses we have many friends amongst the white people" (63).

This professional discrepancy was most entrenched in the Transvaal, where migrant Europeans who worked in the mining industry held the majority of skilled jobs, leaving a large proportion of Africans who came from what was called the high commission territories—Portuguese East Africa and the British Nyasaland Protectorate—to do menial jobs. European and Asian immigrants were considered permanent residents, but Africans were considered temporary residents and encouraged to be so by the mining industry so that Africans would not endanger the privileges of white workers. The Africans' migrant worker status was also sustained by their insignificant wages, which compelled them to return to their villages to assist with the harvest because their families relied on agriculture for their subsistence and to show their loyalty to the community to which they were to return at retirement. Migrant labor was hence the norm in the mining industry, the second most important South African employer.

Since the times of Jan van Riebeeck, who attempted to regulate the treatment of slaves in 1658, Europeans tried, according to van der Horst, to control the relationships between employees and employers through the 1841 Masters, Servants and Apprentices Ordinance and the 1856 Cape Province Masters and Servants Act. There were similar laws in Natal and the Transvaal, and they all attached criminal liability to acts that breached civil contracts, part of an effort to keep both European and native workers from attempting to commit such breaches. The criminality attached to breaching one's contract was extended in later legislation that controlled the recruitment of workers and defined the work conditions of laborers in the mining industry. The three major statutes governing labor conditions and hiring in the mining sector, according to van der Horst, were the Native Labour Regulation Act, the Mines and Works Act, and the Silicosis (Miner's Phthisis) Act.

The Native Labour Regulation Act, no. 15 (1911), protected employers by making a breach of contract a criminal offense and by outlining the minimum requirements for accommodation and food. Participating in a strike was made a criminal offense. This Act also provided compensation for injuries to African laborers. European laborers, on the other hand, were protected by the workmen's compensation legislation, except for cases involving silicosis or tuberculosis. The Mines and Works Act, no. 12 (1911), protected employers in outlining the minimum necessary security measures required for mines and establishments that used machinery. This law was used to facilitate discrimination against Africans in hiring for certain types of jobs that required a certificate, since Africans, unlike Coloreds in the Cape, were barred by the 1926 Mines and Works Amendment Act from obtaining such certificates of competency in engine driving, blasting, surveying, and many other skilled jobs. The Industrial Conciliation Act, no. 36 (1937), provided for the registration and regulation of trade unions and employers' organizations and regulated the means for settling disputes between employers and employees regarding conditions of employment by arbitration or agreement. This Act made provisions also for the establishment of industrial councils and conciliation boards and for the appointment of mediators and arbitrators to assist in settling industrial disputes. Under it, Africans, whose contracts were regulated by the Masters and Servants Acts, were not considered employees and thus were excluded from the industrial agreements unless the Minister of Labour explicitly extended such agreements to include them. According to van der Horst, these extensions were conceived not to protect Africans but to protect European workers who feared that employers might replace whites with Africans when faced with economic duress. European employers and white workers could determine the wages and working conditions of Africans, yet Africans were not represented on industrial councils since they were not employees, unless the Minister of Labour appointed an "inspector," with no voting power, to represent them (148). Trade union pressure could result in agreements with industrial council agreements to raise employee wages, but these raises were related to the workers' efficiency; non-Europeans, barred from obtaining certificates and thus considered low producers, could not be employed. African trade unions, moreover, could not be registered because Africans were not considered employees. They could manifest their discontent only through strikes and lockouts, which were considered criminal acts. Ironically, African women were considered employees and could therefore belong to registered unions because they were not governed by the Masters and Servants Acts.

Cry, the Beloved Country well depicts the South African labor issue through the European debate on the future of South Africa. While some (mainly English-speaking Europeans) desired a republic and advocated the dismantling of the compound system and "the establishment of villages or the labourers in mines and industry" (78), the Afrikaner community desired the creation of segregated white and black states in which, for some, both whites and blacks could farm their own lands and exploit their own mines. Some white South Africans fought for better wages for African workers, while others disapproved of such a move, for it, according to them, would lead to more educated and thus discontented blacks. *Cry, the Beloved Country* also gives us insight into some Europeans' perspectives on trade unions. A dismayed Harrison informs James Jarvis that "the natives are getting out of hand. They've even started Trade Unions, did you know that? . . . They're threatening to strike here in the Mines for ten shillings a day. They get about three shillings a day. They get about three shillings a shift now, and some of the mines are on the verge of closing down" (150). They live, according to him, in accommodations that are so good that he would not mind living in them himself, eat "good balanced" meals, get free medical care, and have a better lifestyle than they would have were they living in their villages. Yet, he claims that if their salaries were to increase, the mines would have to close, so where would the general South African economy be? South Africa would cease to exist, he claims, if it were not for the mines. South Africans, he claims, should stop criticizing the mines, especially Afrikaners, who consider the mining people "foreign to the country, and . . . sucking the blood out of it, ready to clear out when the goose stops laying the eggs" (151).

It is evident from Harrison's venting that the wages of poor Africans are central to the prosperity of the mines; thus, Kumalo asserts, "We know that we do not get enough, Kumalo says. . . . They say that higher wages will cause the mines to close down. Then what is it worth, this mining industry? And why should it be kept alive, if it is only our poverty that keeps it alive? They say it makes the country rich, but what do we see of these riches? Is it we that must be kept poor so that others may stay rich" (184)? John Kumalo claims that it is not equality and the removal of the color bar that Africans seek but simply fair wages. Kumalo's passionate speech, potentially dangerous yet contained, illustrates the need for a revolt by African workers in a country, that does not see them as employees equal to any other.

The Industrial Conciliation (Natives) Bill, published in 1947, did not apply to residential domestic servants and gold- and coalminers. It made special provisions for mediation and conciliation for Africans in classes and areas to be specified by the minister. Registration of African trade unions was mandatory under this Act, which also legalized discrimination and limited Africans' right of association. It also restricted the rights of Africans to strike under Act No. 36.

Despite the lack of legal trade unions, between 1907 and 1922, there was considerable unrest in the mining sector. In September 1917, the Chamber of Mines signed an agreement providing that blacks could not be hired to fill white positions and that two whites would be hired for every seventeen black workers. In 1918, white electrical mechanics went on strike and obtained a raise, but when African sanitary workers went on strike, they received none; instead, they were flogged, threatened, and incarcerated. When the African National Congress protested the ill treatment of Africans, this led to a general call for a strike on the first of July. By 1919, African laborers had formed the Industrial and Commercial Workers' Union, with Clement Kadalie as its secretary, and had organized numerous strikes. When gold prices dipped and mining companies attempted to hire low-paid blacks, white miners rebelled, in 1921, staging what is called the 1921 Rand Revolt of white miners, organized under the banner "For a White South Africa."

In 1928, five unions created the Federation of the Non-Western European Trade Unions, which for the first time brought all South Africans together in one union. Alan Paton refers to the death of six miners in his novel, which evokes the 1919 strike, but when he is writing his novel the 1946 strike is taking place. M. P. Naicker's "The African Miners' Strike of 1946," Victor Leonard Allen's "Wages," and the excerpt from Alex La Guma's *Time of the Butcherbird* provide insight into the conditions of miners during the period in which Paton's book is set.

FROM M. P. NAICKER, "THE AFRICAN MINERS' STRIKE OF 1946"[1]

(Online posting at <http://www.anc.org.za/ancdocs/history/misc/miners.html>)

This article provides information on the history of trade unions and miners' strikes in South Africa. It also gives insight into the work conditions of the miners and the difficulties they experienced voicing their needs. This is an important document, since *Cry, the Beloved Country* speaks of a strike where three people die, the wage discrepancies, and the mechanisms utilized to get the miners to return to work.

> "Two hundred thousand subterranean heroes who, by day and by night, for a mere pittance lay down their lives to the familiar 'fall of rock' and who, at deep levels, ranging from 1,000 to 3,000 feet in the bowels of the earth, sacrifice their lungs to the rock dust which develops miners' phthisis and pneumonia."
>
> —Sol Plaatje, first Secretary of the African National Congress, describing the lives of black miners in 1914

Thirty years ago, on August 12, 1946, the African mine workers of the Witwatersrand came out on strike in support of a demand for higher wages—10 shillings a day. They continued the strike for a week in the face of the most savage police terror, in which officially 1,248 workers were wounded and a very large number—officially only 9—were killed. Lawless police and army violence smashed the strike. The resources of the racist State were mobilised, almost on a war footing, against the unarmed workmen.

But the miners' strike had profound repercussions which are felt until this day. The intense persecution of workers' organisations which began during the strike, when trade union and political offices and homes of officials were raided throughout the country, has not ceased.

The most profound result of the strike, however, was to be the impact it had on the political thinking within the national liberation movement; almost immediately it shifted significantly from a policy of concession to more dynamic and militant forms of struggle.

Birth of the African Mine Workers' Union

Black workers were introduced to trade unionism by the early struggles of white British workers who had begun to form trade unions from 1880 onwards. During the first thirty years of their existence the white workers were occupied in a turbulent struggle for decent wages, union recognition and survival.

Writing about this period Alex Hepple states:

> "It was a struggle of white men, striving for a higher standard of life and inbred with a fiery belief in their cause which carried them into bloody strikes, violence and rebellion. Their main enemy was the Chamber of Mines, a body of men who owned the rich gold mines. The quarrel revolved around the Chamber's low-wage policy. This conflict greatly influenced the pattern and direction of trade unionism in South Africa. It introduced the race factor into labour economics and steered white workers into support of an industrial colour bar, with all its damaging effects on workers' solidarity."

Indeed solidarity between white and black workers was lost in those first thirty years, never to be regained to this day. The result has been that the white workers became the aristocrats of labour in South Africa, being among the highest paid workers in the world, while their black compatriots are, in the main, still living below the breadline. What is worse, the overwhelming majority of white workers in South Africa became the main and the most vociferous supporters of successive racist regimes.

However, they taught the black workers one important lesson, i.e., in order to win their demands they had to organise. The organisation of African mine workers was and remains one of the most difficult—and the most essential—tasks facing the trade union and national movement in South Africa. Recruited from the four corners of the country and beyond its borders . . . the African miners are spread out from Randfontein to Springs in the Witwatersrand, spilling over into the Orange Free State.

They are shut into prison-like compounds, speaking many languages, guarded and spied upon.

Any attempt at organisation exposed them to the wiles of employers, the antagonism of white workers and the ferocious arm of the law.

Many unsuccessful attempts were made to form a trade union prior to 1941. But in that year, on 3 August, a very representative miners' conference was called by the Transvaal Provincial Committee of the African National Congress. The conference was attended not only by workers from many mines, but also by delegates from a large number of African, Indian, Coloured and white organisations, as well as representatives from a number of black unions. Some white unions gave their moral support and even the Paramount Chief of Zululand sent an encouraging message. A broad committee of fifteen was elected to "proceed by every means it thought fit to build up an African Mine Workers' Union in order to raise the standards and guard the interests of all African mine workers."[3] From the first the committee encountered innumerable obstacles. . . . Speakers were arrested and meetings broken up.

Another serious obstacle was the wide-scale use of spies by the mine owners.

Time and again provisional shaft and compound union committees were established, only to end in the victimisation and expulsion from the mines of the officials and committee members. Nevertheless, the organising campaign progressed steadily and the stage was reached where a very representative conference of mine workers was held. . . .

Background to the strike

In 1941, when the decision to launch the Mine Workers' Union was first mooted the wage rate for African workers was R70 per year while white workers received R848. In 1946, the year of the great strike the wages were: Africans R87 and whites R1,106.[4]

In both cases it would be noticed that the wage gap between the white worker and the black worker was 12:1.

With the formal establishment of the Union, organisational work began in earnest in the face of increased harassment, arrests, dismissals, and deportation of workers by the police and the mine management. Nevertheless, the Union grew in strength and influence. The Chamber of Mines, however, refused even to acknowledge the existence of the African Mine Workers' Union, much less to negotiate with its representatives. The Chamber's secretary instructed the office staff not to reply to communications from the Union.[5] Unofficially, of course, the Chamber was acutely conscious of the Union's activities and secret directives were sent out to break the Union. . . .

In order to stave off the growing unrest among the African mine workers, the regime appointed a Commission of Enquiry in 1943, with Judge Lansdowne as its Chairman. . . .

The African Mine Workers' Union presented an unanswerable case before this Commission in support of the workers' claim to a living wage. The Chamber of Mines made no serious attempt to rebut the Union's case, reiterating that its policy was to employ cheap African labour. Meanwhile, however, the *Guardian,* a progressive South African weekly, the only paper which totally supported the strike, was sued by four mining companies for 40,000 pounds for publishing the Unions memorandum on the grounds that it was false and that the recruiting of mine labourers would be hindered. The Court decided against the *Guardian* and awarded 750 pounds damages to each of the four companies. . . .

The report of the Lansdowne Commission which appeared in April 1944 was a shameful document. It accepted the basic premise of the mine owners; all its recommendations were quite frankly made within the framework of preserving the cheap labour system. The miner's wage, said the Commission, was not really intended to be a living wage, but merely a "supplementary income". Supplementary, that is, to the worker's supposed income from his land. The evidence placed before the Commission of acute starvation in the Transkei and other reserves was ignored.

The report of the Commission was received with bitter disappointment by the workers. Even its wretchedly miserly recommendations were rejected, in the main, by both the regime and the mine owners.

The recommendations were:

- an increase of five pence per shift for surface workers and six pence per shift for underground workers, on the basic rate of 22 pence per shift obtained for nearly a generation;
- cost of living allowance of 3 pence per shift;

- boot allowance of 36 pence for 30 shifts;
- two weeks' paid leave per annum for permanent workers; and overtime wages at time and a half.

Towards the end of that year the racist Prime Minister, Field Marshal Smuts, announced that wages were to be raised by 4 pence for surface and 5 pence for underground workers, and that the extra wage would be borne by the State in the form of tax remission to the mines. The Chamber of Mines also agreed to overtime pay. All the other recommendations, miserly though they were, were completely ignored.

Obviously expecting that this would do little to allay the general discontent among the African miners, Smuts issued a Proclamation—War Measure No. 1425—prohibiting gatherings of more than twenty persons on mining property without special permission. . . .

Despite these difficulties the African Mine Workers' Union increased its following in numerous mines throughout the Witwatersrand. And on May 19, 1946, the biggest conference yet held of representatives of the workers instructed the Executive of the Union to make yet one more approach to the Chamber of Mines to place before them the workers' demands for a ten shillings (one Rand) a day wage and other improvements. Failing agreement, decided the Conference, the workers would take strike action.

From May till July the Union redoubled its efforts to get the Chamber to see reason. . . .

Decision to strike

On Sunday, August 4, 1946, over one thousand delegates assembled at an open air conference held in the Newtown Market Square: no hall where Africans could hold meetings was big enough to accommodate those present. The conference carried the following resolution unanimously:

> "Because of the intransigent attitude of the Transvaal Chamber of Mines towards the legitimate demands of the workers for a minimum wage of 10 shillings per day and better conditions of work, this meeting of African miners resolves to embark upon a general strike of all Africans employed on the gold mines, as from August 12, 1946."

Before the decision was adopted, speaker after speaker mounted the platform and demanded immediate action. . . .

After the decision to strike was adopted, the President, J. B. Marks, stressed the gravity of the strike decision and said that the workers must be prepared for repression by possible violence. . . . . There was little doubt, he warned, that the regime would attempt to suppress the strike by brute force.[7]

The Strike and the Terror

A letter conveying the decision of the meeting to the Chamber, and adding a desperate last-minute appeal for negotiations, was as usual ignored. The press and mass media, except the *Guardian,* did not print any news of the decision until the morning of Monday, 12 August, when the *Rand Daily Mail* came out with a front page story that the strike was a "complete failure". The report was obviously mischievous and a lie, as the paper went to bed before midnight, when the strike had not even begun.

The *Star* that evening, however, had a different tale to tell: tens of thousands of workers were out on strike from the East to the West Rand; the Smuts regime had formed a special committee of Cabinet Ministers to "deal with" the situation; and thousands of police were being mobilised and drafted to the area.

They dealt with it by means of bloody violence. The police batoned, bayoneted and fired on the striking workers to force them down the mine shafts. The full extent of police repression is not known but reports from miners and some newspapers reveal intense persecution and terror during the week following Monday, 12 August.

A peaceful procession of workers began to march to Johannesburg on what became known as Bloody Tuesday, 13 August, from the East Rand. They wanted to get their passes and go back home. Police opened fire on the procession and a number of workers were killed. At one mine workers, forced to go down the mine, started a sit-down strike underground. The police drove the workers up—according to the *Star*—"stope by stope, level by level" to the surface. They then started beating them up, chasing them into the veld with baton charges. Then the workers were "re-assembled" in the compound yard and, said the *Star,* "volunteered to go back to work".

In protest against these savage brutalities, a special conference of the Transvaal Council of Non-European Trade Unions (CONETU) decided to call a general strike in Johannesburg on Wednesday, 14 August. The Johannesburg City Council sent a deputation to plead with CONETU to maintain essential services. Many workers heeded the call, but the weakness of the unions generally, and the failure to bring the call home to the workers in factories, resulted in only a partial success of the strike.

CONETU called a mass meeting of workers at the Newtown Market Square on 15 August. The meeting was banned in terms of the Riotous Assemblies Act, and the decision banning the meeting was conveyed by a senior police officer, backed by a large squad of armed police. Those present were given five minutes to disperse. . . .

By Friday, 16 August, all the striking workers—75,000 according to the government "Director of Native Labour" but probably nearer 100,000—were bludgeoned back to work.

Throughout the week hundreds of workers were arrested, tried, imprisoned or deported. Leaders of the African trade unions and the entire Executive Committee of the African Mine Workers' Union, the whole of the Central Committee of the Communist Party and scores of Provincial and local leaders of the African National Congress were arrested and charged in a series of abortive "treason and sedition" trials. Innumerable police raids, not only in the Transvaal but in all the main cities in the country including Durban, Cape Town, Port Elizabeth, Kimberley and East London, were carried out on the offices of trade unions, the Congresses and the Communist Party. The homes of leaders of the ANC, the Communist Party, the Indian and Coloured Congresses and the trade unions were also raided simultaneously. The white South African State was mobilised and rampant in defence of its cheap labour policy and big dividends for the mining magnates and big business. This marked the opening of a phase of intense repression by the racist regime of the day, led by Field Marshal Smuts, against the forces for change in South Africa. This repression continues to this day under the Vorster regime.

The African Mine Workers' Union, mainly because of the very difficult circumstances under which it operated, was never a closely-organised well-knit body. During the strike the central strike committee was effectively cut off from the workers at each mine by massive police action and the workers had to struggle in isolation. . . .

Nevertheless, thousand of miners defied terror, arrest and enemy propaganda and stood out for five days—from 12 to 16 August. During the strike 32 of the 45 mines on the Rand were affected according to one report received by the Union and later confirmed by the Johannesburg *Star.* According to the estimates issued by the Chief Native Commissioner for the Witwatersrand, 21 mines were affected by the strike, 11 wholly and 10 partially. The dead, according to this official, numbered nine, of whom four were trampled to death, three died in the hospital, one was shot dead and one "killed himself by running into a dustbin".

The regime called the strike a failure. But no great movement of this character is really a "failure", even though it might not succeed in its immediate aim. . . .

The brave miners of 1946 gave birth to the ANC Youth League's Programme of Action adopted in 1949; they were the forerunners of the freedom strikers of May 1, 1950, against the Suppression of Communism Act, and the tens of thousands who joined the 26 June nation-wide protest strike that followed the killing of sixteen people during the May Day strike . . . ; they inspired the mood that led to the upsurge in 1960 and to the emergence of *Umkhonto we Sizwe* (Spear of the Nation)—the military wing of the African National Congress.

FROM VICTOR LEONARD ALLEN, "WAGES" (STATEMENT TO THE WITTWATERSAND GOLD MINES NATIVE WAGES COMMITTEE, BY THE AFRICAN MINE WORKERS UNION), FROM *THE HISTORY OF BLACK MINEWORKERS IN SOUTH AFRICA,* VOL. 1

(NEW YORKSHIRE, UK: MERLIN PRESS, 1992: 433)

John Kumalo's speech in *Cry, the Beloved Country* emphasizes wages. This document provides insight into the wage discrepancies among mineworkers in the 1940s.

We have discussed the effect of the recruiting system on miners' wages. The miner has no say when he enters into his contract with the Chamber of Mines. He is told that he will be paid at the rates prevailing on the mine for the class of work to which he is put. There is no way of labour utilising a period of labour shortage to ask for higher wages. There is no machinery through which the African miner can inform his employer, peacefully, that the cost of living has rendered it impossible for him to manage on his minute earnings. The decision lies only with the employer, whose answer is only too clear: wage rates do not rise over a period of twenty years. Many men who have been on the mines for twenty years are still earning 2s. a day.

We wish to draw your attention to the following facts:

1. In 1931 86 per cent of underground and surface workers were earning less than 2/6d per shift. The same percentage were earning less than 2/6d per shift in *1938.*
2. A comparison of the wages and benefits given by the Mines to their European and non-European employees reveals the following startling facts:

In 1940, 37 826 European employees received in wages alone £18 974 600—an average wage of £1.11.10 per shift (312 shifts per annum). In addition they received benefits equal to £4.18.2 per month per head. In addition they received paid leave, with provision for long leave, cost of living allowance and a grant to the Mines Benefit Society from the Chamber of Mines of £30 000. Further the Mines pay contributions to National Unemployment Insurance in respect of European employees.

In the same year the 344 897 non-Europeans received £12 418 106, an average wage of 2s. 3d and two-thirds pence per shift. The only additional benefit they received was thirteen and a half pence per day, the "cost of keep".

FROM ALEX LA GUMA, *TIME OF THE BUTCHERBIRD*

LONDON: HEINEMANN, 1987: 29–36)

This excerpt provides information on the 1922 White Rand miner's revolt and the 1946 black miners strike; the bus boycott depicted in the novel; and the relationships among the different South African racial groups.

A long time ago it had been the perpetual scene of mine dumps and the grease-stained and rusty remains of machinery, the dark skeletons of disused mineheads. Beyond all that you came into the untidy old streets, the shabby hotels with iron balconies, rows of one storey cottages. After the big strike the white miners who lived there had trickled away, but her father had stayed on, as if it would have been an act of indecency to abandon the little shop with its barricades of tins of jam, the sharp-smelling bars of washing soap, the ranked bottles of cooking oil.

The artillery of the government, the rifles, shot-guns and sticks of dynamite of the defeated miners had passed into history books, but the little shop still stood. Her father had sometimes pointed out the old bullet holes in the wall outside, as if he had actually taken part in the fighting. But he had actually locked up the place and, safe upstairs in the tiny flat, he had peeped bravely through the gap in the window shutter while his wife had crouched terrified by the wardrobe.

Afterwards he would remark with pride that he'd seen it all, or that he'd even taken part, gone through it all. Sometimes he lied and claimed he'd known Taffy Long. The fact of the matter was that at that time he had recently bought the little store, lock, stock, and barrel, from the estate of an old Syrian who had passed on, and since he had nothing to do with strikes and miners and the bloody government, what the hell was there to be scared of? Why should he not stay?

Gradually the Whites drifted away from the area to settle in other spots, but Barends stuck, even though the coolies and coloureds and the bloody Chinamen moved into surround them. They had to eat too, didn't they? They needed condensed milk and curry powder and hair-nets, didn't they?

But it was not really the same. A man couldn't get into proper conversation with the population. What could you talk to a damn applesammy about? When his wife died of something to do with her bowels, Barends seemed to surrender completely and he began to care less about the shop. The years passed. The stacked products gathered dust—he wasn't selling well because on top of it all there were coolie shops around too . . . ; the cheese got mixed up with soap; the tobacco with the tins of sardines. It was like fortifications left to crumble after a war. Upstairs the little flat grew shabbier and the sherry bottles began to gather on the untidy sideboard.

'You've got to pull your socks up, man,' his brother admonished whenever he visited. His brother worked on the railways. He had started as a shunter when the government had decided to replace Black workers more and more with Whites. They called it Civilised Labour. Later he'd become a ganger and *now* was a foreman. 'Time's passing, things are looking up, and here you are wasting away in this godforsaken place. Look at all these bloody coolies and coons around you, why, *they* seem even better off.'

'Well, at least I'm in business, aren't I?'

'Ach, business is all very well, but this one is going to the dogs. I tell you what, you need to marry again, man. True as God, that's the thing old man.'

It was his brother who introduced him to Elizabeth Gray. The three of them spent a few evenings in a hotel lounge, chatting idly. She wore big dentures that seemed to clatter when she talked. Her husband had died of phthisis, she was lonely too, but in a different way. A formidable woman, with red hair and a face like a limestone crag, she needed things to regulate, people to dominate. Before he knew it, Barends was swept up along with his shop.

Business picked up, everything became spick and span, severely orderly, under her firm, almost grim direction, and they thrived even in that area. Most of the groceries disappeared—-they could he purchased elsewhere—to be replaced by bottles of soft drinks; magazines appeared, comic papers, pulp novels, most of the daily newspapers, even those which started catering for the Blacks, film and fashion magazines. . . . For the rest, everything was run by the former widow, now Missus Elizabeth Barends. . . . He became like some shade haunting the premises, the traditional ghost that went with the castle: a little, withdrawn man more like a hanger-on around the store than anybody to do with ownership.

So it might have come as a surprise to him, as it was to everybody else—most of the friends were his wife's—when the daughter was born. It was as if his wife had timed and ordered the conception too, like *arranging* the delivery of a side of veal. 'We'll call her Maisie,' his wife said in the hospital bed. 'That's a nice name.' Barends wondered why, but did not disagree, sitting humbly at the bedside, with the packet of bananas and the box of assorted biscuits he had brought her held awkwardly on his lap. . . .

The War passed, then there was a strike by the black miners and Barends remembered the old days. But it didn't come this way and he read the newspaper accounts. It wasn't the same, and though the soldiers and police had been turned out with fixed bayonets the blacks did not have the shot-guns and dynamite as in those times. They could be handled and the police had rounded up a lot of Communists.

'I'm not interested in politics,' his new wife said. 'That's awright for the government and the kaffirs. There's the business to see to.'

The child was kept upstairs, among the fairly new modernistic furniture—the sideboard and the old wardrobe where the first Mrs. Barends had cowered had all gone—because all the children in the neighbourhood were a lot of coons. When the time came for her to go to school Barends escorted her to the distant White school, taking her there in the morning and fetching her in the afternoon, travelling on the segregated tramcars. . . . She did not complete high school; primary had been passable. . . .

'She'll be a help in the shop,' Mrs Barends said. 'It's not such a hard job giving change, even though arithmetic ain't her best subject.'

It wasn't so bad helping in the shop. In between counting money she could sit and read the film magazines or look at the latest fashions in the girls' clothes. But it could be a bore too. Luckily the shop closed Saturday afternoons and she went to the bioscope, the one for Europeans Only. . . .

'God,' her mother scolded sometimes. 'Don't you think of anything else but bioscope and blerry film actresses? We've got a business to run, and it's for your benefit. You'll have it when we're gone.'

'What's so wonderful about this?' Maisie would venture to retort petulantly. 'Serving a lot of niggers.' She imagined the bright lights, the flashing neon signs of the city centre.

'You got no 'preciation, like your pa.'

Past the shop windows the dark people went by outside and there was a perpetual smell of oriental spices in the air.

There were boys now and then, men in the foyers of cinemas. But petting in the dark auditorium depended on what film hero the particular choice resembled. There would be Tony Curtis, but soon the Tony Curtis hairstyle became too common. That one looked a little like Alan Ladd, that one like Audie Murphy. . . .

'We'll have to keep you in hand, young lady,' more than once snapped the large and looming Mrs. Barends, clashing her dentures. 'In future it'll be straight home from the pitchers for you. One night the Kaffirs will get you, you'll see. If there was any pertickler young man, there's no need to be afraid of bringing him here for us to have a look at, like any respectable girl.' . . .

God, how could she bring any fellow home? Right on the edge of coolieland? During the day the white sherry tramps drank from bottles in alleyways, Indian women in saris jabbered on the pavements. She usually came alone on the tramcar that stopped a little distance away, running the few blocks, so the boys really didn't have to see where she lived.

Then came the time Edgar Stopes made his appearance. The regular salesman came in one afternoon and said cheerfully, . . .

So there he was coming in regularly each month to fill in the order book so Missus Barends could top up the supplies of the shop. 'Nice little business you got here, ladies,' he smiled, licking the point of his pencil. . . . 'You've got to have it *here* to run a nice place like this.' He tapped his dark blond hair with the pencil. 'In God we trust and all others cash, that's my motto.' . . .

It was a few weeks later and he was scribbling an order in his book. 'It'll be a pleasure to escort the delightful Miss Barends.' He ran a surreptitious eye over the healthy bustline, then asked: 'Business okay?'

'Getting on awright. This is a steady thing, you know, hey.'

'It is, it is. You sell the things people need and keep the customers happy, that's the thing. But don't let 'em get the upper hand. You can't afford to do any favours. Like credit for instance.' He shut his order book and snapped the elastic band around it. 'People don't appreciate favours. Look at those stupid natives, refusing to ride their bloody buses—begging your pardon. They got their own buses and then they go an' boycott them because of fares. We all got to pay fares. So what do they get as a result? Sore feet.'

'Well, they are kind of poor, aren't they?' Maisie said, looking up from the cover of a magazine. 'The fares went up, it said so in the papers.'

Stopes shrugged. 'Poor; there's no need to be poor. Are you poor, am I poor? No, because we got initiative, hey. We got *brains*. Look after number one, that's what I say. If it wasn't for people like us, why the country would never be civilised.'

TOPICS FOR ORAL OR WRITTEN EXPLORATION

1. Are South African laws conceived to promote the welfare of all citizens?

2. After reading the documents relating the status and conditions of African workers, to what extent are John Kumalo's demands justified? Did you have much empathy for him after reading *Cry, the Beloved Country*? Has the additional information on the work conditions of miners and the labor strikes given you a better and more sympathetic understanding of John Kumalo?

3. Research the history of black miners in the United States. Is their experience similar to or different from that of South African miners, and were they allowed to have trade unions?

4. Imagine that you are an American newspaper reporter; write an article on the 1946 strike exposing the laws of South Africa and the oppressive South African regime.

5. Read "The Freedom Charter," and write an essay denouncing the treatment of South African miners on the basis of their experience and the demands of the Charter.

NOTES

1. From "Notes and Documents," No. 21/76, September 1976.
3. E. Roux, *Time Longer than Rope.* University of Wisconsin Press, p. 335.
4. Annual Reports of the South African Government Mining Engineers.
5. "The Impending Strike of African Mine Workers," a statement by the African Mine Workers' Union, August 1946.
7. Ibid.

SUGGESTIONS FOR FURTHER READING

Abrahams, Peter. *Mine Boy.* London: Faber and Faber, 1946.

Allen, Victor Leonard. *The History of Black Mineworkers in South Africa.* Vol. 1. New Yorkshire, UK: Merlin Press, 1992.

Van der Horst, Sheila. "Labour." In *Handbook on Race Relations in South Africa.* Ed. Ellen Hellman. New York: Octagon Books, 1975.

WORKS CITED

Allen, Victor Leonard. *The History of Black Mineworkers in South Africa.* Vol. 1. New Yorkshire, UK: Merlin Press, 1992.

La Guma, Alex. *Time of the Butcherbird.* London: Heinemann, 1987.

Naicker, M. P. "The African Miners' Strike of 1946," online posting at <http://www.anc.org.za/ancdocs/history/misc/miners.html>.

Paton, Alan. *The Land and People of South Africa.* Philadelphia and New York: J. B. Lippincott, 1955.

Van der Horst, Sheila. "Labour." In *Handbook on Race Relations in South Africa.* Ed. Ellen Hellman. New York: Octagon Books, 1975.

6

Social and Economic Conditions in the City

Alan Paton's representation of urban Africans in *Cry, the Beloved Country* is sordid and bleak. Although Reverend Kumalo is mesmerized by the city and is portrayed as a country bumpkin when he attempts to cross the street, urban life is far from glamorous. As the reader travels with Reverend Kumalo from Sophiatown to Claredon, Shanty Town, Alexandra, and so on, it is not the shining lights of Johannesburg on which the narrator focuses but the squalor, the poverty, the crime, and the despair of the urbanites. Likewise, as Paton guides the reader through South Africa in *The Land and People of South Africa,* his descriptions of the slums of Newclare, Orlando, Sophiatown, and the Shanty Towns are anything but beautiful, even though he seeks to find explanations for the ugliness of Orlando.

The laborers who come to the city leave their wives and children behind, according to John Kumalo, to live in the compounds. In this promiscuous city, there are also no morals, fidelity, or customs. When some African men, according to Msimangu, become powerful and wealthy, they are great men if they have not been corrupted. But when they begin to enjoy their wealth and power, they often gratify their lusts, arrange to have access to European liquor, but have no real power, for it is corrupt (39). The areas outside Johannesburg where they live, such as Alexandra, are not cared for, not lighted, "and so great is the demand for accommodation that every man, if he could, built rooms in his yard and sublet them to others. Many of these rooms were the hideouts for thieves and robbers, and there was much prostitution and brewing of illicit liquor" (44).

These urban areas were, moreover, nests of crime. Africans were a menace to whites, according to the narrator of *Cry, the Beloved Country,* for they robbed and assaulted them. The Africans themselves are insecure in this overpopulated, crime-ridden city. When they are relocated from white areas, they have to live in settlements and in houses made of planks, sacks, tins, and poles. In these makeshift shantytown houses with no sanitation and water, they brave the cold and the rain. And, in all this misery, children are dying of epidemics. When they are not living in settlements, they are squatters in shantytowns outside black townships or in single-sex hostels, which house domestic workers, widows, orphans, unmarried women, and people working in industries. In these hostels, consisting of shared rooms, they live in harsh and oppressive conditions.

The city, as opposed to the peaceful, romanticized rural area, is a frightening place to live. Unlike the peaceful village of Ndotsheni, it is a place where children grow up "without a home or school or custom" (67). This is a sad place where the family is disintegrating and children are being driven to crime because only four out of ten children attend school. Moreover, these city dwellers have lost their freedom, since they must carry passes, and a "hundred thousand natives" fill prisons (77). Even their leisure and recreation are controlled and promiscuous, since men spend most of their time drinking the illicit beer of shebbeens.

Before the creation of the Union, African settlement in urban spaces was haphazard, according to Ellen Hellman, since the colony applied a laissez-faire policy under which Africans were allowed, except in the Free State, to acquire land according to their means. Asians and Europeans were ready, according to her, to build iron huts to lease to Africans. Although the local authorities in Cape Town had the right to determine where Africans could live and the sanitary facilities required, these powers were not put into effect. The 1913 Land Act gave Europeans control of the urban areas, and the 1945 Natives (Urban Areas) Consolidation Act and its subsequent amendments gave them increased control over the influx of Africans into towns. Documents in this chapter that provide a glimpse of life in South Africa's cities include excerpts from Modisane's *Blame Me on History;* "The First Group Areas Proclamations in Contentious Areas"; *Kaffir Boy,* by Mark Mathabane; "Kwashiokor," from Can Themba's *The Will to Die;* Paton's "Modern Industry and Tribal Life," from his book *South Africa Today;* and Desmond Tutu's writings.

FROM BLOKE MODISANE, *BLAME ME ON HISTORY*

(LONDON: THAMES AND HUDSON, 1963, 5–15)

One of the settings of Alan Paton's *Cry, the Beloved Country* is Sophia Town. This excerpt from Modisane's *Blame Me on History* describes the state of Sophia Town and how it was destroyed for political reasons.

Chapter One

SOMETHING in me died, a piece of me died, with the dying of Sophiatown; it was in the winter of 1958, the sky was a cold blue veil which had been immersed in a bleaching solution and then spread out against a concave, the blue filtering through, and tinted by, a powder screen of grey; the sun, like the moon of the day, gave off more light than heat, mocking me with its promise of warmth—a fixture against the grey—blue sky—a mirror deflecting the heat and concentrating upon me in my Sophiatown only a reflection. . . .

In the name of slum clearance they had brought the bulldozers and gored into her body, and for a brief moment, looking down Good Street, Sophiatown was like one of its own many victims; a man gored by the knives of Sophiatown, lying in the open gutters, a raisin in the smelling drains, dying of multiple stab wounds, gaping wells gushing forth blood; the look of shock and bewilderment, of horror and incredulity, on the face of the dying man. . . .

Perhaps the concentrated impact had not crystallized in my mind; at the time it had seemed the heroic thing to do, but standing there on the ruins of the house in which I was born I seemed to be looking at my whole life, the body which contained that life reduced to dust; I kept remembering a line of Omar Khayyám: 'I came like water, and like wind I go.' Sophiatown and I were reduced to the basic elements, both of us for the same reason: we were black spots.

Sophiatown died, not because it was a social embarrassment, but because it was a political corn inside the apartheid boot. The then Minister of Bantu Administration and Development, Dr Verwoerd, condemned Sophiatown because it was a slum; true there were no parks, playgrounds, civic halls, libraries; true that a large number of people lived in what was described as 'appalling conditions', in corrugated iron shanties, subdivided by cardboard walls; true that on 50 by 100 feet areas, up to eighty people were huddled in back-yard shacks; but it is also true that Moroka was an approved shanty started in 1946 as an emergency camp where every family was housed in hessian shacks.

If the Government was concerned with alleviating the living conditions of the Africans, the shanties of Moroka, Edenvale, Eastern Township, deserved this consideration far more than did Sophiatown, where the real problem was overcrowding; the shanties of Sophiatown were erected behind solid houses; but the politicians saw political gains and the sociologists and the race relationists saw only textbook solutions—new townships, with recreation centres, parks, schools, libraries, playgrounds; poverty it seems is less disturbing to the public conscience if it is suffocated in model housing estates.

Sophiatown belonged to me; when we were not shaking hands or chasing the same girl or sharing a bottle of brandy, we were sticking knives into each other's backs. The land was bought with the sweat, the scrounging, the doing without, and it not only was mine, but a piece of me; the house was mine even if the rain leaked through the roof and the cold seemed to creep through the cracks in the ceiling, and crawled through the rattling window-frames and under the door.

It was widely conceded that Sophiatown was a slum, and slum clearance was a programme the principles of which were generally accepted; but it was Sophiatown the 'black spot' which had to be ravaged, and as Can Temba said: 'I have long stopped arguing the injustice, the vindictiveness, the strong-arm authority of which prostrate Sophiatown is a loud symbol.'

MURIEL HORRELL, "THE FIRST GROUP AREAS PROCLAMATIONS IN CONTENTIOUS AREAS," FROM *THE GROUP AREAS ACT. ITS EFFECT ON HUMAN BEINGS*

(JOHANNESBURG: THE SOUTH AFRICAN INSTITUTE OF RACE RELATIONS, 1956: 135–140)

This excerpt, giving extensive information on the lives of South African Colored minority groups, shows the extent to which Africans were discriminated against in segregated and apartheid South Africa. It explains why Reverend Kumalo's search for his family in *Cry, the Beloved Country* is limited to black areas.

Johannesburg

SINCE the discovery of gold on the Witwatersrand in 1886 and, subsequently, the extraordinarily rapid development there of secondary industry, people of a very large variety of languages and racial groups have flocked to the Reef. Johannesburg is now the largest city in Southern Africa, 80 square miles in extent, with an estimated population, in 1956, of 387,800 Whites, 45,100 Coloured people, 2,500 Chinese, 25,600 Indians, and some 663,000 Africans—including those Africans who are accommodated on the mines or who live in pen-urban areas but work in the city. The economic activities of all these people are extremely varied. . . .

Where the People Live[6]

Johannesburg grew in a haphazard way, and the provision of housing, especially for the Non-White groups, has always lagged very far indeed behind the demand.

(a) The White Group

The residential areas were originally near the railway line and belt of mining ground which run through the southern part of the municipal area. As time went by, the better-off White citizens moved further to the north. Suburbs near the mines gradually deteriorated into slums, and, in later years, have become industrialized. White residential areas now extend some ten miles to the north, well beyond the municipal boundary; and have been developed also to the south of the belt of gold mines. In some cases they now surround areas which had been set aside for Non-Whites.

(b) Asiatics

Because of the restrictions on land rights to which Asiatics in the Transvaal have always been subjected. most of the Indian-owned property in Johannesburg is in defined areas which from time to time were allocated to them under the legislation of 1885 and 1946, described in the first chapter of this booklet. There are, however, large numbers of individual traders and small groups of Indians scattered through very many of the suburbs of Johannesburg, living mainly in rented accommodation; and some 2,500 Indians who live in pen-urban areas around the city.

A few of the townships between the main railway line and the gold mining area, for example City and Suburban and Ferreirastown, were "exempted" areas where Asiatics could own land. But these have since become largely industrialized, and although the Indian owners received good prices, their many tenants were forced to seek other accommodation.

The same process is now occurring in other predominantly Indian areas in this locality, for example parts of Fordsburg, Newtown West and Burghersdorp. Indians retain much property in these areas, however, and also in Pageview (adjoining Burghersdorp but to the north of the railway line), and in certain suburbs near the western boundary of Johannesburg, especially in Newclare and to a lesser extent in Martindale, Sophiatown and Newlands. . . .

It is said that the Indians of Johannesburg own property worth some £10-million; but this property is probably held by about 200 individuals at most. There are four or five very wealthy land-owning families. The vast majority of the Indians are very poor people, employed as small traders, shop assistants, factory workers, waiters, hawkers and so on, and are forced to rent accommodation from the property owners. Johannesburg has never provided a housing scheme for Asiatics.

The population in the predominantly Indian-owned areas is extraordinarily mixed. In the Burghersdorp—Newtown West—Diagonal Street area, for example, it is estimated that there are 4,759 Asiatics, 2,363 Africans, 1,951 Coloured people and 695 Whites. In Pageview there are 3,680 Asiatics, 2,949 Africans, 1,922 Cape Coloured people, 1,474 Malays and one or two Whites. In Newclare there are some 1,500 Indians and Chinese, 1,000 Coloured, 100 Malays and 14,000 Africans.

Because of the restrictions on Non-European land rights, the absence of municipal housing schemes for Indians, the very acute shortage of housing for Coloured people and Africans, and the industrialization of parts of the town, which is displacing many hundreds of families, land in the "exempted" areas fetches famine prices.

More and more shacks have been erected in back yards until there is hardly a square inch of ground left unoccupied. Increasingly high rentals are charged, and, in some cases, "key money" is demanded from new tenants. Overcrowding has reached such a stage that Indian and Coloured families who are displaced because of factory development have literally no hope, at present, of acquiring other homes.

According to evidence by the City Council before the Group Areas Board during *1955,* 200 Indian and 200 Coloured families were then in desperate need of accommodation. Since then many more have been ejected from their homes. Some of them have lived in tents for many months. . . .

Pageview, about *95* per cent Indian-owned,[7] is part of the old Malay location allocated to Coloured people and Asiatics by the Transvaal Republican Government in 1887. It was made an "exempted" Indian area in 1937, and this position was confirmed by a resolution of both Houses of Parliament in 1941. . . . Very many Europeans, especially in the lower income-groups, come for long distances to do their shopping in Pageview, partly because they are given generous credit terms, and partly because many of the stores specialize in remnants and "off-cut" materials which are sold at cut prices.

For the reasons given earlier, Pageview has become a dreadfully overcrowded slum area. In the northern part, occupied predominantly by Indians and Coloured people, there are some substantial buildings and some houses in fair condition which are interspersed with shacks; but in the lower portion, where large numbers of Africans live, the housing is deplorable. Very high rentals are charged. The only place where the children can play is in the extremely narrow streets. . . .

For years there have been bitter disputes over possible areas for Indian expansion. Leaders of the Indian Congress have fiercely rejected any suggestion of segregation, fearing that if a segregated area was provided, they would all be forced to move there, in the meanwhile the municipal area has been increasingly built-up, and overcrowding among the poorer classes of Indians, who form the vast majority, has become well-nigh intolerable.

When giving evidence before the Group Areas Board, the City Council's representatives said that the only way in which the Indian and Chinese people could be decently rehoused, in areas reasonably close to the city, would be to erect numbers of six-story blocks of flats in central areas such as Burghersdorp; but such schemes would be too expensive for most of them.

(c) Coloured people

The Coloured people of Johannesburg are slightly better off than the Indians so far as housing is concerned; but their needs, too, are clamant.

Some 3,500 Cape Coloured people and 600 Malays live in a suburb named Albertville, in the Western Areas of Johannesburg. This township was developed about 21 years ago. The stands were at first offered to Europeans, but, as there was little response, were subsequently made available for purchase by Coloured people, who have invested large sums in property there. It has become the most prized Coloured suburb, catering for the good middle classes. Most of the houses are well above average, while many of them are excellently-built, worth £4,000 or more, and set in attractive gardens.

About 8,000 Coloured people live in two municipal housing schemes, at Coronationville in the Western Areas, and at Noordgesig away to the south-west of the city, adjoining the African area of Orlando. The houses are of brick, set in their own gardens, and there is a very long waiting-list for admission to these schemes. The British Empire Service League has built a number of flats for Coloured people at Coronationville.

Some 500 of the Coloured population have moved to a developing freehold township at Protea, about 17 miles by road to the south-west of the city, beyond the African areas. The rest, numbering over 32.000, live in hopelessly overcrowded conditions in the slums of Pageview, Newclare, Fordsburg. Vrededorp and elsewhere, or in homes scattered throughout 28 other suburbs.

(d) Avns

As in so many other towns, the Africans of Johannesburg have gradually been forced to move further and further out from the business centre. The Municipality has developed large numbers of housing schemes for them: but at no time in recent years has it been possible to catch up with the backlog.

Three of the earliest Municipal schemes were Western Native Township, adjoining Newclare in the Western Areas of the city, Eastern Native Township near the industrial area in the east, and at Pimville, about twelve miles south-west of the city. Many Africans were allowed to erect their own dwellings at Pimville, on leased land; and this township has become much overcrowded.

There are two areas where Africans have been able to own land in freehold. The first is in the Western Areas, in Sophiatown, Martindale and Newclare. Sophiatown, the largest, was originally owned by a Mr. Tobiansky. He obtained authority to develop it as a township, and, after unsuccessfully offering plots for sale to Europeans, finally disposed of them to Non-Whites before the days when control over acquisition of land by Africans was imposed.

There were most complicated arrangements for the sale of stands. Some Africans had perpetual mortgages; others bought on small-payment hire purchase terms; and there were even more complex agreements. In consequence, although Mr. Tobiansky died some twenty years ago, his estate is still in process of liquidation. Recent racial zoning decisions have added to the confusion.

For the same reasons as obtained in Pageview, appalling slum areas developed in Sophiatown. Homeless families were willing to pay outrageous prices to rent single rooms or hastily- erected shacks in back yards. There are still stands 50 by 100 feet in size on which about 80 people are living in rough corrugated iron shanties, subdivided, in some cases, by cardboard walls. Until recently, some 200 Indian and 50 Chinese traders operated in the area. The estimated total value of the township is about £2-million.

The other area where Africans own land in freehold, in which much the same conditions apply, is Alexandra Township, outside the municipal area and some twelve miles north of the centre of the city. It has a population of about 70,000, mainly Africans, and is governed by its own Health Committee. As is to be expected, there has been much crime and delinquency in all these congested areas.

There had been fairly satisfactory progress in the provision of housing for Africans until the outbreak of the last war. From 1939 onwards, due to war needs and the consequent shortage of manpower and materials, building virtually stopped. But the war also gave a great impetus to industrialization and Africans flocked to Johannesburg to provide the labour required.

For a number of reasons—financial difficulties, the then customary use of White artisans to build houses for Africans, the indifference and apathy of the City Council itself—the housing question was not energetically taken in hand after the war had ended. Apart from one scheme of 5,100 units passed in 1947, other schemes were trifling in the face of the need until some three years ago, when a Division of Native Housing under an able Director was established and real progress made.

During the war and post-war period overcrowding, sub-letting and rent-racketeering mounted alarmingly. European land-owners in pen-urban areas took advantage of the situation to entice homeless African workers to pay large sums in order to rent small strips of ground, on which they erected their own tin shanties, European and Indian property owners in town, in areas such as Pageview, Newclare, Martindale and others, erected still more shacks on already overcrowded stands. Very large numbers of Africans live, illegally and surreptitiously, in the back yards of private European householders.

Extensive sub-letting, and in consequence overcrowding, occurred in the municipal locations, as well as in the freehold areas. Tensions mounted. Not only were African sub-tenants well-nigh desperate: but there was increasing resentment among European residents of suburbs which had most short-sightedly been allowed to develop around the Non-White townships. The Europeans objected to the slums they had to pass, to the crime that was an inevitable concomitant of these conditions, to the very fact that Non-Whites were in their midst.

In 1944 a large number of African sub-tenants in Orlando, who claimed that conditions had become unbearable, moved out of the township and put up hessian shacks on undeveloped municipal land nearby. It was over a year before the authorities took any action. Eventually rough "breezeblock" shelters were erected for occupation by the squatters. This was intended to be purely a temporary measure—but these shelters are still in use.

A similar exodus of sub-tenants took place in Alexandra Township in 1946. Johannesburg Municipality then laid out an emergency camp at Moroka, some distance to the south-west of Orlando. to which squatters were moved from Alexandra Township, Orlando, Newclare and other areas. They were provided with stands 20 feet by 20 feet in size and rudimentary services, and were required to erect their own dwellings. It was intended that the population of Moroka, should gradually be thinned out and larger stands the provided. But this has not yet been achieved.

Only during the last few years has the housing programme really been adequately accelerated. Building costs have been reduced, employers of Africans have been required to contribute to the Services Levy Fund, used for the provision of roads, water, etc. . . .

African Removal Schemes

. . . In 1954 it [the Johannesburg City Council] created a native Resettlement Board to buy up properties in the areas concerned [slum properties] and to rehouse the Africans at Meadowlands, to the west of Orlando.

Possibly up to 17,000 Africans have now been moved to new homes at Meadowlands; but no startling difference can yet be seen in Pageview, Sophiatown and Newclare. Here and there are gaps where houses have been demolished, and numbers of overcrowded back yards have been cleared; but the Government's self-imposed task remains a stupendous one.

Secondly, an inter-departmental Native Areas Zoning Committee (the Mentz Committee) was appointed in 1953 to draw up plans for the siting of African townships in the Southern Transvaal. It recommended that there should be three African areas only for Johannesburg: Alexandra Township (with reduced population), Eastern Native Township, and the large Meadowlands-OrlandoMoroka area. These proposals would mean the total clearance of Pimville (population 27,000) and of Western Native Township (some 20,000).

No decision has been made public. At the sitting of the Group Areas Board in Johannesburg, the City Council's representatives pleaded for the retention of Pimville; but it seems to be likely that Western Native Township is to go.

Thirdly, the Natives (Urban Areas) Amendment Act of 1954 provided that no owner of a building in a town or city may allow more than five Africans to live in it unless special permission is obtained. If strictly implemented in Johannesburg, between 10,000 and 18,000 Africans might have to leave their present accommodation in flats, boarding houses and hotels, and be rehoused in the African townships.

Group Areas

The logical solution of Johannesburg's problem would seem to be to erect housing schemes for the homeless or overcrowded families, as near to the centre of town as possible. This would relieve the position in slum areas. The shortage of housing for Non-Whites is so acute that the task would tax the authorities' resources to the uttermost for years to come. Even if fully economic rentals were charged, or hire-purchase agreements made, the people concerned would be better off than they are at present, paying high rentals and, often, "key-money" for shacks or rooms in evil slums.

But such a scheme did not satisfy the Government. It is determined to demarcate completely separate, self-contained areas for each racial group. And it has decided that many of the "mixed" areas of the town, and also some Non-White suburbs which are surrounded by White areas, shall be allocated to Whites, the Non-Europeans to move considerable distances out of town.

ALAN PATON, "MODERN INDUSTRY AND TRIBAL LIFE," FROM *SOUTH AFRICA TODAY*

(NEW YORK: THE PHELPS STOKES FUND, 1951:14–18)

This excerpt shows the effects of industrialization on Africans and also elaborates Alan Paton's theory of urban crime and the disintegration of the African way of life.

Modern Industry and Tribal Life

MEANWHILE in these forty years of Union, the country has undergone an industrial revolution, which at the moment is proceeding unabated. It has had one outstanding consequence. The rapidly growing cities drew to themselves a never-ending stream of African laborers from the reserved lands which both British and Afrikaner Governments had in the course of time set aside for them.

The African population of the Union is about nine millions, and of these roughly one third has been drawn to the cities, one third lives and labors on the white man's farms, and one third lives in the reserved lands, where some form of tribal organization still exists. The impact of the mines and industrialism on the inhabitants of these reserved lands has been very great. The mines largely confine themselves to migrant labor, and have built great compounds to house their African miners. The mines have made great efforts to soften the effects of this pernicious system, which separates men from their families, and denudes the reserved lands of much of their male population. They pay to the ordinary miner a net wage of £ 3 per month, and this is supplemented by benefits, amounting in value to about one-third of the wages. The mines attract the more primitive and ignorant amongst the tribesmen, those who have been influenced relatively little by the missions or the schools. It is important to understand clearly this situation. While it is true to say that there would be no gold-mining at all without this cheap labor, it is equally true to say that the more primitive and ignorant would earn nothing at all but for the mines, and that the influx to the cities would have been greater and more uncontrollable than ever.

Industry has also had its great effect on the reserved lands, but its labor is only partly migratory. It is responsible, together with the white city homes with their native servants, for attracting a steady stream of laborers from the overcrowded, eroded reserved lands, and for causing many of them to decide to settle in the cities. Industry with its higher wages has also drawn away labor from the farms, and this in its minor way has further accentuated the cleavage between the two white racial groups, for industry is mainly British in origin, and farmers are mainly Afrikaans-speaking. This great influx to the cities has caused a most acute housing situation in the native city townships, called "locations," and I should state here that it has always been the practice of white settlers, both English- and Afrikaans-speaking, to set aside these locations in every white settlement. These locations have in many places filled to the bursting point, and have spilled over into what are called the "Shanty Towns."

All this development has taken place without plan or regulation. The present government is determined to bring this to an end, to plan further development, and to separate all racial groups from one another. Some Nationalists even talk of applying the separation policy to the tribes themselves, and of separating Xosa-speaking, Zulu-speaking, Sesuto-speaking Africans from one another. This is however a refinement we need not consider now; the main task is sufficiently immense.

Many of these native locations are nothing but slums. Others are model townships of their kind. Some of the municipalities (whose chief authorities are always white men) are making great efforts to cope with the industrial revolution. In general it can be said that some municipalities can take pride in what they have done in the face of tremendous difficulties. It can also be said that many of these difficulties would have been swept aside if there had been a greater will to it.

Crime and Disintegration

African crime is a serious problem in the cities, not only to the white inhabitants, but to the law-abiding Africans in the locations themselves. One must consider here the simple organization of the tribes. They were, if savage, disciplined; if war-like, obedient; if heathen, moral; if simple, efficient. Crime was no serious problem and children were respectful and docile. It was, of course, the system of custom and tradition and order that sustained the individual. Many urban African parents are at a total loss to understand the wayward behavior of their children, being too simple to recognize how they themselves were sustained.

The truth is that the impact of the cities on tribal life was shattering. Both fathers and mothers had to go out to work, the schools were full, and most children were educated in the streets. Prostitution began, and illicit liquor was obtainable (the illicit liquor being in part white man's liquor which a black man may not buy, and in part home-made concoctions which a black man may not brew).

The tribes themselves were hopelessly mixed in a thousand "location" streets, and law and custom began to wither away. The maintenance of law and order was no longer a tribal matter, but one for a separate body called the police, some white, some black, but all enforcing many unpalatable laws, notably those which pertained to liquor, and those which pertained to "passes," which certificates had long before been introduced to control migration, vagrancy, and crime. Next to the locations were the white man's shops and houses, full of goods beyond the reach of the black man's purse. Theft and housebreaking became the occupations of the shiftless, often carried out with violence and murder. Even in the locations themselves decent black people were not safe from these callous criminals, many of them mere boys.

It is not then to be wondered at that African tribal life has undergone a process of disintegration, and that crime, illegitimacy, and drunkeness [*sic*]disfigure African urban life. A whole nation has been rocked to its foundations. It was struck by the giant forces of what we call "Western civilization," but not with any plan or concert. The trekker brought subjugation, the missionary brought religion, the teacher education, the trader goods, the wastrel liquor, the womanizer veneral [*sic*] disease; . . .

FROM MARK MATHABANE, *KAFFIR BOY*

(NEW YORK: PLUME BOOKS, 1986: 3–5)

Mathabane's excerpt gives insight into how pass laws regulated the lives of Africans, how Africans moved to the city, and the conditions in which they lived. Alan Paton's *Cry, the Beloved Country* depicts life in Alexandra, so this excerpt gives another perspective on life in this township.

1 WARNING

THIS Road PASSES THROUGH PROCLAIMED BANTU LOCATIONS, ANY PERSON WHO ENTERS

THE LOCATIONS WITHOUT A PERMIT RENDERS

HIMSELF LIABLE FOR PROSECUTION FOR CONTRAVENING THE BANTU (URBAN AREAS) CONSOLIDATION ACT 1945, AND THE LOCATION REGULATION

ACT OF THE CITY OF JOHANNESBURG.

The above message can be found written on larger-than-life signs staked on every road leading into Alexandra, where I was born and raised, or for that matter, into any other black ghetto of South Africa. It is meant to dissuade white people from entering the black world. As a result, more than 90 percent of white South Africans go through a lifetime without seeing firsthand the inhuman conditions under which blacks have to survive.

Yet the white man of South Africa claims to the rest of the world that he knows what is good for black people and what it takes for a black child to grow up to adulthood. He vaunts aloud that "his blacks" in South Africa are well fed and materially better off under the chains of apartheid than their liberated brothers and sisters in the rest of Africa. But, in truth, these claims and boasts are hollow.

The white man of South Africa certainly does not know me. He certainly does not know the conditions under which I was born and had to live for eighteen years. So my story is intended to show him with words a world he would otherwise not see because of a sign and a conscience racked with guilt and to make him feel what I felt when he contemptuously called me a "Kaffir boy."

At the writing of this book the ghetto of Alexandra had just been saved from extinction by Bishop Desmond Tutu, winner of the 1984 Nobel Peace Prize, and a group of clergymen. When the reprieve came over half of Alexandra had already been destroyed, for the ghetto had been on death row since 1962 when the South African government first decreed that it had to go because it occupied land onto which whites wished to expand.

The remains of Alexandra can be found about ten miles north of Johannesburg. You will not mistake those remains for anything else. They occupy a one-square-mile pit constantly shrouded by a heav blanket of smog. It is the only such pit in an enclave of spacious, fresh-aired, verdant white suburbs sporting such melodious names as Northcliff, Rosebank, Lower Houghton, Bramley, Killarney and Edenvale.

The Alexandra of my childhood and youth was a shantytown of mostly shacks, a few decent houses, lots of gutters and lots of unpaved, potholed streets with numbers from First to Twenty-third. First Avenue was where Indians—the cream of Alexandra's quarantined society—lived, behind their sell-everything stores and produce stalls, which were the ghetto's main shopping centre. Indians first came to South Africa in 1860, as indentured servants, to work the sugarcane fields of Natal.

Second, Third and Fourth avenues were inhabited mostly by Coloureds, the mulatto race which came into being nine months after white settlers arrived in South Africa in 1652—without women. The rest of Alexandra's streets were filled by black faces, many of them as black as coal, full-blooded Africans. Many of these blacks were as poor as church mice. In South Africa there's a saying that to be black is to be at the end of the line when anything of significance is to be had. So these people were considered and treated as the dregs of society, aliens in the land of their birth. Such labelling and treatment made them an angry and embittered lot.

The Alexandra of my childhood and youth was one of the oldest shantytowns in the Witwatersrand—the area where black miners toil night and day to tear gold from the bowels of the earth so that the white man of South Africa can enjoy one of the highest standards of living in the world. Many of Alexandra's first settlers came from the tribal reserves, where they could no longer eke out a living, to seek work in the city of gold. Work was plentiful in those days: in mines, factories and white people's homes. As a result these black pioneers stayed, some bought plots of land, established families and called Alexandra home, sweet home. Many shed their tribal cloth and embraced Western culture, a way of life over 350 years of white oppression had deluded them into believing was better than their own. And so it was that in the mid-1950s Alexandra boasted a population of over one hundred thousand blacks, Coloureds and Indians—all squeezed into a space of one square mile.

My parents, a generation or so removed from these earliest settlers of Alexandra, had, too, come from the tribal reserves. My father came from what is now the so-called independent homeland of the Vendas in the northwestern corner of the Transvaal. Venda's specious independence (no other country but South Africa recognizes it) was imposed by the Pretoria regime in 1979, thus at the time making three (Transkei and Bophuthatswana were the other two) the number of these archipelagos of poverty, suffering and corruption, where blacks are supposed to exercise their political rights. Since "independence" the Venda people have been under the clutches of the Pretoria-anointed dictator, Patrick Mphephu, who, despite the loss of two elections, continues clinging to power through untempered repression and brutality.

My mother came from Gazankulu, the tribal reserve for the Tsongas in the Northeastern Transvaal. Gazankulu is also being pressured into "independence." My parents met and married in Alexandra. Immediately following marriage they rented a shack in one of the squalid yards of the ghetto. And in that shack I was born, a few months before sixty-nine unarmed black protesters were massacred—many shot in the back as they fled for safety—by South African policemen during a peaceful demonstration against the pass laws in Sharpeville on March 21, 1960. Pass laws regulate the movement of blacks in so-called white South Africa. And it was the pass laws that, in those not so long ago days of my childhood and youth, first awakened me to the realities of life as a Kaffir boy in South Africa.

FROM CAN THEMBA, "KWASHIORKOR" *THE WILL TO DIE* (LONDON: HEINEMANN, 1983: 14–18)

This excerpt shows the physical and psychological misery of the Alexandra residents depicted in Alan Paton's *Cry, the Beloved Country.*

'Here's another interesting case . . . '

My sister flicked over the pages of the file of one of her case studies, arid I wondered what other shipwrecked human being had there been recorded, catalogued, statisticized and analysed. My sister is a social worker with the Social Welfare Department of the Non-European Section of the Municipality of Johannesburg. In other words, she probes into the derelict lives of the unfortunate poor in Johannesburg. She studies their living habits, their recreational habits, their sporting habits, their drinking habits, the incidence of crime, neglect, malnutrition, divorce, aberration, and she records all this in cyclostyled forms that ask the questions ready-made. She has got so good that she could tell without looking whether such-and-such a query falls under paragraph so-and-so. She has got so clinical that no particular case rattles her, for she has met its like before and knows how and where to classify it.

Her only trouble was ferocious Alexandra Township, that hell-hole in Johannesburg where it was never safe for a woman to walk the streets unchaperoned or to go from house to house asking testing questions. This is where I come in. Often I have to escort: her on her rounds just so that no township rough-neck molests her. We arranged it lovely so that she only went to Alexandra on Saturday afternoons when I was half-day-off and could tag along.

'Dave,' she said, 'here's another interesting case. I'm sure you would love to hear about it. It's Alex again. I'm interested in the psychological motivations and the statistical significance, but I think you'll get you a human-interest story. I know you can't be objective, but do, I beg you, do take it all quietly and don't mess me up with your sentimental reactions. We'll meet at two o'clock on Saturday, okay?'

That is how we went to that battered house in 3rd Avenue, Alexandra. It was just a lot of wood and tin knocked together gawkily to make four rooms. The house stood precariously a few yards from the sour, cider-tasting gutter, and in the back there was a row of out-rooms constructed like a train and let to smaller families or bachelor men and women. This was the main source of income for the Mabiletsa family—mother, daughter and daughter's daughter.

But let me refer to my sister Eileen's records to get my facts straight.

Mother: Mrs Sarah Mabiletsa, age 62, widow, husband Abner Mabiletsa died 1953 in motor-car accident. Sarah does not work. Medical Report says chronic arthritis. Her sole sources of support are rent from out-rooms and working daughter, Maria. Sarah is dually illiterate.

Daughter:	Maria Mabiletsa, age 17, Reference Book No. F/V 118/32N1682. Domestic servant. Educational standard: Reads and writes English, Afrikaans, Sepedi. Convictions: 30 days for shoplifting. One illegitimate child unmaintained and of disputed paternity.
Child:	Sekgametse Daphne Lorraine Mabiletsa, Maria's child, age 3 years. Father undetermined. Free clinic attendance. Medical Report: Advanced Kwashiorkor.
Other relatives:	Sarah's brother, Edgar Mokgomane, serving jail sentence, 15 years, murder and robbery.
Remarks (Eileen's verdict):	This family is desperate.
Mother:	Ineffectual care for child. Child: showing malnutrition effects. Overall quantitative and qualitative nutritional deficiency. Maria: good-time girl, seldom at home, spends earnings mostly on self and parties. Recommend urgent welfare aid and/or intervention.

Although Eileen talks about these things clinically, *objectively,* she told me the story and I somehow got the feel of it.

Abner Mabiletsa was one of those people who was not content with life in the reserves in Pietersburg district where he was born and grew up. He did not see where the tribal set-up of chief and kgotla—the tribal council—and customs, taboos, superstitions, witchcraft and the lackadaisical dreariness of rotating with the sun from morn till eve, would take the people and would take him. . . . So he upped and went to Johannesburg . . .

Abner made it. . . . He had escapades, fun, riotous living . . . Until one day one of his escapades became pregnant and bore him a daughter. . . .

But life in Johannesburg was such that he did not find much time to look after his family. . . . Then suddenly, one crash! He died in a motor–car accident . . .

His daughter, Maria, grew up in the streets of Alexandra. The spectre of poverty was always looming over her life. . . .

First, Marie shed all her love—that is, the anguish and pain she suffered, the bitterness, the humiliation, the sense of desolation and collapse of her tinsel world—upon this infant. But people either perish or recover *from* wounds; even the worst afflictions do not gnaw at you forever. Maria recovered. She went back to her domestic work, leaving the baby with her mother. She would come home every Thursday—Sheila's Day—or the day-off for all the domestics in Johannesburg. She came to her baby, bringing clothing, blankets, pampering little goodies and smothering treacly love.

But she was young still, and the blood burst inside her once she recovered. Johannesburg was outside there calling, calling, first wooingly, alluringly, then more and more stridently, irresistibly. She came home less often, but remorsefully, and would crush the child to her in those brief moments. Even as she hugged the rose, the thorns tore at her. Then suddenly she came home no more. . . .

'It is quite a typical case of recidivism,' Eileen explained scholastically to me on our way to Alexandra. 'You see, there's a moment's panic as a result of the trauma. The reaction varies according to the victim. One way is that for most of our girls there's a stubborn residue of moral up-bringing from home or school or church, sometimes really only from mamma's personality, and mamma probably comes from an older, steadier, more inhibited and tribe-controlled environment . . .' Eileen shrugged helplessly, ' . . . and detribalization, modernization, adaptation, acculturation, call it what you like, has to tear its way into their psychological pattern, brute-like. At first, before the shock, these girls really just float loosely about in the new freedoms, not really willing evil, not consciously flouting the order, but they're nevertheless playing with fire, and there's no-one knows how to tell them no. Their parents themselves are baffled by what the world's come to and there's no invisible reality like tribe, or comprehensible code like custom or taboo, to keep some kind of balance. Meanwhile, the new dispensation—the superior culture, they call it; the diabolical shadow-life, I call it—pounds at them relentlessly. Suddenly, some traumatic event, a jail sentence, a sudden encounter with brute, bloody death, or a first pregnancy, pulverizes them into what we credulous monitors consider repentance. It's really the startled whimper of a frightened child vaguely remembering that in some remote distance mamma or tribe or school or church has whispered, "Thou shalt not," and the horror that it's too late.

'But,' Eileen almost cursed out the words, 'the superior culture keeps pounding at them, and it's a matter of time before your repentant maiden sings again, "Jo'burg, here I come".'

I was shaken, 'Eileen, you know that much and yet you continue tinkering with statistics!'

She pulled herself together with an effort. But though she spoke confidently, it sounded unconvincing: 'Lad, I'm a social scientist, not a conjuress.'

FROM DESMOND TUTU, *THE WORDS OF DESMOND TUTU* (ED. NAOMI TUTU. LONDON: SPIRE, 1989: 58)

This excerpt reinforces Alan Paton's account of the squatters and how Christian love should move European Christians to change their circumstances.

Every day in a squatter camp near Cape Town, called K.T.C., the authorities have been demolishing flimsy plastic shelters that black mothers have erected because they were taking their marriage vows seriously. They have been reduced to sitting on soaking mattresses, with their household effects strewn round their feet, and whimpering babies on their laps, in the cold Cape winter rain. Every day the authorities have carried out these callous demolitions. What heinous crime have these women committed, to be hounded like criminals in this manner? All they have wanted is to be with their husbands, the fathers of their children. Everywhere else in the world they would be highly commended, but in South Africa, a land that claims to be Christian, and that boasts a public holiday called Family Day, these gallant women are treated so inhumanely, and yet all they want is to have a decent and stable family life. Unfortunately, in the land of their birth, it is a criminal offense for them to live happily with their husbands and fathers of their children. Black family life is thus being undermined, not accidentally, but by deliberate government policy. It is part of the price human beings, God's children, are called to pay for apartheid. An unacceptable price.

TOPICS FOR ORAL OR WRITTEN EXPLORATION

1. Research the Urban Areas Acts, and show the extent to which these acts have had an impact on the lives of Africans and have disenfranchised them.

2. Space is a means to control people. Are American cities also spatially divided like those of apartheid South Africa? Write an essay demonstrating whether space is an important factor in our lives and whether race alone determines spatial divisions.

3. Imagine that your town has been destroyed to accommodate our inhabitants. Write an essay capturing the essence of your town and the loss and injustice you have incurred.

4. After reading Bloke Modisane and Can Themba's texts, do you believe that Alan Paton has well rendered the condition and status of the people of these townships? Give textual evidence to support your comments.

NOTES

6. Much of the information in this chapter has been obtained from articles written at various times by Ellen Hellman.

7. Much of the information in this chapter has been obtained from articles written at various times by Ellen Hellman.

SUGGESTIONS FOR FURTHER READING

Abrahams, Peter. *Tell Freedom.* London: Faber and Faber, 1951.

———. *Return to Goli.* London: Faber and Faber, 1952.

———. *Mine Boy.* London: Heinemann, 1946.

Dikobe, Modikwe. *The Marabi Dance.* London: Heinemann, 1873.

Hellman, Ellen. "Urban Areas." *Handbook on Race Relations in South Africa.* New York: Octagon Books, 1975.

Huddleson, Trevor, *Naught for Your Comfort.* London: Collins, 1956.

Mphahlele, Es'kia [Ezekiel]. *Down Second Avenue.* London: Faber, 1959.

Phillips, Ray E. *The Bantu in the City.* Lovedale, South Africa: Alice Lovedale Press, 1938.

Whittington. G. *Land and People of South Africa.* London: Methuen Educational LTD, 1974.

WORKS CITED

Hellman, Ellen. "Urban Areas." *Handbook on Race Relations in South Africa.* New York: Octagon Books, 1975.

Horrell, Muriel. *The Group Areas Act. Its Effect on Human Beings.* Johannesburg: The South African Institute of Race Relations, 1956: 135–140.

Modisane, Bloke. *Blame Me on History.* London: Thames and Hudson, 1963.
Paton, Alan. "Modern Industry and Tribal Life." *South Africa Today.* New York: The Phelps Stokes Fund, 1951.
———. *The People and Land of South Africa.* Philadelphia and New York: J. B. Lippincott, 1955.
Themba, Can. *The Will to Die.* London: Heinemann, 1983.
Tutu, Desmond. *The Words of Desmond Tutu.* Ed. Naomi Tutu. London: Spire, 1989.

7

Social and Economic Conditions in Rural Communities

Alan Paton well depicts life in rural South Africa in the 1940s in *Cry, the Beloved Country.* Traditional South African life has changed through its contact with the Western world, so modernity and Western aspects of life are very much part of everyday rural experience. The Africans have adopted Western clothing and technology, for, as the narrator in *Cry, the Beloved Country* clearly states, when Reverend Kumalo observes his fellow countrymen on the train, the majority have donned Western clothes, except for the women who wear "blankets over the semi-nudity of their primitive dress" (13). Despite the narrator's romantization of the rural environment—associated with innocence and good—rural South Africa has also been contaminated by the corruption of the city, which destroys the family and values, and also needs to be mended. According to the narrator, "The white man has broken the tribe. And it is my belief—," writes the narrator, "that it cannot be mended again. But the house that is broken, and the man that falls apart when the house is broken, these are the tragic things" (25–26). Even though rural areas are described poetically as places of beauty and innocence, they are places of overwhelming poverty, disease, and death. James Jarvis's world from the top of the mountain, a symbol of status and class, is full of prosperity. The dry world of Ndotsheni, on the other hand, lacks water and food. The villagers do not even have milk for the children; their place of worship cannot even shelter them from the pouring rain seeping through the roof of the church full of holes. James Jarvis's world is opulent like the "green rich hills that he inherited from his father" (131). But, in Kumalo's world, there are no refrigerators or water.

Africans were constricted to nine areas that together made up just 13.5 percent of the country. The lands were infertile and had very little water, no ports, no industries, and no urban infrastructures. Yet they were supposedly to sustain the autonomy and development of the Africans. Because the lands did not produce much, the homelands depended on food imported from outside the reserves, and Africans, especially males, were compelled to seek work outside. A large percentage of women, children, and elderly suffered numerous material deprivations and emotional separation from their spouses, sons, or fathers.

Africans were entitled to own land only on reserves—Ciskei, Transkei, Bechuanaland, Natal reserves, Zululand, Transvaal reserves, and the Orange Free State reserves. The 1913 Natives Land Act unequally distributed land between whites and blacks. Apart from Pondoland and the Transkei, the reserves had medium to poor fertility. Because of the paucity of traditional farming methods, overstocking of animals, and overpopulation, malnutrition was elevated in the homelands. The South African government attempted to redress the situation through the 1936 Land Act, but, with the mounting opposition of white farmers' organizations, it never managed to purchase land for natives or convert white-owned land; most of the released land was also of poor quality. The government also attempted to redress the situation, even though it did not heavily invest financially in the project, by providing Africans agricultural education to convert them to modern farming. In 1949, there were four agriculture schools that formed agricultural demonstrators. In 1944 and 1945, according to Edward Roux, there were 413 agricultural demonstrators.

Those Africans who worked on white farms were no better off, since they too suffered from malnutrition. Their employers gave them meager salaries and rations, but these often proved to be insufficient, so they had to live off their own crops or purchased food. Some farmers gave their workers milk, but the majority of Africans were often not given sufficient proteins. Each year, they generally received a pair of khaki trousers and a shirt. Sometimes, more generous patrons provided their employees two of each and, infrequently, boots and overcoats. Although employers were contracted to give their laborers medical care, the paternalistic farming system gave owners much freedom to determine how much money they would spend, and when and how, to assist their ailing employees and their families. The African laborers worked from sun down to sunrise; they were beaten, mistreated, or harshly treated by the police. They were allowed to brew only 40 gallons of "Kaffir beer," which they could drink only at the discretion of their employers. Interfarm visits were controlled, and the farmer had the freedom to use the entire family's labor. Because white farmers needed labor, the children living on the farm did not get an education, especially since education for African children was not mandatory. This may explain, according to some analysts, why South Africa had more girls in school than boys. Younger teenagers who wished to go to the city could not travel without their fathers' employers' passes, which the white farmers did not always give readily when the offspring of their employees desired to work in the city temporarily. Youngsters were, at times, ordered to leave the premises forever, and their families were also, at times, expelled from the farm. The laborers also had little access to churches.

The excerpt from Desmond Tutu, *The Words of Desmond Tutu,* illustrates how Africans have become dispossessed. The excerpt from Sol Plaatje's *Native Life in South Africa* describes the impact of the 1913 Land Act on the African population; Es'kia Mphahlele's "People Leave the Land" provides a snapshot of life in the rural area; and the excerpt from Nelson Mandela's *Long Walk to Freedom* shows the impact of the West on traditional life and the subsequent loss of traditional values.

FROM DESMOND TUTU, *THE WORDS OF DESMOND TUTU*

(ED. NAOMI TUTU. LONDON: SPIRE, 1989, 73)

Desmond Tutu's excerpt speaks to the "arid poverty-stricken Ndotsheni" and describes how Africans, who have no political rights, have become dispossessed within their own country.

People have been turned into aliens in the land of their birth, because aliens cannot claim any rights, least of all political rights. Millions have been deprived of their birthright, their South African citizenship; stable black communities have been destroyed, and those who have been uprooted have been dumped as you dump not people but things, in arid poverty-striken [*sic*] Bantustan homeland resettlement camps. Three and a half million people are treated in such a callous and heartless fashion in a land whose newest constitution invokes the name of God to sanctify a vicious, evil, and totally immoral and utterly un-Christian system, a system as evil, as immoral, as un-Christian as communism and Nazism.

SOL PLAATJE, "ONE NIGHT WITH THE FUGITIVES," FROM *NATIVE LIFE IN SOUTH AFRICA* (1982)

(online posting at <http://www.anc.org.za/books/nlife04.html>)

Sol Plaatje's excerpt provides insight into the fate of Africans after passage of the Land Act of 1913, which confiscated lands owned by Africans, and into the degradation that followed this dispossession. It also shows how pass laws affected the lives of Africans and the oppressive farming system within the rural area. The inhabitants of Ndotsheni, in *Cry, the Beloved Country,* are incapable of providing their children milk. Sol Plaatje's text explains how Africans who were pastoralists or mixed farmers lost their cattle and why their lands failed to yield food. It also discusses the issue of love and hatred raised in Alan Paton's novel.

> *Es ist unkoeniglich zu weinen—ach, Und hier nicht weinen ist unvaeterlich.*
>
> —Schiller

"Pray that your flight be not in winter," said Jesus Christ; but it was only during the winter of 1913 that the full significance of this New Testament passage was revealed to us. We left Kimberley by the early morning train during the first week in July, on a tour of observation regarding the operation of the Natives' Land Act; and we arrived at Bloemhof, in Transvaal, at about noon. On the River Diggings there were no actual cases representing the effects of the Act, but traces of these effects were everywhere manifest. Some fugitives of the Natives' Land Act had crossed the river in full flight. The fact that they reached the diggings a fortnight before our visit would seem to show that while the debates were proceeding in Parliament some farmers already viewed with eager eyes the impending opportunity for at once making slaves of their tenants and appropriating their stock; for, acting on the powers conferred on them by an Act signed by Lord Gladstone, so lately as June 16, they had during that very week (probably a couple of days after, and in some cases, it would seem, a couple of days before the actual signing of the Bill) approached their tenants with stories about a new Act which makes it criminal for any one to have black tenants and lawful to have black servants. Few of these Natives, of course, would object to be servants, especially if the white man is worth working for, but this is where the shoe pinches: one of the conditions is that the black man's (that is the servant's) cattle shall henceforth work for the landlord free of charge. Then the Natives would decide to leave the farm rather than make the landlord a present of all their life's savings, and some of them had passed through the diggings in search of a place in the Transvaal. But the higher up they went the more gloomy was their prospect as the news about the new law was now penetrating every part of the country.

One farmer met a wandering native family in the town of Bloemhof a week before our visit. He was willing to employ the Native and many more homeless families as follows: A monthly wage of £2 10s. for each such family, the husband working in the fields, the wife in the house, with an additional 10s. a month for each son, and 5s. for each daughter, but on condition that the Native's cattle were also handed over to work for him. It must be clearly understood, we are told that the Dutchman added, that occasionally the Native would have to leave his family at work on the farm, and go out with his wagon and his oxen to earn money whenever and wherever he was told to go, in order that the master may be enabled to pay the stipulated wage. The Natives were at first inclined to laugh at the idea of working for a master with their families and goods and chattels, and then to have the additional pleasure of paying their own small wages, besides bringing money to pay the "Baas" for employing them. But the Dutchman's serious demeanour told them that his suggestion was "no joke". He himself had for some time been in need of a native cattle owner, to assist him as transport rider between Bloemhof, Mooifontein, London, and other diggings, in return for the occupation and cultivation of some of his waste lands in the district, but that was now illegal. He could only "employ" them; but, as he had no money to pay wages, their cattle would have to go out and earn it for him. Had they not heard of the law before? he inquired. Of course they had; in fact that is why they left the other place, but as they thought that it was but a "Free" State law, they took the anomalous situation for one of the multifarious aspects of the freedom of the "Free" State whence they came; they had scarcely thought that the Transvaal was similarly afflicted.

Needless to say the Natives did not see their way to agree with such a one-sided bargain. They moved up country, but only to find the next farmer offering the same terms, however, with a good many more disturbing details—and the next farmer and the next—so that after this native farmer had wandered from farm to farm, occasionally getting into trouble for travelling with unknown stock, "across my ground without my permission", and at times escaping arrest for he knew not what, and further, being abused for the crimes of having a black skin and no master, he sold some of his stock along the way, beside losing many which died of cold and starvation; and after thus having lost much of his substance, he eventually worked his way back to Bloemhof with the remainder, sold them for anything they could fetch, and went to work for a digger.

The experience of another native sufferer was similar to the above, except that instead of working for a digger he sold his stock for a mere bagatelle, and left with his family by the Johannesburg night train for an unknown destination. More native families crossed the river and went inland during the previous week, and as nothing had since been heard of them, it would seem that they were still wandering somewhere, and incidentally becoming well versed in the law that was responsible for their compulsory unsettlement.

Well, we knew that this law was as harsh as its instigators were callous, and we knew that it would, if passed, render many poor people homeless, but it must be confessed that we were scarcely prepared for such a rapid and widespread crash as it caused in the lives of the Natives in this neighbourhood. We left our luggage the next morning with the local Mission School teacher, and crossed the river to find out some more about this wonderful law of extermination. It was about 10 A.M. when we landed on the south bank of the Vaal River—the picturesque Vaal River, upon whose banks a hundred miles farther west we spent the best and happiest days of our boyhood. It was interesting to walk on one portion of the banks of that beautiful river—a portion which we had never traversed except as an infant in mother's arms more than thirty years before. How the subsequent happy days at Barkly West, so long past, came crowding upon our memory!—days when there were no railways, no bridges, and no system of irrigation. In rainy seasons, which at that time were far more regular and certain, the river used to overflow its high banks and flood the surrounding valleys to such an extent, that no punt could carry the wagons across. Thereby the transport service used to be hung up, and numbers of wagons would congregate for weeks on both sides of the river until the floods subsided. At such times the price of fresh milk used to mount up to 1s. per pint. There being next to no competition, we boys had a monopoly over the milk trade. We recalled the number of haversacks full of bottles of milk we youngsters often carried to those wagons, how we returned with empty bottles and with just that number of shillings. Mother and our elder brothers had leather bags full of gold and did not care for the "boy's money"; and unlike the boys of the neighbouring village, having no sisters of our own, we gave away some of our money to fair cousins, and jingled the rest in our pockets. We had been told from boyhood that sweets were injurious to the teeth, and so spurning these delights we had hardly any use for money, for all we wanted to eat, drink and wear was at hand in plenty. We could then get six or eight shillings every morning from the pastime of washing that number of bottles, filling them with fresh milk and carrying them down to the wagons; there was always such an abundance of the liquid that our shepherd's hunting dog could not possibly miss what we took, for while the flocks were feeding on the luscious buds of the haak-doorns and the orange-coloured blossoms of the rich mimosa and other wild vegetation that abounded on the banks of the Vaal River, the cows, similarly engaged, were gathering more and more milk.

The gods are cruel, and one of their cruellest acts of omission was that of giving us no hint that in very much less than a quarter of a century all those hundreds of heads of cattle, and sheep and horses belonging to the family would vanish like a morning mist, and that we ourselves would live to pay 30s. per month for a daily supply of this same precious fluid, and in very limited quantities. They might have warned us that Englishmen would agree with Dutchmen to make it unlawful for black men to keep milch cows of their own on the banks of that river, and gradually have prepared us for the shock.

Crossing the river from the Transvaal side brings one into the Province of the Orange "Free" State, in which, in the adjoining division of Boshof, we were born thirty-six years back. We remember the name of the farm, but not having been in this neighbourhood since infancy, we could not tell its whereabouts, nor could we say whether the present owner was a Dutchman, his lawyer, or a Hebrew merchant; one thing we do know, however: it is that even if we had the money and the owner was willing to sell the spot upon which we first saw the light of day and breathed the pure air of heaven, the sale would be followed with a fine of one hundred pounds. The law of the country forbids the sale of land to a Native. Russia is one of the most abused countries in the world, but it is extremely doubtful if the statute book of that Empire contains a law debarring the peasant from purchasing the land whereon he was born, or from building a home wherein he might end his days.

At this time we felt something rising from our heels along our back, gripping us in a spasm, as we were cycling along; a needlelike pang, too, pierced our heart with a sharp thrill. What was it? We remembered feeling something nearly like it when our father died eighteen years ago; but at that time our physical organs were fresh and grief was easily thrown off in tears, but then we lived in a happy South Africa that was full of pleasant anticipations, and now—what changes for the worse have we undergone! For to crown all our calamities, South Africa has by law ceased to be the home of any of her native children whose skins are dyed with a pigment that does not conform with the regulation hue.

We are told to forgive our enemies and not to let the sun go down upon our wrath, so we breathe the prayer that peace may be to the white races, and that they, including our present persecutors of the Union Parliament, may never live to find themselves deprived of all occupation and property rights in their native country as is now the case with the Native. History does not tell us of any other continent where the Bantu lived besides Africa, and if this systematic ill-treatment of the Natives by the colonists is to be the guiding principle of Europe's scramble for Africa, slavery is our only alternative; for now it is only as serfs that the Natives are legally entitled to live here. Is it to be thought that God is using the South African Parliament to hound us out of our ancestral homes in order to quicken our pace heavenward? But go from where to heaven? In the beginning, we are told, God created heaven and earth, and peopled the earth, for people do not shoot up to heaven from nowhere. They must have had an earthly home. Enoch, Melchizedek, Elijah, and other saints, came to heaven from earth. God did not say to the Israelites in their bondage: "Cheer up, boys; bear it all in good part for I have bright mansions on high awaiting you all." But he said: "I have surely seen the affliction of my people which are in Egypt, and have heard their cry by reason of their taskmasters; for I know their sorrows, and I am come down to bring them out of the hands of the Egyptians, and to bring them up out of that land unto a good land and a large, unto a land flowing with milk and honey." And He used Moses to carry out the promise He made to their ancestor Abraham in Canaan, that "unto thy seed will I give this land." It is to be hoped that in the Boer churches, entrance to which is barred against coloured people during divine service, they also read the Pentateuch.

It is doubtful if we ever thought so much on a single bicycle ride as we did on this journey; however, the sight of a policeman ahead of us disturbed these meditations and gave place to thoughts of quite another kind, for—we had no pass. Dutchmen, Englishmen, Jews, Germans, and other foreigners may roam the "Free" State without permission—but not Natives. To us it would mean a fine and imprisonment to be without a pass. The "pass" law was first instituted to check the movement of livestock over sparsely populated areas. In a sense it was a wise provision, in that it served to identify the livestock which one happened to be driving along the high road, to prove the *bona fides* of the driver and his title to the stock. Although white men still steal large droves of horses in Basutoland and sell them in Natal or in East Griqualand, they, of course, are not required to carry any passes. These white horse-thieves, to escape the clutches of the police, employ Natives to go and sell the stolen stock and write the passes for these Natives, forging the names of Magistrates and Justices of the Peace. Such native thieves in some instances ceasing to be hirelings in the criminal business, trade on their own, but it is not clear what purpose it is intended to serve by subjecting native pedestrians to the degrading requirement of carrying passes when they are not in charge of any stock. In a few moments the policeman was before us and we alighted in presence of the representative of the law, with our feet on the accursed soil of the district in which we were born. The policeman stopped. By his looks and his familiar "Dag jong" we noticed that the policeman was Dutch, and the embodiment of affability. He spoke and we were glad to notice that he had no intention of dragging an innocent man to prison. We were many miles from the nearest police station, and in such a case one is generally able to gather the real views of the man on patrol, as distinct from the written code of his office, but our friend was becoming very companionable. Naturally we asked him about the operation of the plague law. He was a Transvaaler, he said, and he knew that Kafirs were inferior beings, but they had rights, and were always left in undisturbed possession of their property when Paul Kruger was alive. "The poor devils must be sorry now," he said, "that they ever sang 'God save the Queen' when the British troops came into the Transvaal, for I have seen, in the course of my duties, that a Kafir's life nowadays was not worth a——, and I believe that no man regretted the change of flags now more than the Kafirs of Transvaal." This information was superfluous, for personal contact with the Natives of Transvaal had convinced us of the fact. They say it is only the criminal who has any reason to rejoice over the presence of the Union Jack, because in his case the cat-o'-nine-tails, except for very serious crimes, has been abolished.

"Some of the poor creatures," continued the policeman, "I knew to be fairly comfortable, if not rich, and they enjoyed the possession of their stock, living in many instances just like Dutchmen. Many of these are now being forced to leave their homes. Cycling along this road you will meet several of them in search of new homes, and if ever there was a fool's errand, it is that of a Kafir trying to find a new home for his stock and family just now."

"And what do you think, Baas Officer, must eventually be the lot of a people under such unfortunate circumstances?" we asked.

"I think," said the policeman, "that it must serve them right. They had no business to hanker after British rule, to cheat and plot with the enemies of their Republic for the overthrow of their Government. Why did they not assist the forces of their Republic during the war instead of supplying the English with scouts and intelligence? Oom Paul would not have died of a broken heart and he would still be there to protect them. Serve them right, I say." . . .

It was cold that afternoon as we cycled into the "Free" State from Transvaal, and towards evening the southern winds rose. A cutting blizzard raged during the night, and native mothers evicted from their homes shivered with their babies by their sides. When we saw on that night the teeth of the little children clattering through the cold, we thought of our own little ones in their Kimberley home of an evening after gambolling in their winter frocks with their schoolmates, and we wondered what these little mites had done that a home should suddenly become to them a thing of the past. . . .

Numerous details narrated by these victims of an Act of Parliament kept us awake all that night, and by next morning we were glad enough to hear no more of the sickening procedure of extermination voluntarily instituted by the South African Parliament. We had spent a hideous night under a bitterly cold sky, conditions to which hundreds of our unfortunate countrymen and countrywomen in various parts of the country are condemned by the provisions of this Parliamentary land plague. At five o'clock in the morning the cold seemed to redouble its energies; and never before did we so fully appreciate the Master's saying: "But pray ye that your flight be not in the winter."

ES'KIA MPHAHLELE, "PEOPLE LEAVE THE LAND," FROM *FATHER COME HOME*

(JOHANNESBURG: RAVEN PRESS, 1992)

This excerpt shows how the rural area was a reserve for urban labor; it also describes the impact of the Land Act of 1913 and the ways rural areas were changed by European ways of life and commodities. The transformation of traditional African life is indirectly delineated in *Cry, the Beloved Country.*

In the early 1920s, soon after the First World War of 1914–1918, the mines, especially the gold mines, clamoured for more labour. By 'labour' was meant African workers who were not skilled to do anything other than work that needed a strong body, strong arms and legs, and a willingness. This cry for more workers came from all the mines, including diamond, coal, copper and platinum mines. Giant factories like the iron and Steel Works in Pretoria also wanted more and still more workers. White farmers added their own voices to the call that filled the air everywhere in the country; the call for more African workers.

In 1913 the Land Act had been passed. Thousands of black people had been driven off the land and one could buy land only in areas that were set aside for black people. One could buy land only from another African, not from a white man. Like everywhere else, land in the Transvaal Bushveld was shrinking, right before the people's eyes, like land that the water claims: now in big chunks, now in nibbles.

It seemed nothing was ever going to break the cycle: less and less land, greater and greater poverty, more of a willingness to be recruited by white farmers and the mines, by business firms, and then more recruitment. With the young men gone away to seek work for cash wages, the little land they left behind went untilled for lack of strong bodies and strong arms, it yielded less and less food for wives and children; and then more poverty and a greater willingness to be recruited or simply to *go* and seek other pastures. . . .

Maredi observed all this in the Bushveld. Indeed, his people's plot needed a strong man's hand. The young men were leaving, young women were going to Pietersburg, Pretoria, and the Reef to find work as domestics. Here in the Bushveld Maredi saw mostly children under sixteen, middle-aged women like his own mother, and old men and women. Young men and women who did not go to the towns and cities went to teacher-training schools when they finished Standard Six. Or the women got married.

When Christmas time came, the villages were again back to normal. Men and women flaunted their higher education along with the fabrics and styles of dress they had picked up in the towns: gramophones that you had to wind every so often and which gave out high-pitched music; men's caps of various colours: jackets that had sleeves with fish-tails: tinned foods and loaves of bread enough to feed multitudes: food items that came only once a year, or at the most twice.

Only those who had moved to the farms of white folks as labour tenants did not return. Some squatted on the farms, cultivating little plots lent to them, in return for which they gave the farmers their labour. Later, the law put an end to this squatting. The workers all became labour tenants then. They could not grow food on plots lent to them as they had done before. Instead, they received rations of maize meal, salt, sugar, some meat, arid a little cash for their work.

Come Christmas time, Maredi's people would have little to show for it. And his uncle Namedi, who worked in Pretoria. was responsible for whatever cheer they had over the season. Loyal down to his toe-nails, the uncle was known never to miss a Christmas visit to Sedibeng. He brought all the good things Maredi could imagine: rare and staple foods like condensed milk, loaves of white bread, mealie meal, sugar, tea, coffee, jams, rice, vegetables, and new clothes, cotton and silk fabrics for the whole family. . . .

They seldom had money to buy clothes or blankets during the year. But occasionally, when someone was visiting Sedibeng on two-weeks' leave, he or she brought a blanket or two from Namedi.

Unlike Hunadi's Sedibeng brother Namedi was not loudmouthed. He never boasted about his generous heart. . . .

It was useless asking him about Hunadi's man or her *so,* rumoured to be in Johannesburg. Rumour even had it that the youth had become one of the *malata.* These were boxing gangs who marched to some open ground on the edge of town every Sunday afternoon for their bouts of fisticuffs. . . . Hunadi was really alarmed when it was reported that her son had become a bum, a drunk; that he had become a hole-digger. This meant that he was being kept by a beerbrewing queen who gave him food and sleeping room in return for digging holes in the yard to conceal tins of beer against police raids. A hole-digger was considered to have sunk to the lowest level of self-hate—beyond all hope. Once a hole-digger, only bodily decay and death await you, and there is never a return to the decent life.

FROM NELSON MANDELA, *LONG WALK TO FREEDOM: THE AUTOBIOGRAPHY OF NELSON MANDELA*

(BOSTON: LITTLE BROWN, 1994)

Nelson Mandela's autobiography illustrates the positive aspects of rural life, which are touted in *Cry, the Beloved Country.* While rural life is sordid and rampant with poverty, this text emphasizes the every day experiences of children in rural communities, the values that shape their vision of the world, their interactions with the white community, and the type of education they receive, which Reverend Kumalo wished his son had had.

Part One

A Country Childhood

THE VILLAGE OF QUNU was situated in a narrow, grassy valley crisscrossed by clear streams, and overlooked by green hills. It consisted of no more than a few hundred people who lived in huts, known as rondavels, which were beehive-shaped structures of mud walls, with a wooden pole in the center holding up a peaked, grass roof. The floor was made of crushed ant-heap, the hard dome of excavated earth above an ant colony, and was kept smooth by smearing it regularly with fresh cow dung. The smoke from the hearth escaped through the roof, and the only opening was a low doorway one had to stoop to walk through. The rondavels were generally grouped together in a residential area that was some distance away from the maize fields. There were no roads, only paths through the grass worn away by barefooted boys and women. The women and children of the village wore blankets dyed in ocher; only the few Christians in the village wore Western-style clothing. Cattle, sheep, goats, and horses grazed together in common pastures. The land around Qunu was mostly treeless except for a cluster of poplars on a hill overlooking the village. The land itself was owned by the state. With very few exceptions, Africans at the time did not enjoy private title to land in South Africa but were tenants paying rent annually to the government. In the area, there were two small primary schools, a general store, and a dipping tank to rid the cattle of ticks and diseases. Maize (what we called mealies and people in the West call corn), sorghum, beans, and pumpkins formed the largest portion of our diet, not because of any inherent preference for these foods, but because the people could not afford anything richer. The wealthier families in our village supplemented their diets with tea, coffee, and sugar, but for most people in Qunu these were exotic luxuries far beyond their means. The water used for farming, cooking, and washing had to be fetched in buckets from streams and springs. This was woman's work, and indeed, Qunu was a village of women and children: most of the men spent the greater part of the year working on remote farms or in the mines along the Reef, the great ridge of gold-bearing rock and shale that forms the southern boundary of Johannesburg. They returned perhaps twice a year, mainly to plow their fields. The hoeing, weeding, and harvesting were left to the women and children. Few if any of the people in the village knew how to read or write, and the concept of education was still a foreign one to many.

My mother presided over three rondavels at Qunu which, as I remember, were always filled with the babies and children of my relations. In fact, I hardly recall any occasion as a child when I was alone. In African culture, the sons and daughters of one's aunts or uncles are considered brothers and sisters, not cousins. We do not make the same distinctions among relations practiced by Europeans. We have no half brothers or half sisters. My mother's sister is my mother; my uncle's son is my brother; my brother's child is my son, my daughter.

Of my mother's three huts, one was used for cooking, one for sleeping, and one for storage. In the hut in which we slept, there was no furniture in the Western sense. We slept on mats and sat on the ground. I did not discover pillows until I went away to school. The stove on which my mother cooked was a three-legged iron pot that rested on a grate over a hole in the ground. Everything we ate we grew and made ourselves. . . . From an early age, I spent most of my free time in the veld playing and fighting with the other boys of the village. A boy who remained at home tied to his mother's apron strings was regarded as a sissy. At night, I shared my food and blanket with these same boys. I was no more than five when I became a herd-boy, looking after sheep and calves in the fields. I discovered the almost mystical attachment that the Xhosa have for cattle, not only as a source of food and wealth, but as a blessing from God and a source of happiness. . . . I learned to stick-fight—essential knowledge to any rural African boy—and became adept at its various techniques, parrying blows, feinting in one direction and striking in another, breaking away from an opponent with quick footwork. . . .

I learned my lesson one day from an unruly donkey. We had been taking turns climbing up and down its back and when my chance came I jumped on and the donkey bolted into a nearby thornbush. It bent its head, trying to unseat me, which it did, but not before the thorns had pricked and scratched my face, embarrassing me in front of my friends. Like the people of the East, Africans have a highly developed sense of dignity, or what the Chinese call "face". I had lost face among my friends. Even though it was a donkey that unseated me, I learned that to humiliate another person is to make him suffer an unnecessarily cruel fate. Even as a boy, I defeated my opponents without dishonoring them. . . .

As we grew older, we organized matches against boys from neighboring villages, and those who distinguished themselves in these fraternal battles were greatly admired, as generals who achieve great victories in war are justly celebrated.

After games such as these, I would return to my mother's kraal where she was preparing supper. Whereas my father once told stories of historic battles and heroic Xhosa warriors, my mother would enchant us with Xhosa legends and fables that had come down from numberless generations. These tales stimulated my childish imagination, and usually contained some moral lesson. I recall one story my mother told us about a traveler who was approached by an old woman with terrible cataracts on her eyes. . . .

It is a simple tale, but its message is an enduring one: virtue and generosity will be rewarded in ways that one cannot know. . . .

My life, and that of most Xhosas at the time, was shaped by custom, ritual, and taboo. This was the alpha and omega of our existence, and went unquestioned. . . .

I came across few whites as a boy at Qunu. The local magistrate, of course, was white, as was the nearest shopkeeper. Occasionally white travelers or policemen passed through our area. These whites appeared as grand as gods to me, and I was aware that they were to be treated with a mixture of fear and respect. But their role in my life was a distant one, and I thought little if at all about the white man in general or relations between my own people and these curious and remote figures.

The only rivalry between different clans or tribes in our small world at Qunu was that between the Xhosas and the Mfengu, a small number of whom lived in our village. The Mfengu arrived on the eastern Cape after fleeing from Shaka Zulu's armies in a period known as the Mfecane, the great wave of battles and migrations between 1820 and 1840 set in motion by the rise of Shaka and the Zulu state, during which the Zulu warrior sought to conquer and then unite all the tribes under military rule. The Mfengu, who were not originally Xhosa-speakers, were refugees from the Mfecane and were forced to do jobs that no other African would do. They worked on white farms and in white businesses, something that was looked down upon by the more established Xhosa tribes. But the Mfengu were an industrious people, and because of their contact with Europeans, they were often more educated and "Western" than other Africans.

When I was a boy, the Mfengu were the most advanced section of the community and furnished our clergymen, policemen, teachers, clerks, and interpreters. They were also amongst the first to become Christians, to build better houses, and to use scientific methods of agriculture, and they were wealthier than their Xhosa compatriots. They confirmed the missionaries' axiom, that to be Christian was to be civilized, and to be civilized was to be Christian. There still existed some hostility toward the Mfengu, but in retrospect, I would attribute this more to jealousy than tribal animosity. This local form of tribalism that I observed as a boy was relatively harmless. At that stage, I did not witness nor even suspect the violent tribal rivalries that would subsequently be promoted by the white rulers of South Africa.

My father did not subscribe to local prejudice toward the Mfengu and befriended two Mfengu brothers, George and Ben Mbekela. The brothers were an exception in Qunu: they were educated and Christian. George, the older of the two, was a retired teacher and Ben was a police sergeant. Despite the proselytizing of the Mbekela brothers, my father remained aloof from Christianity and instead reserved his own faith for the great spirit of the Xhosas, Qamata, the God of his fathers. . . .

While the faith of the Mbekela brothers did not rub off on my father, it did inspire my mother, who became a Christian. In fact, Fanny was literally her Christian name, for she had been given it in church. It was due to the influence of the Mbekela brothers that I myself was baptized into the Methodist, or Wesleyan Church as it was then known, and sent to school. The brothers would often see me playing or minding sheep and come over to talk to me. One day, George Mbekela paid a visit to my mother. "Your son is a clever young fellow," he said. "He should go to school." My mother remained silent. No one in my family had ever attended school and my mother was unprepared for Mbekela's suggestion. But she did relay it to my father, who despite—or perhaps because of—his own lack of education immediately decided that his youngest son should go to school.

The schoolhouse consisted of a single room, with a Western-style roof, on the other side of the hill from Qunu. I was seven years old, and on the day before I was to begin, my father took me aside and told me that I must be dressed properly for school. Until that time, I, like all the other boys in Qunu, had worn only a blanket, which was wrapped around one shoulder and pinned at the waist. My father took a pair of his trousers and cut them at the knee. He told me to put them on, which I did, and they were roughly the correct length, although the waist was far too large. My father then took a piece of string and cinched the trousers at the waist. I must have been a comical sight, but I have never owned a suit I was prouder to wear than my father's cut-off pants.

On the first day of school, my teacher, Miss Mdingane, gave each of us an English name and said that from thenceforth that was the name we would answer to in school. This was the custom among Africans in those days and was undoubtedly due to the British bias of our education. The education I received was a British education, in which British ideas, British culture, British institutions, were automatically assumed to be superior. There was no such thing as African culture.

Africans of my generation—and even today—generally have both an English and an African name. Whites were either unable or unwilling to pronounce an African name, and considered it uncivilized to have one. That day, Miss Mdingane told me that my new name was Nelson. Why she bestowed this particular name upon me I have no idea. Perhaps it had something to do with the great British sea captain Lord Nelson, but that would be only a guess.

TOPICS FOR ORAL OR WRITTEN EXPLORATION

1. Does *Cry, the Beloved Country* adequately depict the lives of the people of Ndotsheni? What, according to you, should be included in Paton's portrayal of rural life to give readers outside South Africa a better or deeper understanding of the lives of the people of Ndotsheni?

2. Read the 1913 Land Act, and explain how this Act lays the groundwork for apartheid and how it divests Africans of their citizenship.

3. How is traditional power depicted in *Cry, the Beloved Country*? Do you believe the chiefs still have power, and can they continue to be powerful within the colonial context?

4. Research South African homelands. What is the rational behind the creation of the Bantustans? Do you believe that they were created to protect African cultures and traditions?

5. Imagine you are a woman living in the rural area during the implementation of the 1913 Land Act. Write what you experienced as you sought refuge across the border.

SUGGESTIONS FOR FURTHER READING

Gordimer, Nadine. *July's People.* New York: Penguin Books, 1981.

Ngcobo, Lauretta. *They Didn't Die.* Johannesburg: Skotaville; London: Virago, 1990.

Roux, Edward. "Land and Agriculture in the Native Reserves." *Handbook on Race Relations in South Africa.* New York: Octagon Books, 1975.

WORKS CITED

Mandela, Nelson. *Long Walk to Freedom: The Autobiography of Nelson Mandela.* Boston: Little Brown, 1994.

Mphahlele, Es'kia. *Father Come Home.* Johannesburg: Raven Press, 1992.

Plaatje, Sol. "One Night with the Fugitives." Chapter 4 in *Native Life in South Africa.* Athens: University Press, 1991, and online at <http://www.anc.orh.za/books/nlife04.htm>.

Roux, Edward. "Land and Agriculture in the Native Reserves." *Handbook on Race Relations in South Africa.* New York: Octagon Books, 1975:171–205.

Tutu, Desmond. *The Words of Desmond Tutu.* Ed. Naomi Tutu. London: Spire, 1989.

8

The Condition of South African Women

Women in Alan Paton's *Cry, the Beloved Country,* whether white or black, do not hold a seminal position in their society. From the onset, Mrs. Kumalo is associated with food and service; the white women also occupy solely domestic spaces. Most of what is heard about Mrs. James Jarvis, even when she attends her son's funeral, is learned indirectly; the reader is given insight into her sorrow, but she never articulates it herself. Reverend Kumalo's wife has also lost a son, but she, too, apart from expressing her public humiliation, never expresses her thoughts. How could she have done so? As the narrator claims, even when Reverend Kumalo angrily projects his frustration on her, she sits quietly at the table, "with the patient suffering of black women, with the suffering of oxen, with the suffering of any that are mute" (10). The African woman is not only mute but also invisible, as attested to by Mrs. Kumalo's lack of maiden name, especially since traditionally African women did not take their husband's names. This invisibility is again manifested in *Cry, the Beloved Country* with the marginalization of Gertrude's saga, supposedly the reason behind Reverend Kumalo's quest.

Both white and black women in *Cry, the Beloved Country* are represented as either good, married women or evil, single prostitutes. The good women are associated with domesticity, whereas the bad—the prostitutes—are associated with their bodies. Although the main white women in the novel are both presented as married women, there is nonetheless also an indirect allusion in the novel to a white female with lax morals, mentioned during a discussion of urban crime. The good African women, like Mrs. Lithebe and Mrs. Kumalo, are married women. Absalom Kumalo's promiscuous girlfriend is turned into a dignified woman through marriage and the tutelage of Reverend Kumalo. Gertrude and the Shebbeen Queens, on the other hand, are single women castigated for their prostitution and laxity. The actions of both white and black women are also materialized through men; it is James Jarvis who puts into action his spouse's aspirations for the church of Ndotsheni, and it is Reverend Kumalo who must save Gertrude, although she is of another mind. Both black and white females seem to be subjected to circumstances; they are secondary characters who are not historical actresses.

Because *Cry, the Beloved Country* is interested primarily in the African community, white women are not depicted in depth, but it should be noted that white women, just like their African counterparts, did not have much leverage within their society. They were also second-class citizens, with the exception that they were primarily consumers. According to Adele van der Spuy, the lives of European South African women, like those of all Western women during this period, were regulated by Roman law, which considered them minors and put them under the tutelage of the father of the house, or *pater familias.* Moreover, white women had no alternative, under Dutch law, to common-property marriages, so they and their possessions were controlled by their spouses. Years later, thanks to some legislative amendments, they were able to control their property, but these required an exception. Unlike their African counterparts, they did not have to endure the monotonous tasks of mothering and domesticity, which were entrusted to African women. Except for those who were poor, white women had the opportunity to socially enrich their lives and to play sports. They commanded higher salaries than their black counterparts and worked as skilled service workers in industries. On the other hand, African women who were married under separate-property laws were not any better off than their white counterparts, because they were not allowed to own land and were also subject to the authority of their spouses. They did not have the leisure to go to swimming pools, and, unlike white South African women, who later were allowed to exercise greater control over their bodies and their property, they faced the double bind of colonialism and patriarchy.

The generally held assumption is that African women have been oppressed by tradition and have had no rights throughout history. This is far from the truth, for the status of African women varied according to their traditions. Nguni women (Hxosa-speaking people of the Ciskei and Transkei) are said, according to Monica Wilson, to have had the right to own individual property, such as a cow, which could not be seized in payment of a spouse's debt. They also had status in their traditional societies as chieftainness, herbalists, and diviners and had the right to own land, which was plentiful. Even in cases of polygamy, they had the right to own fields, produce, and cattle. However, over the years, she says, women lost the right to individual property because men, notably traditional chiefs, ensured that they were no longer entitled to it when land became scarce, around the 1950s. Although African women also had the right to consent to their marriages, arranged marriages were the norm, thus jeopardizing their freedom. Oppressed by tradition, they became doubly oppressed with the introduction of colonization and Western patriarchy.

Education is one of the main elements necessary for women's social and political independence. South African women, unlike some of their African counterparts, were given access to education from the time missionary schools were established, according to Wilson. From 1868 on, they were trained, along with men, at Lovedale to be schoolteachers; from 1903, they were trained to be nurses. In 1916, when Fort Hare University was established, two women were among the first students.

African women made advancements in their increasingly Westernized world, but their disenfranchisement by the South African segregation and apartheid systems contributed much to their oppression. First, migrant labor laws mandated that men abandon their spouses and families in the Bantustans to work in the cities; this regulation destroyed families. Women frequently had to spend numerous years alone, without their spouses, and when they did join the men, they were not always able to reside with them. Although historically they had had their own spheres of activity and were not in competition with men in traditional society, in the modern Bantustans, according to Hilda Bernstein, they were forced to be heads of families yet subject to many restrictions. They had to feed their families despite the barren land and spent enormous amounts of time collecting firewood and fetching water. The lack of employment in the homelands, the increasing overpopulation, and the poverty ultimately drew some of the women to the city, where, like Gertrude in *Cry, the Beloved Country,* they lived in insecurity, since they had very few professional choices.

The few professional choices available to African women—teaching or being a seamstress—were low-paying jobs. And even when they were housewives, they often had to supplement their spouses' meager earnings by engaging in some informal trade; they sold used clothing, cooked foods, and milk farm products and also sublet rooms in their homes, like Mrs. Lithebe of *Cry, the Beloved Country.* Those who sublet their homes were, in times of prosperity, capable of making more than half the salary of a female domestic. Although domestic work in most African colonies was a man's job, in South Africa it was primarily done by women. In 1910, African women were increasingly pressured to get into domestic work. They cooked, cleaned, ironed, and nursed.

They raised European children while they were separated from their own children, and, since spouses were not allowed to live together on the premises of their employers, even though a husband was working in the same town, they did not have the privilege of living together. A good number of women also chose to work as laundresses. They did laundry at the river until 1906, when laundry houses were constructed, but, in order to use these facilities, they had to purchase permits. They were also allowed to do some limited brewing in the early days of the city but, as shown in *Cry, the Beloved Country* and in Peter Abrahams's *Mine Boy,* brewing later became a felony.

The most oppressive laws for African women were the Urban Areas Acts of 1945. Women lived in great insecurity since the majority of them were not able to meet residency requirements and were easily expelled from the city. Because their residency in the city was determined on the basis of their marital status, they could easily lose their residential status if they were abandoned by their spouses or became widowed or divorced. Even having been born in the city to an urban dweller did not entitle one necessarily to live in the city if one's future spouse was not also eligible. African women were also dependent on the goodwill of the municipal or district labor officers, who determined their work eligibility and the status of a contract, to obtain employment. They were also forced to live in single-sex hostels, married or not. African women, like their male counterparts, also suffered much from the pass laws. Highly educated African men did not have to carry passes, but their spouses had to submit to the humiliation of carrying them. Even Africans who were exempt from the mandatory oppressive pass laws had to carry them after the Town Council of Bloemfontein decided that they would be required in order to help authorities control prostitution. Ironically, the women who suffered most from this law were women engaged in informal trades and not lewd women, since prostitution generally involved African women and European men, who were able to write passes for the prostitutes.

Because South African women's oppression was very much intertwined with their political oppression, women contributed to the political liberation of their country. When African men created the South African Native National Congress (SANNC), in 1912, the women who attended also quickly organized themselves into the Bantu Women's League. In 1913, they sent a delegation to Cape Town with a petition, signed by 5,000 women, protesting the implementation of a provision requiring women to carry passes. They organized marches, which were not taken seriously by the European administration, but during which women were incarcerated and had to brave a repressive police. This strike took on a life of its own and soon became a major force that was extinguished only with South Africa's participation in World War I. After

1948 and through the 1950s, women were involved in other demonstrations protesting the imposition of pass requirements on women.

African women were also very much involved in trade unions. In 1920, South African women were considered employees and did not have to carry passes. They organized themselves in the laundry, clothing, baking, and mattress industries; numerous national black federations were created, but these were later dissolved. In the 1930s and 1940s, when there was greater demand for labor, more African women moved to the city and became involved in union movements. In 1944, Christina Okolo, who worked in the clothing industry and represented other female workers, asked the court to declare that women were employees, which they were according to the law. The suit was supported by female workers of all races in the industry, and the court ruled in the women's favor, so that black women were granted the rights extended to white, Coloured, and Indian women. Unfortunately, through the 1953 Bantu Labour Law (settlement of disputes), they were stripped of these rights.

South African women, as the documents highlighting their conditions during the segregation and the apartheid eras prove, were victims of a system but also very much actors in history. Nelson Mandela, Oliver Tambo, and Archbishop Desmond Tutu are rightly considered the architects of the new South Africa, but the road to freedom could not have been realized without the numerous South African women who played vital roles in protests, marches, and the underground resistance. Winnie Mandela, despite the controversial figure she became toward the end of the struggle, is one among the many women who dedicated their lives and those of their children and spouses to building a more inclusive and moral democracy. The Winnie Mandela Solidarity Coalition's *Black Women in South Africa and the Case of Winnie Mandela,*" Monica Wilson's "The Changing Status of African Women," Julia C. Wells's piece, *We Are Done with Pleading,* Frene Ginwala's "Women and the African National Congress: 1912–1943," and Hilda Bernstein's *For Their Triumphs and for Their Tears* well illustrate the suffering and social obstacles African women have had to overcome in both their traditional and their Westernized worlds.

FROM WINNIE MANDELA SOLIDARITY COALITION, *BLACK WOMEN IN SOUTH AFRICA AND THE CASE OF WINNIE MANDELA*

(BOSTON: WINNIE MANDELA SOLIDARITY COALITION, 1980: 6–10)

This excerpt gives an in-depth understanding of the roles and nature of the South African female. Alan Paton's *Cry, the Beloved Country* depicts strong women but does not show how these women are affected by their political environment. The focus is on good and bad women and the subservience of African women; but the novel fails to provide an in-depth understanding of African women's contribution to the struggle for independence, and the strength they showed during that struggle.

The Life of Black Women in the Reserves

> "Widowhood—a life of void and loneliness; a period of tension, unbalance, and strenuous adjustment. And what can it be to those thousands of African women—those adolescent girls married before they reach womanhood, thrown into a life of responsibility before they have completely passed from childhood to adulthood; those young women in the prime of early womanhood left to face life alone, burdened with the task of building a home and rearing a family; those young women doomed to nurse alone their sick babies, weep alone for their dead babies, dress and bury alone their corpses? What can it mean to those young brides whose purpose has been snatched away, overnight, leaving them bewildered and lost, leaving them with a thirst and hunger that cannot be stilled?
>
> And yet this is the daily lot of tens of thousands of African women whose husbands are torn away from them to go and work in the cities, mines, and farms—husbands who because of the migratory labor system cannot take their wives with them and because of the starvation wages they receive, are forced to remain in the work centers for long periods—strangers in a strange land—but equally strangers at home to their wives and children."

Phyllis Ntantala, "The Oppression of Women in South Africa"

In the reserves, those who can, get passes for work and leave to take jobs in industry, in the mines, or on white-owned farms. The worker is generally a man, who leaves his wife and children in the reserve—not because he wants to, but because the apartheid law does not allow 'useless appendages' to live in 'white' South Africa. Thus, both South African employers and multinational corporations can keep wages down and profits high by separating families, paying men a wage only just sufficient for their own upkeep, and forcing the rest of the family to rely on meager farming in the reserves. With the family in the reserve, an 'independent' country, the South African government can shrug off the responsibility of providing basic social, health, education, and sanitation services.

The burden of survival and of raising the next generation of workers falls on the women. Separated from their men, they have to scratch out a living from the poor land—if they are lucky enough to have land. They must also care for the old and the sick—those who have no legal place in South African society. In this situation, women become isolated and lonely. They are uncertain about family members who become caught up in the struggle for survival in town—a struggle that can lead to alcoholism, prostitution, and the breakup of families. Often these women in the reserves suffer severe emotional anguish.

In The Urban Areas

Faced with this situation, some women will go to town to find their husbands or other loved ones who are on labor contracts. Often, women are traveling illegally because the government will not allow such visits, or will allow only extremely restricted visits. For example, more than 20,000 wives and children of men on 11 month contracts left their 'tribal homelands' to settle in a squatter camp called Crossroads. They wanted to be near their husbands who worked in Cape town. In September, 1978, the police arrived at night to try to bulldoze the camp. When the squatters resisted, one man was killed. Women, including pregnant women, were beaten, and 300 people were arrested.

Women also go to 'white' towns to look for work. They are forced to leave their children behind, often in the care of another woman, who may be too old or overburdened to cope. Most working women find jobs as servants living in tiny quarters in their 'madam's' backyard. They typically work 60-hour weeks and are not allowed to have overnight visitors, even if the visitor is their husband or child. For such work, African women receive around $50 a month.

If women can't find other kinds of work, they desperately try to make ends meet by doing white people's laundry (without the help of any machines) or by brewing and selling traditional beer, which is illegal. A small percentage of women find slightly better paying jobs in industry, hospitals, or as clerical workers. As Africans they face legal and enforced wage and job discrimination; as African women, they also receive the lowest wages.

Many women, like men, are forced to live in single-sex hostels for the period of their contracts. These 'hostels' are like concentration camps—bleak, cramped, cold, guarded, and isolated from outside contact. Even the few women who are allowed to live with their families in the Black townships have a very insecure position. A woman has no right to rent a house in her own name. If her husband dies, she is likely to get evicted—even if she is working and can pay rent. Only if she has a son, she may escape eviction by registering the house in his name.

Thus apartheid means not only inequality and separation of Black from white, but also separation of Black men and women workers from each other and their families. . . .

Role of Women in The Liberation Struggle

Black women in South Africa are faced with the double oppression of being Black and female. One Black woman, active in the political struggle in South Africa, has commented on the relationship between national liberation and women's struggle for dignity and equality:

> "*In* different parts of the world today women are demanding equal recognition *with men in all walks of life and* rejecting a *home-shackled* existence. *But* we are *behind* everyone else in the *world—where* other women are rejecting the *home-centered* life, our women are denied even that. . . .
>
> *But what have our men* done to reduce the impact of *this double* load of oppression on their *women? Admittedly, in many spheres* of social *life* they *are powerless* to please us and give us our *rights. They cannot, for instance, give us a better quality education; they could not save us from crime and violence; they could not give us greater justice and greater dignity, better homes and better social institutions; . . . Were our women to launch a frontal attack on men and join hands with all the women of the world at this stage, would they attain their liberation? . . . Do our women wish to share the dismal position of their men? . . . We are left with one option only, and that is to fight side by side with our men for our National liberation."*
>
> *Women's Conference on Women in South Africa, Botswana, 1976*

FROM MONICA WILSON, "THE CHANGING STATUS OF AFRICAN WOMEN," NATIONAL COUNCIL OF WOMEN OF SOUTH AFRICA

(FIFTH BERTHA SOLOMON MEMORIAL LECTURE. PORT ELIZABETH: NATIONAL COUNCIL OF WOMEN OF SOUTH AFRICA, 1974: 8–9)

This excerpt supports Alan Paton's thesis of the disintegration of the African family in *Cry, the Beloved Country.* It shows the emotional impact of labor laws that prevent families from living together and the oppression of African women.

The disabilities of African women in the Republic are many, but it seems to me that their disabilities are far more because they are part of a disenfranchised community than because they are women. There are disabilities peculiar to women but these are much less than the disabilities of the black community as a whole. The most pressing disability on African women is the restriction on the right of movement and residence, which prohibits their joining their husbands who are working in towns. Surely the National Council of Women must be concerned with the right of all women to live with their husbands at their place of work. As the situation is in South Africa, more and more women are prevented from doing so. To say that a man has the choice whether to work away from home or not is dishonest: the choice for the great majority of African men is between taking work as a contract labourer working in town or mine or farm away from home, and seeing his family starve. In order to feed them he must leave his wife and children in a so-called 'home land' and take work elsewhere. Wife and children are forbidden to join him. This is the cancer gnawing the heart of South Africa: this is the destruction of the basic unit of society, the family. And make no mistake, South Africa will reap the whirlwind, for when families are destroyed, children are not trained, and disorder follows. Even expectation becomes corrupted, and people begin to take it for granted that husband and wife should live separately. Because of these implications, some educated African women are rejecting marriage altogether. Why be tied to a man who will continually be absent?

Because this basic right, the right to be with the husbands to whom they are legally married, is so widely destroyed for African women by the laws of the Republic, I cannot feel that other limitations on women's rights are of comparable importance. But there are other limitations. African women share with men exclusion from many occupations either by law or by convention. They share with African men lower salaries paid for comparable work and qualifications, simply because of race.

FROM JULIA C. WELLS, *WE ARE DONE WITH PLEADING* (JOHANNESBURG: RAVEN PRESS, 1991: 27)

This excerpt, supposedly written by Ms. Bauman, shows the difference in the lifestyles of white and black women. White women, in the passage, support the strike by African women, but essentially for selfish reasons: were the black women not allowed to work, the white women would be overwhelmed with domestic work.

"Common Justice"

Sir,

Our Town Councillors have made a pretty mess of things here. They have been persecuting the native women in the location for the past three months because the women have struck—quite justly, we white women think—against carrying a pass for which they have to pay what amounts to about five per cent of their wages. Many of the girls have already been hauled before the magistrate and awarded, under the Council's iniquitous by-law, fines or terms of imprisonment in default of payment, but one and all have, with commendable courage, chosen to go to prison rather than pay. Fines have been increased and terms of imprisonment lengthened and rendered more terrifying by the addition of hard labour, without avail; for they all declare that, come what will, they will not take out another pass!

But this is not the worst. The council, baffled and beaten, and angry because their august will has been flouted, have now decided to turn out of the location all maids who fail to take out a pass!

Fellow housewives, do you realise what this means to us? It means that, if the council be permitted to work their will, we shall all shortly be deprived of our female servants, and faced with the alternative of doing all nursing and housework ourselves, or allowing it to go undone. Can we allow the councillors thus to tyrannise over us with impunity? I think not.

Sisters, I appeal to you, I implore you to join me in attempting to compel the Municipal Council to abandon their plan. A number of us are to meet at Vet River Drift on Wednesday next, the 15th instant, at 2.30 pm, and we urgently appeal to all the white women of Winburg to join us, and to bring appropriately worded banners with them. At 3 o'clock we shall march in procession to Market Square, via Bell's Pass, and there we shall hold a mass meeting. No violence will be attempted or countenanced unless the councillors interfere with us, when let them beware!

When the hour comes my identity shall be disclosed; till then I prefer to hide it in the nom-de-plume. I am, etc,

COMMON JUSTICE,

Winburg, 8 October 1913

FROM FRENE GINWALA, "WOMEN AND THE AFRICAN NATIONAL CONGRESS: 1912–1943"

(online posting at <http://www.anc.org.za/ancdocs/history/misc/fatima.html>)

This excerpt demonstrates that, despite Alan Paton's claim that African women were submissive, African women have been actors within history. They not only were spoken for and directed by men but played a pivotal role in the liberation of South Africa.

While all Africans were subjected to conquest, colonial rule and dispossession, the way in which women and men experienced these differed as did their political, economic and legal status. These differences shaped their particular response, helped to determine the issues they took up, and the methods of struggle adopted.

In the wake of the conquest, there emerged a group of Africans, mostly mission educated, who turning their backs on traditional African society sought entry into the colonial one. The liberal values as proclaimed by British Imperial and colonial governments, and adopted by Africans, had led to a not unreasonable expectations that Africans would be admitted into the new society being established in South Africa. Though the expectations of the African people had been repeatedly frustrated, they continued to hope and form organisations to protect and expand African interests and rights from within the constitutional framework and institutions of the new system. These organisations adopted the style of the conquerors and addressed the authorities in ways that would be considered acceptable by whites, and would not alienate them. They saw the franchise as a gateway to this society and focused their political demands on it. As a consequence, the leadership and membership of the organisations inevitably came from those who would qualify for the franchise: men of property and education.

While sharing the overall objectives, women, and those without property and education, did not feel it necessary to operate only within the parameters laid down by colonial society and were less inclined to comply with or accommodate settler rules and sensitivities. While some women saw themselves as gender images, "the wives and daughters" of the ANC leadership, most of those who participated in resistance differed in the issues they took up, their organisation, mobilisation and methods, as well as economic status and educational levels. To a greater extent than the SANNC, the women's resistance was shaped from below.

Because women chose to engage in issues of immediate and direct relevance to their daily lives, they found it easy to mobilise support and mount campaigns. In the context of colonialism and the nature of the oppression of the African people, these issues were relatively easy to resolve. But they were not linked to long term goals, the campaigns did not lead to lasting organisational formations. Men assumed, and women conceded, that defining and achieving the long term goals was men's territory.

When dealing with officials women were handicapped by a lack of fluency in European languages, and of confidence. These handicaps were made worse by the frequent refusal of white officials to meet with or listen to women.

Men, sometimes national leaders, were requested to act as go-betweens or interpreters. Generally they tried to control women's initiatives and steer them away from militant and direct action. It was not so much that they were opposed to such methods in principle, but rather that they were concerned to ensure that an 'acceptable' and reassuring image of Africans were always presented to whites. . . .

The issues around which women mobilised before and after the formation of the Union of South Africa, were materially based. In the Transvaal in 1910, women protested at the lack of employment opportunities. . . .

The trigger for the militant Orange Free State anti-pass campaign was the enforcement of the regulation requiring women to purchase permits to use the municipal wash house, which further limited their ability to retain economic independence.

These were very different concerns from those that prevailed amongst the founding fathers of the SANNC who met in Bloemfontein on 8 January 1912.

They clearly conceived of it as an organisation of men in which women's participation would be limited to their stereotyped 'traditional' domestic roles. The draft constitution placed before the founding Congress refers to three classes of membership. The prevailing patriarchal notions of women's roles in society were inscribed in the constitutional provisions for and duties of a category of "auxiliary" members, automatically enrolled without fee and hence with no vote. . . .

However, by 1912, women had been participating in a number of overtly political Associations and Congresses which were later to constitute the SANNC. . . .

The Anti-Pass Campaign

The Free State Anti-Pass Campaign highlighted the different approaches of women and men in pursuance of a common demand, and serves to illustrate aspects of women's relationship with the male dominated political organisations.

Opposition to passes for African women had featured regularly in most of the representation that were made to the authorities, and the 1912 SANNC Conference passed a resolution urging the repeal of all laws which compelled African women to carry passes. Less than a month later, women in the province began collecting signatures for a petition which they decided to present directly to the authorities in Cape Town. Within weeks they had collected over 5000 signatures (no mean accomplishment) and began to prepare to go to Cape Town. (Wells, 1982).

The authorities as well as the political organisations were discomforted by women who took initiatives, especially at national level. The Minister of Native Affairs wrote to the President of the SANNC, John Dube, advising the male African leaders to prevent the women's deputation from coming to Cape Town, as he feared such a deputation would lead to further agitation and excitement amongst whites that would make it more difficult for the SANNC other representations to succeed. However, the women would not be dissuaded and in the event Walter Rubusana assisted in the presentation of the petition and accompanied the women's deputation to the Minister (Wells, 1982).

In the Afrikaner Republics no distinctions had been made between Africans and Coloureds and the communities lived together in the same locations and under the same restrictions. Coloured women who were also required to carry passes, were involved in the campaigns against them. Their independent actions caused the African People's Organisation (APO) to express it [*sic*] concerns and its paper chided them: "We think the deputation might have awaited the Native Congress. It is also regrettable that Coloured women of the Orange Free State did not consult the executive of the APO's Women's Guild. We feel sure that no deputation of Coloured men of the APO would come to Cape Town without first acquainting the Executive with the object of its mission" (APO 6 April 1912). . . .

The ORCNC however called a special general meeting of its members to hear a report from the deputation after its return from Cape Town. Later, many centers elected one man and one woman as their delegates to the Annual Conference, where one of the women's leaders, Katie Louw, reported on the progress of the anti-pass campaign. (Odendaal, 1984)

The Free State women did not confine themselves to making representations, and in May 1913 decided to stop carrying passes or buying permits. The action spread across the provinces and there were numerous confrontations with the police as they tried to rescue those being taken to prison after sentence. The women who went to prison for refusing to carry passes lived in the urban centers, but were not all from amongst the elite. . . .

Initially women had mobilised through manyanaos [women's section of church], but as the campaign spread across the province and the number of women in prisons grew, women from the Orange Free State Congress and the APO Women's Guild came together and set up the NCWA to oversee the campaign (Wells, 1982). The NCWA tried to mobilise support, and raised funds to provide for those in prison and for medical treatment after they completed their sentence. . . .

As the campaign progressed, the earlier misgivings about women's independence and militancy had given way to admiration and a general pride in the women's achievements. The Secretary General of the SANNC Sol Plaatje visited the women in prison, expressed his admiration (and surprise at their determination), and tried to publicise the resistance and mobilise support.

The African press rallied to the support of those who were imprisoned, as did the APO journal and the Indian Opinion.

The NCWA addressed an appeal to "many Europeans friends in the provinces" urging them to use their influence to get legislation introduced in Parliament abolishing passes for women. They also addressed a petition to Governor Gladstone. These were initiatives similar to those of the SANNC, but there they were being undertaken in a context where women were continuing to go to prison for refusing to carry passes. Also the content and approach in the representations differed from those made by men. . . .

HILDA BERNSTEIN, "WOMEN IN TOWNS," FROM *FOR THEIR TRIUMPHS AND FOR THEIR TEARS*

(London: International Defence and Aid Fund, 1985; also <http:www.anc.org.za/books/triumphs.html>)

This excerpt illuminates Alan Paton's discussion of the family. It also provides information on the lives of urban African females.

Even with legal rights to reside in towns, black women live under the strains of great insecurity. Their legal status may be rescinded on a large variety of pretexts. A woman must avoid the misfortune of being left without a husband, whether through desertion, divorce or death. She often loses her home as well as her husband. A divorced woman may be given permission to stay in her home only if she was not the guilty party in the divorce suit, and has been granted custody of the children; if she qualifies in her own right to remain in town; if she can pay the rent; and if her former husband has agreed to vacate the house. If he has remarried immediately, he may choose to remain in the house with his new wife.

African women who are living lawfully in an urban area outside a bantustan may only obtain work through the municipal or district labour officer, from whom they must obtain a permit. Labour officers can refuse to issue a permit for many reasons, or they may refuse a permit for a specific job that a woman wishes to take and refer her to another somewhere; or they may require women, with their dependents, to leave the area. A labour officer can also cancel an existing labour contract, a provision that hangs over the head of those African workers (male or female) who may participate in trade union or political activities. . . .

A work permit may also be refused to a woman if she is unable to find housing, and the women are under severe difficulties as houses are not usually available for women. Hostels and compound accommodations are for men, with the exception of a few township hostels. . . .

An African woman is even subject to arrest for living with her husband if he stays with her in domestic servant's quarters, of if she cohabits with him in his quarters, or if she cohabits with him in his quarters when she is not qualified to have his family with him.

Independence

A Johannesburg journalist, Percy Quboza, maintains that the picture painted of the black woman as a depressed, voiceless, subservient person is misleading and often dangerous. He describes the historical background of their militant struggles against political oppression, and says black women are not the subservient objects many people take them to be.

> We continue to insult their dignity and motherhood in various ways. Getting them to clean pavements in Soweto is an affront to their dignity . . . throwing them in jail in Hilibrow for not having passes degrades their dignity. Their silent endurance of these insults must not be taken for subservience.

The truth is that to survive, black women have had to develop a high degree of independence and to exert great strength of character. Sociologists have commented on the emergence of the single, independent, black woman. Speaking on the changing status of African women' Professor Monica Wilson of the University of Cape Town said that women's rights were destroyed more by the fact that they were part of a disenfranchised community than that they were women. 'The most pressing disability of African women is the restriction on the rights of movement and residence which prohibits their joining their husbands who are working in the towns. . . . Why be tied to a man who will be continually absent?'

A black newspaper editor, Mr Tom Moerane, reports on research undertaken by his daughter among African women.

A significant number of young women regarded marriage in an entirely negative manner. They said they did not care about marriage as an institution, nor did they think it was of any particular use to them. Some indicated that they desired to bear children and that this made it necessary to cohabit with a man, but 'the baby is going to be my baby'.

In both town and country numbers of African women see dubious advantages in marriage and more and more young women show a preference for staying single. 'Girls who are married and have husbands in cities', comments a rural woman, are struggling as I do. Many are suffering as I do and yet have husbands.' Joanne Yawitch says this tendency can be interpreted in many ways, but it does seem clear that the economic rewards of marriage are steadily declining. Furthermore, the fact that there is a gross contradiction in terms of who is *supposed* to take responsibility and decisions, and who *actually* does, often makes marriage an unviable option for rural women. Their reaction to the idea of marriage is 'highly ambiguous, contradictory and often aggressive'.

The overcrowding, crime, poverty and increasing unemployment that are the features of township life impose massive strains on individuals. 'The family functions as a soak pit to absorb expressions of anger that are not allowed elsewhere. Often, men have had a hard day at work, get drunk and take it out on their wives and children. Batter and alcoholism are the most common results of this situation. In Soweto 60 per cent of children are illegitimate, and while parents may often marry after they are born, more women are choosing not to marry.

Whatever the complexity of reasons (including, in the urban areas, the tendency for women to be able to enter better-paid work than domestic service, decreasing their economic dependence on men) more and more women are finding marriage a burden to them.

TOPICS FOR ORAL OR WRITTEN EXPLORATION

1. How has the status of African women been affected by colonization?

2. Are South African women all feminists, and have African women embraced this ideology in the same manner as Western females? Also, was it possible for white and South African women to bond?

3. After reading the excerpts on the experience of South African women, write a paper analyzing Alan Paton's female characters. What additional information would you have provided to give the reader a more in-depth understanding of the status of women in this country?

4. Imagine you are Absalom's wife. Write a letter to a friend explaining your circumstances and your happiness upon hearing that you will be going with Reverend Kumalo to Ndotsheni.

5. African women are supposedly inferior, according to popular opinion, but do you consider them helpless and childlike, considering their political and social actions?

SUGGESTIONS FOR FURTHER READING

Head, Bessie. *A Woman Alone.* Oxford: Portsmouth, NH: Heinemann, 1990.

Kuzwayo, Ellen. *Call Me Woman.* San Francisco: Aunt Lute Books, 1991.

Ngcobo, Lauretta. *Let It Be Told: Essays by Black Women Writers in Britain.* London: Virago, 1988.

Shostak, Marjorie. *Nisa.* New York: Vintage Books, 1983.

WORKS CITED

Bernstein, Hilda. *For Their Triumphs and for Their Tears. Women in Apartheid South Africa.* London: International Defence and Aid Fund for Southern Africa, 1985.

Ginnwala, Frene. "Women and the African National Congress: 1912–1943"; online posting at <http://www.anc.org.za/ancdocs/history/misc/fatima.html>.

Winnie Mandela Solidarity Coalition. *Black Women in South Africa and the Case of Winnie Mandela.* Boston: Winnie Mandela Solidarity Coalition, 1980.

Spuy, Adele van der. *South African Women—The Other Discrimination.* Pasadena, CA: Munger African Library, California Institute of Technology, 1978.

Wells, Julia C. *We Are Done with Pleading.* Johannesburg: Raven Press, 1991: 27.

Wilson, Monica. *The Changing Status of African Women.* Fifth Bertha Solomon memorial lecture. Port Elizabeth: National Council of Women of South Africa Conference, 1974.

9

Contemporary Applications: Life after Apartheid

Alan Paton's *Cry, the Beloved Country* ends with a rising dawn. What type of day this dawn will bring is unknown. It is, however, evident from its message of hope and from Mr. Jarvis's attempt to bring about social justice that the dawn will bring equanimity and justice to the South African landscape. Equanimity was the slogan under which the ANC ran during the 1994 election. Mandela's election was a symbol of a new South Africa, in which Africans would have rights to better housing, jobs, salaries, and education. In the new South Africa, Africans would have the power not only to determine their own future but also to gain access to the wealth and resources of their country.

But, as in all political transitional processes, achieving the dream of black South Africans has not been an easy task. Some analysts of South Africa contend that the ANC has failed to deliver on its electoral promises. It has succeeded in establishing democracy but has failed the poor and the African population; poverty has increased, unemployment is higher, and the gap between the rich and the poor has widened. White South Africans earn higher wages than before apartheid, whereas Africans' wages have not improved. According to John Saul, the ANC adopted an economic policy that encouraged privatization of government services. At times, the ANC contends, these services are not privatized but run by the government in a business-like style.

When the Mandela ANC government began its tenure, the African population had much hope for the future and for the redress of past labor injustices.

It adopted the economic strategy termed Growth, Employment, and Redistribution (GEAR), which predicted employment growth. According to some analysts, the contentions that there has virtually been no economic growth is unfounded, for the data utilized in the majority of these researches are incomplete since the informal economic sectors are not included. The demand for employment has not kept up with economic growth. The percentage of unemployed women and educated South African has risen, and this growth continues to disadvantage Africans, with white and Coloured men and women having the lowest unemployment. There has been much growth in the informal sector, and, according to Stein Inge Nesvag, street trading, once restricted and prohibited during the apartheid regime, has flourished. It is the source of employment among the marginalized poor.

South Africa is frequently referred to as the "miracle nation," but life in this nation is far from perfect. Poverty, crime, and inequality continue to be major problems. Despite these hurdles, there have been some improvements: the criminalization of racism, the establishment of an acclaimed constitution, and the establishment of systems and institutions that protect human rights. Unfortunately, along with these improvements, negative new trends have also emerged: xenophobic hostility to strangers, the appearance of crime-fighting vigilantes, and social and economic struggles around land and services. Crime, during this period, has been redefined. During the apartheid era, it was construed as the result of the violent apartheid regime and as a form of resistance; today it is considered a crime, but, unfortunately, the state has legitimized crime-fighting vigilantes, accessible only to the wealthy.

Postapartheid South Africa did not racialize South African spaces by dissolving the Group Act, since space (geographic boundaries) continue to determine who has access to resources, services, and land. Space also continues to shape identity. Race is not contextualized historically in present-day South Africa, but it certainly continues to define South African social interactions. There has been some migration between the formally designated racial residential areas; more Indians have moved to white suburbs, and more affluent Africans are leaving townships such as Soweto. These migrations have, however, engendered racial tensions and violence. African immigrants are known to experience similar hostility from their hosts. Contemporary South Africa continues to be a site of socioeconomic exclusion, community marginalization, eroding family relationships, increasing crime, and increasing mistrust among communities. Resources have yet to be equally distributed, and corruption and abuse of power are creating new centers of resistance.

These are the various problems that confront South Africa today; yet one needs to understand that, like all transitional governments, the ANC-led government does not have an easy task. The country acquired political independence but not economic independence. Perhaps, this is the new struggle that will ultimately diminish the poverty of Africans in capitalist South Africa. The excerpt from Rian Malan's "Book I. Life in This Strange Place," from *My Traitor's Heart,* speaks to the fear felt by European South Africans in Alan Paton's *Cry, the Beloved Country.* It also speaks to the ways individuals internalize racialist ideas even when they resist them and how loyalty to one's group can inhibit one from acting or supporting actions that might undo past wrongs. The excerpt from Desmond Tutu's "God Believes in Us" reflects the spirit of the new South Africa; John Saul's "Cry for the Beloved Country: The Post-Apartheid Denouement" and Jeremy Cronin's "Post-Apartheid South Africa: A Reply to John Saul—Exchange"analyze the social and economic context. "*Interview with Kabengele,*" Anne Paton's "Why I'm Fleeing South Africa," and Nelson Mandela's *Cry, the Beloved Country*: Miramax World Premiere speech provide insight into contemporary sociopolitical issues.

RIAN MALAN, "BOOK I. LIFE IN THIS STRANGE PLACE," FROM *MY TRAITOR'S HEART*

(NEW YORK: GROVE PRESS, 1990: 5–6)

Rian Malan's text speaks to Europeans' fear of Africans. A "Kaffirboetie," he has difficulties taking a strong position against apartheid for fear of betraying his own group, even as he loves Africans. It also speaks to the internalized racialism evinced by Mr. Jarvis, whose behavior toward blacks is informed by European paternalism.

> We are betrayed by what is false within.
>
> —George Meredith

And that, my friend, is why I ran away. I ran away because I was scared of the coming changes, and scared of the consequences of not changing. I ran because I wouldn't carry a gun for apartheid, and because I wouldn't carry a gun against it. I ran away because I hated Afrikaners and loved blacks. I ran away because I was an Afrikaner and feared blacks. You could say, I suppose, that I ran away from the paradox.

How do you render a paradox? I just don't seem able to get it down right, and yet I know it in my mind. On the beach near where I live today, a rocky promontory presents a square, blunt face to the sea. At high tide, a big wave sometimes charges the cliff, climbs halfway up it, then turns and rushes back to the sea. Twenty yards out, it meets the incoming wave, and they defeat one another in a great clash of spray. Both waves simply disappear, and for a few moments the sea lies still and hissing. It is that state of quandary that I am trying to describe, but I can't get it; I can only feel it.

And that is how it has been all my life, from the moment my eyes first opened. It was quite clear, even to a little boy, that blacks were violent, and inscrutable, and yet I loved them. It was also clear that they were capable, kind, and generous, and yet I was afraid of them. The paradox was a given in my life, part of the natural order of things. It was only later, when I was old enough to be aware of what was happening around me that the paradox started eating me. I'd been born into an agony of polarization and felt I had to commit myself one way or the other. I couldn't just stand there, paralyzed by the paradox.

So I fell into the habit of saying that I loved blacks, and I sided with them against my own people. I did my best to act accordingly, but in truth, I was always riddled with doubt. The instant I stepped beyond rhetoric and into bed with a black woman, I felt as though I had broken a very law of nature, and yet, thinking such thoughts, I was simultaneously stricken by another shame and disgust, a traitor's shame, the shame of discovering that I was capable of harboring such ideas. Because I truly did love them.

You want to know my true position in the revolution? Look at this photograph, which comes from *Die Vaderland,* an Afrikaans daily. Those are my outstretched arms, and those are my cheekbones, jutting out over the layout artist's crop line. This picture was taken in July or August 1976, just after the riots of June. Soweto's students had the temerity to board trains and come into white Johannesburg, where they paraded through the streets with their placards. The Boers fell on them, of course. That snarling white traffic cop with a whip in his hand is trying to get at this black teenager here in the left-hand corner, and that's me in the middle, with arms akimbo and spiral-bound notebook between my teeth, trying to keep them apart. Trying to make them stop it. That was my position—in the middle, skewered by the paradox. It was a stupid position to be in, and untenable. In South Africa, you had to be true to one side or the other, but I belonged to neither, and that is why I ran away.

As I shook Mike's hand for the last time, he said, "So you're leaving us to the Boers' mercy, hey *boeniie?*" Langa said, "You're doing the right thing. Don't come back." Miriam wept and said, "Why are you going? You a good somebody." At the airport, my Afrikaner father said, "You have given nothing to this country. You have just taken, and now you are running away."

And then I got on a plane, and ran away.

I'd sworn not to inflict further disgrace on my long-suffering father by applying for political asylum as a draft dodger, so I roamed Europe for a few years, prodded onward by the unsympathetic immigration services of half a dozen countries. Canada didn't want me either, so I wound up in the United States in 1979, with no money and no working papers. I washed dishes, picked crops, sold my blood, rode freight trains and Greyhounds, cowering in bus-station toilets during stopovers for fear that *la migra* would nail me. No, I'm not whining. It was great adventure, and besides, I considered myself a socialist. I imagined that I was finally seeing the sole of the boot as it ground the working man down. I was certainly as low as you can go. There came a day when I had no money at all, not a cent. I was stranding on the side of a highway in the Cascades in Washington State, all alone on a continent on which I knew nobody, with nowhere to go and little hope of getting there before dark. . . .

DESMOND TUTU, "GOD BELIEVES IN US," FROM *GOD HAS A DREAM*

(NEW YORK: DOUBLEDAY, 2004: 4–7)

Alan Paton wonders, at the end of *Cry, the Beloved Country,* what type of day the dawn will bring. Desmond Tutu's excerpt speaks to a day when whites see themselves as a minority that is no longer in a hegemonic position and how the freedom of all South Africans also liberates European South Africans.

As I sat in the priory garden I thought of our desperate political situation in the light of this principle of transfiguration, and from that moment on, it has helped me to see with new eyes. I have witnessed time and again the improbable redemptions that are possible in our world. Let me give you just one example from our struggle in South Africa, which I know best, but such transfigurations are not limited to one country or one people. This story took place almost twenty-five years after that first experience in the priory.

It was just before April 1994 and we were on the verge of disaster, literally on the brink of civil war and threatened with being overwhelmed by a bloodbath. We had witnessed the stunning release of Nelson Mandela and other leaders in 1990 and the miraculous move toward universal elections, but between 1990 and 1994 we had been on a roller-coaster ride, exhilarated at one moment, in the depths of despair the next. Thousands of people had died in massacres during the transition, such as one at Boipatong, near Johannesburg, in which about forty-five people were killed in one night. The province of KwaZulu-Natal was a running sore as a result of rivalry between the Inkatha Freedom Party and the African National Congress. Some of us said that a sinister Third Force, including elements of the government's security forces, was behind a spate of indiscriminate killings on trains, at taxi ranks and bus stops. We were usually pooh-poohed by the authorities. Just before the election, there was an insurrection in one of the so-called independent homelands, which was run by black leaders who were prepared to work within the apartheid policy. A neo-Nazi Afrikaner group who wanted to sabotage the transition intervened in the rebellion. Inkatha, a major party in KwaZulu, was boycotting the election. Attempts were made to destabilize and intimidate the black community and to scare them away from voting. Our impending election looked like a disaster waiting to happen. We were all gritting our teeth, expecting the worst. But in the weeks leading up to the election, the insurrection failed and the neo-Nazi group was ignominiously routed. At the proverbial eleventh hour, we heaved a sigh of relief as Inkatha was persuaded to join the election.

Elections are usually just secular political events in most parts of the world. Our elections turned out to be a spiritual even a religious, experience. We won't so quickly forget the images of those long queues snaking their way slowly into the polling booths. People waited a very long time. John Allen, my media secretary, said there was a new status symbol at the time in South Africa. Someone would say, "I stood for two hours before I could vote!" And someone else would say, "Oh, that's nothing—I waited four hours. . . ." There was chaos in many places, not enough ballot papers or ink or whatever. It was a catastrophe about to take place. It never did. After I had cast my vote, having waited all of sixty-two years to do so for the first time, I toured some of the voting stations. The people had come out in droves and they looked so utterly vulnerable. It would have taken just two or three people with AK-47s to sow the most awful mayhem. It did not happen. What took place can only be described as a miracle. People stood in those long lines, people of all races in South Africa that had known separation and apartheid for so long—black and white, colored and Indian, farmer, laborer, educated, unschooled, poor, rich—they stood in those lines and the scales fell from their eyes. South Africans made an earth-shattering discovery—hey, we are all fellow South Africans. We are compatriots. People shared newspapers, picnic lunches, stories—and they discovered (what a profound discovery!) that they were human together and that they actually seemed to want much the same things—a nice house in a secure and safe neighborhood, a steady job, good schools for the children, and, yes, skin color and race were indeed thoroughly irrelevant.

People entered the booth one person and emerged on the other side a totally different person. The black person went in burdened with all the anguish of having had his or her dignity trampled underfoot and being treated as a nonperson—and then voted. And said, "Hey, I'm free—my dignity has been restored, my humanity has been acknowledged. I'm free!" She emerged a changed person, a transformed, a transfigured person.

The white person entered the booth one person, burdened by the weight of guilt for having enjoyed many privileges unjustly, voted, and emerged on the other side a new person. "Hey, I'm free. The burden has been lifted. I'm free!" She emerged a new, a different, a transformed, a transfigured person. Many white people confessed that they too were voting for the first time—for the first time as really free people. Now they realized what we had been trying to tell them for so long, that freedom was indivisible, that they would never be free until we were free.

Yes, our first election turned out to be a deeply spiritual event, a religious experience, a transfiguration experience, a mountaintop experience. We had won a spectacular victory over injustice, oppression, and evil. There we were—people who as a matter of public policy were deliberately tearing one another apart, declaring that human fellowship, togetherness, friendship, laughter, joy, caring, that these were impossible for us as one nation, and now here we were becoming, from all the different tribes and languages, diverse cultures, and faiths, so utterly improbably, we were becoming one nation. Now who could ever believe that that was possible?

JOHN SAUL, "CRY FOR THE BELOVED COUNTRY: THE POST-APARTHEID DENOUEMENT," FROM *MONTHLY REVIEW* (JANUARY 2001): 1–64

(online posting at <http://www.findarticles.com/p/articles/mi_m1132/is_8_52/ai_70397123/pg_2>)

John S. Saul's essay contends that life after apartheid has not improved and that the new ANC leaders are undemocratic leaders who do not heed criticism. It also claims that South African leaders have failed to bring about change since poverty is rampant and the leaders are interested primarily in their own material gain.

A tragedy is being enacted in South Africa, as much a metaphor for our times as Rwanda and Yugoslavia and, even if not so immediately searing of the spirit, it is perhaps a more revealing one. For in the teeth of high expectations arising from the successful struggle against a malignant apartheid state, a very large percentage of the population—among them many of the most desperately poor in the world—are being sacrificed on the altar of the neoliberal logic of global capitalism. Moreover, as I had occasion to remark during a recent stint spent teaching in that country, the most striking thing I personally discovered about the New South Africa is just how easy it has now become to find oneself considered an ultra-leftist! For to talk with opinion leaders or to read their public statements was to be drowned in a sea of smug: this is the way the world works; competitiveness is good; get with the program; get real. One does not know whether to laugh or cry at this kind of realism—"magical market realism," as I have termed it elsewhere.

For there is absolutely no reason to assume that the vast majority of people in South Africa will find their lives improved by the policies that are being adopted in their name by the present African National Congress (ANC) government. Indeed, something quite the reverse is the far more likely outcome.

Why this sad denouement? Are we mourning here the state of the world of globalization, marking soberly the wisdom of Adam Przeworski's famously bleak aphorism—"Capitalism is irrational; socialism is unfeasible; in the real world people starve: the conclusions we have reached are not encouraging"—and accepting (albeit with less glee than some of them do) the oft-stated premise of many members of the new South African elite: There Is No Alternative (TINA)? Or are we marking, instead, the failure of South Africa's popular movement or even, as some would have it, a betrayal on the part of the ANC itself? The answer may well be that both emphases contain some truth, although just how one weights them will depend a great deal on what one believes regarding the art of the possible for nationally-based political movements and parties under present worldwide (and continental) conditions generally—or in South Africa more specifically. . . .

To highlight such negatives, it is sometimes said in South Africa, is to indulge in "Afro-pessimism." But it can much more easily be argued that the real Afro-pessimists are those who state that South Africa has little choice but to tag along behind a global capitalism that actually offers it very little by way of development prospect. . . .

For all the fears that resentful ANC socialists would confiscate wealth, the new breed shares the same capitalist aspirations as the old. Though black incomes are barely a sixth of white ones, a black elite is rising on the back of government jobs and the promotion of black business. It is moving into the leafy suburbs, such as Kelvin and Sandton, and adopting the outward symbols of prestige—the BMW, swimming pool, golf handicap and black maid—that so mesmerize status-conscious whites. . . .

The majority of South Africans know that the road to freedom and a better life will not take just five (or ten) years . . . [this is] not fatalistic patience . . . but the residues of knowledge accumulated through countless personal and collective struggles.

The country did not actually feel like that to me during my stay there, I must confess. On the left, there was the sense that the road, however long, is not actually running in a very promising direction. But more generally, and even more striking, was, yes, quite a lot of fatalism (and/or cynicism). And, equally marked, the weakness, not the strength, of any sense of shared purpose—together with clear signs that the ANC, reluctant to facilitate a substantial mobilization of people for any more transformative purpose than fairly passive vote delivery, is content to allow the profoundly individualizing logic of a market society to help actively to demobilize and to neutralize the mass of the population. . . .

Starting from Scratch?

In focusing upon the terms of ANC hegemony, we should avoid any underestimation of the hard edge that Mbeki and his party also maintain in order to lock their project firmly into place—the iron fist beneath the velvet glove of their undoubted legitimacy, as it were. The truth is that many members of that leadership group are people of limited democratic sensibility who simply do not like to be crossed. . . . As president, Mbeki has further centralized things in his own hands, the fact that virtually no leading ANC politician would publicly critique his stubborn attempt to contradict progressive consensus on the question of the link between HIV and AIDs may provide some indication of just how far the writ of his own authority runs. . . .

It is, of course, far too early to evaluate the prospects of any such attempt by various forces in South African civil society-including trade unions but also organizations of women, the church, the environmentally engaged, and those focused on issues of land or education or community concerns, among others—to link up more self-consciously, within and across sectors, in a popular alliance from below. . . .

JEREMY CRONIN, "POST-APARTHEID SOUTH AFRICA: A REPLY TO JOHN SAUL—EXCHANGE," FROM *MONTHLY REVIEW* (DECEMBER 2002): 1–9

(online posting at <http://www.findarticles.com/p/articles/mi_m1132/is_7_54/ai_95551899/print>)

Jeremy Cronin's article is a response to John S. Saul's article "Cry the Beloved Country," just presented. It shows us that the future about which Alan Paton reflected is not as bad as some claim.

John Saul has had an extensive and committed involvement with Southern Africa. His analyses are taken seriously in left circles in South Africa. Sadly, perhaps understandably, his most recent extended visit to this country has left him feeling deeply disappointed ("Cry for the Beloved Country: The Post-Apartheid Denouement," *Monthly Review* 52, no. 8, January 2001, pp. 1–51). This sense of disappointment is rooted, I would guess, partly in the intellectual, organizational and even emotional energies that Saul, like many others, invested in the solidarity struggle against apartheid, and in legitimate expectations for a post-apartheid South Africa. There is also, and I want to underline my own empathy with his irritation on this score, a hint of personal hurt: "The most startling thing I personally discovered about the New South Africa is just how easy it has become to find oneself considered an ultraleftist!" (p. 1). This sense of disappointment, even of betrayal, is also present in many progressive circles within South Africa, and indeed among many cadres of our movement. Despite all of this there is, I believe, something seriously off-beam in Saul's analysis. . . .

There is much by way of emphasis and detail that I would want to qualify or amend, but I agree substantially with the broad analysis of the last twelve years or so in South Africa that Saul makes in his pessimism-of-the-intellect mode. So what's the problem? The problem is that this general analysis is continuously trumped by another paradigm, another sensibility. This second approach is announced in the very title of the article, "Cry for the Beloved Country: The Post-Apartheid Denouement," and in the opening paragraph: "A tragedy is being enacted in South Africa, as much a metaphor for our times as Rwanda and Yugoslavia . . . " (p. 1). Note the literary and rhetorical flourishes: "denouement," "tragedy," "metaphor," and a title that evokes the novel (*Cry, the Beloved Country*) by the doyen of white South African liberalism, Alan Paton. They announce a paradigm of imminent closure, the revolution that is about to be (has always been about to be) betrayed. This is Greek tragedy, and as Brecht said of such tragedy, it renders the spectator a passive observer. All we can do is emote, as Saul himself says: "One does not know whether to laugh or cry" (p. 1).

But the imposition of this tragic reading onto what is, in my opinion, still a relatively open-ended, complex, and highly contested reality results in a number of internal disjunctures in the course of Saul's article. . . .

There is one more reason, a seemingly anomalous but perhaps, in this case, genuinely tragic reason to disagree with Saul. By a cruel twist of fate, the newly independent South Africa finds itself in the midst of an AIDS pandemic, with possibly one of the highest HIV infection rates in the world. Many, including the World Health Organization and UNAIDS, agree that the ANC-led government, generally speaking, has an admirable, integrated, and comprehensive program to address the pandemic. In particular, the awareness and prevention sides of the campaign have been enlightened and relatively effective. (There are also very strong, self-mobilized social movements of people infected and directly affected by the pandemic.) However, the treatment side of the program has suffered from considerable prevarication and incoherence. A small but well-placed minority within the ANC/government leadership, publicly led by the late Peter Mokaba, were convinced by the AIDS dissident argument that there is no HIV virus. These comrades have argued that AIDS is caused primarily by poverty and the diseases of poverty—repeated exposure to a barrage of infectious diseases (malaria, TB, STDs). Furthermore, so this argument goes, the case for HIV is being pushed by powerful, transnational pharmaceutical corporations. According to this view, HIV is a profit-seeking ideological construct, not a proven medical fact. This is not the official ANC or government position—both have emphasized on numerous occasions that our policies and programs are actively premised on the "assumption that AIDS is caused by HIV." But there have been hesitations, uncertainties, and incoherence in the implementation of treatment measures, particularly in regard to antiretrovirals.

If we are to evoke the notion of a tragedy, or of tragic irony, then it is here, but strictly only here, that it is applicable. The dissident view within our ranks is not held out of some venal opportunism, still less out of a desire to pander to neoliberal circles in the North. Quite the contrary, the hesitations around antiretroviral treatment have cost the ANC government considerable credibility in those quarters. To compound the tragic irony, the dissident view in our ranks is generally advanced by those who have been least sympathetic to any "dissidence" on the economic policy front. All of this underlines that, contrary to Saul's frozen penultimate assumptions about an inevitable betrayal to [*sic*] neoliberalism, anti-imperialist sensibilities run deep within the ANC, and they are liable to emerge, sometimes in surprising and, in this case, perhaps in tragically misguided ways. . . .

Interview with Kabengele

This interview, in April 2006, of a postapartheid immigrant, E. Kabengele, a teacher and engineer currently working in South Africa, provides an outsider/insider perspective on apartheid and life in postapartheid South Africa. This interview highlights the international perception of apartheid, provides an immigrant South African's perception of the continuing social devastations of apartheid, and offers insight into South Africans' current perception of the new South Africa.

1) What does apartheid mean to you?

It is a legalized form of discrimination, in South Africa, that existed from 1948 to 1994 when laws were passed to make sure that people of different colors did not mix. These laws, in essence, gave many opportunities and unfair advantages to the white race. Ironically, the then government of South Africa was officially calling it "separate development."

2) How did your racial (Black African, white, Indian or Coloured , immigrant etc.) identity shape your everyday experience?

As an Immigrant South African, I did not experience apartheid during its peak years since, at that time, I was outside South Africa. However I did suffer a psychological strain as I was connected to a South African family in the 80's when I worked at the University of Zambia. Ms. Sikozi , an ANC member, and her daughter used to come to our flat in Lusaka, Zambia and told us all the atrocities committed upon her extended family back home by the apartheid government machine. She was a student at the University of Zambia and got divorced from another ANC member when my spouse and I met her. I can summarize my own experience as follows: the system was the basis of the destruction of the fundamental unit of society that is the family, for the native South Africans. Even today, its effects are being felt in the South-African society. Specifically, Blacks were coached to believe that their purpose on earth was to serve Whites and it is in that context during 1976, the year of the Soweto pupils uprising, that the NP government tried to impose Afrikaans as a medium of instruction in Black schools and that law lead [*sic*] *to the Soweto Uprising. For adults coming from other areas of South Africa to work in big urban areas, it was required that they live in hostels around the big mining towns and that they leave their families either in their villages or townships not far from their villages. Those who did not accept apartheid (males or females) had to leave the country and more often left behind their partners or their children since they were ANC freedom fighters. The obvious consequence of this situation was a total collapse of the family life: infidelity, divorces, domestic violence, and passion crimes, which were and are still strife in South African society even today although at a decreased intensity.*

3) Have racial issues and social conditions improved since the demise of apartheid?

Definitely especially due to the fact that the reconciliation process under the Truth and Reconciliation Commission was genuine and candid. If you do not mind, I can answer this question as I am also officially a South African for the past two years, have listened to the general feeling of Black South Africans on the progress since the freedom Day of 1994, and also discussed candidly on several occasions with my current countrymen the situation of the country.

Progress has been made in urban areas in the sense that people have access to any part of the country and people can express any view they wish. Sometimes some citizens even complain that there is too much freedom in this country, and irresponsible persons and the media abuse it (One white citizen even took the then active President Mandela to court because he believed Mandela did not apply his mind properly about a decision the Presidency took.; and to set the example the President spent a whole day in the court himself to convince the judge of the contrary). Thus politically the country is on the right track. Economically, however people complain that the requirement imposed by the government on companies to create conditions to empower disadvantaged segments of our society, namely females of all races and Blacks, though partnerships and shareholding seem to create a class of super rich black elite (both sexes) in a blink of time and do not really improve the condition of the mass as the employment rate is still very high among the Blacks. There is also the question of delivery; although a lot of money is available for basic services, i.e. sanitation, water, electricity and housing, some municipalities are unable to convert that money into the effective delivery of those services and at the end of the fiscal year the government has always remained with a huge amount of unused money. That means that on the ground things are not happening at the rate of progress wished by the national government, especially in rural areas.

There is also the problem of HIV/AIDS, which is quite worrisome as it drains a lot of resources and cause damages even among the young population (Remember what I said about the collapse of the family: in fact most of the kids were raised by their grandparents). There is, however, a lot being done about prevention such distribution of condoms free of charge at all clinics of the republic and educating people to come forward and take the medical test to determine their HIV status. This helps people to lead a responsible life according to their status and to take the retroviral cocktail drug if required. South Africa is also active in a well advanced research to come out with a vaccine to prevent the pandemic.

And finally there is a pocket of white South Africans that does not recognize the wrongdoing of apartheid and jump at any opportunity to undermine the current effort of this new nation using the courts of the land. . . .

6) Have you read or seen a film adaptation of Alan Paton's *Cry, the Beloved Country?* What is your reaction to either?

Not as far as I recall.

ANNE PATON, "WHY I'M FLEEING SOUTH AFRICA," FROM THE *LONDON SUNDAY TIMES*—DISPATCHES, SUNDAY, NOVEMBER 29, 1998

(online posting at http://www.ourcivilisation.com/cry.htm)

This article by Alan Paton's widow explains her reasons for leaving South Africa and provides information on the increasing insecurity among South Africans in the new South Africa as the police struggle to ensure the safety of all citizens. Alan Paton highlights crime and violence in *Cry, the Beloved Country.*

I am leaving South Africa. I have lived here for 35 years, and I shall leave with anguish. My home and my friends are here, but I am terrified. I know I shall be in trouble for saying so, because I am the widow of Alan Paton.

Fifty years ago he wrote *Cry, The Beloved Country.* He was an unknown schoolmaster and it was his first book, but it became a bestseller overnight. It was eventually translated into more than 20 languages and became a set book in schools all over the world. It has sold more than 15 million copies and still sells 100,000 copies a year.

As a result of the startling success of this book, my husband became famous for his impassioned speeches and writings, which brought to the notice of the world the suffering of the black man under apartheid.

He campaigned for Nelson Mandela's release from prison and he worked all his life for black majority rule. He was incredibly hopeful about the new South Africa that would follow the end of apartheid, but he died in 1988, aged 85.

I was so sorry he did not witness the euphoria and love at the time of the election in 1994. But I am glad he is not alive now. He would have been so distressed to see what has happened to his beloved country.

I love this country with a passion, but I cannot live here any more. I can no longer live slung about with panic buttons and gear locks. I am tired of driving with my car windows closed and the doors locked, tired of being afraid of stopping at red lights. I am tired of being constantly on the alert, having that sudden frisson of fear at the sight of a shadow by the gate, of a group of youths approaching—although nine times out of 10 they are innocent of harmful intent. Such is the suspicion that dogs us all.

Among my friends and the friends of my friends, I know of nine people who have been murdered in the past four years.

An old friend, an elderly lady, was raped and murdered by someone who broke into her home for no reason at all; another was shot at a garage.

We have a saying, "*Don't fire the gardener*", because of the belief that it is so often an inside job—the gardener who comes back and does you in.

All this may sound like paranoia, but it is not without reason. I have been hijacked, mugged and terrorised. A few years ago my car was taken from me at gunpoint. I was forced into the passenger seat. I sat there frozen. But just as one man jumped into the back and the other fumbled with the starter I opened the door and ran away. To this day I do not know how I did this. But I got away, still clutching my handbag.

On May 1 this year I was mugged in my home at three in the afternoon. I used to live in a community of big houses with big grounds in the countryside. It's still beautiful and green, but the big houses have been knocked down and people have moved into fenced complexes like the one in which I now live. Mine is in the suburbs of Durban, but they're springing up everywhere.

That afternoon I came home and omitted to close the security door. I went upstairs to lie down. After a while I thought I'd heard a noise, perhaps a bird or something. Without a qualm I got up and went to the landing; outside was a man. I screamed and two other men appeared. I was seized by the throat and almost throttled; I could feel myself losing consciousness.

My mouth was bound with Sellotape and I was threatened with my own knife (Girl Guide issue from long ago) and told: "If you make a sound, you die." My hands were tied tightly behind my back and I was thrown into the guest room and the door was shut. They took all the electronic equipment they could find, except the computer. They also, of course, took the car.

A few weeks later my new car was locked up in my fenced carport when I was woken by its alarm in the early hours of the morning. The thieves had removed the radio, having cut through the padlocks in order to bypass the electric control on the gates.

The last straw came a few weeks ago, shortly before my 71st birthday. I returned home in the middle of the afternoon and walked into my sitting room. Outside the window two men were breaking in. I retreated to the hall and pressed the panic alarm.

This time I had shut the front door on entering. By now I had become more cautious. Yet one of the men ran around the house, jumped over the fence and tried to batter down the front door. Meanwhile, his accomplice was breaking my sitting- room window with a hammer.

This took place while the sirens were shrieking, which was the frightening part. They kept coming, in broad daylight, while the alarm was going. They knew that there had to be a time lag of a few minutes before help arrived—enough time to dash off with the television and video recorder. In fact, the front-door assailant was caught and taken off to the cells. Recently I telephoned to ask the magistrate when I would be called as a witness. She told me she had let him off for lack of evidence. She said that banging on my door was not an offence, and how could I prove that his intent was hostile?

I have been careless in the past—razor wire and electric gates give one a feeling of security. Or at least, they did. But I am careless no longer. No fence—be it electric or not—no wall, no razor wire is really a deterrent to the determined intruder. Now my alarm is on all the time and my panic button hung round my neck. While some people say I have been unlucky, others say: "*You are lucky not to have been raped or murdered.*" What kind of a society is this where one is considered "*lucky*" not to have been raped or murdered—yet?

A character in *Cry, the Beloved Country* says: "I have one great fear in my heart, that one day when they are turned to loving they will find we are turned to hating."

And so it has come to pass. There is now more racial tension in this country than I have ever known.

But it is not just about black-on-white crime. It is about general lawlessness. Black people suffer more than the whites. They do not have access to private security firms, and there are no police stations near them in the townships and rural areas. They are the victims of most of the hijackings, rapes and murders. They cannot run away like the whites, who are streaming out of this country in their thousands.

President Mandela has referred to us who leave as "cowards" and says the country can do without us. So be it. But it takes a great deal of courage to uproot and start again. We are leaving because crime is rampaging through the land. The evils that beset this country now are blamed on the legacy of apartheid. One of the worst legacies of that time is that of the Bantu Education Act, which deliberately gave black people an inferior education.

The situation is exacerbated by the fact that criminals know that their chances of being caught are negligible; and if they are caught they will be free almost at once. So what is the answer? The government needs to get its priorities right. We need a powerful, well-trained and well-equipped police force.

Recently there was a robbery at a shopping centre in the afternoon. A call to the police station elicited the reply: "We have no transport." "Just walk then," said the caller; the police station is about a two-minute sprint from the shop in question. "We have no transport," came the reply again. Nobody arrived.

There is a quote from my husband's book: "Cry, the beloved country, for the unborn child that is the inheritor of our fear. Let him not love the earth too deeply. Let him not laugh too gladly when the water runs through his fingers, nor stand too silent when the setting sun makes red the veld with fire. Let him not be too moved when the birds of his land are singing, nor give too much of his heart to a mountain or a valley. For fear will rob him of all if he gives too much."

What has changed in half a century? A lot of people who were convinced that everything would be all right are disillusioned, though they don't want to admit it.

The government has many excellent schemes for improving the lot of the black man, who has been disadvantaged for so long. A great deal of money is spent in this direction. However, nothing can succeed while people live in such fear. Last week, about 10km from my home, an old couple were taken out and murdered in the garden. The wife had only one leg and was in a wheelchair. Yet they were stabbed and strangled—for very little money. They were the second old couple to be killed last week. It goes on and on, all the time; we have become a killing society.

As I prepare to return to England, a young man asked me the other day, in all innocence, if things were more peaceful there. "You see," he said, "I know of no other way of life than this. I cannot imagine anything different." What a tragic statement on the beloved country today. "Because the white man has power, we too want power," says Msimangu.

"But when a black man gets power, when he gets money, he is a great man if he is not corrupted. I have seen it often. He seeks power and money to put right what is wrong, and when he gets them, why, he enjoys the power and the money.

Now he can gratify his lusts, now he can arrange ways to get white man's liquor. I see only one hope for our country, and that is when white men and black men, desiring neither power nor money, but desiring only the good of their country, come together to work for it.

I have one great fear in my heart, that one day when they are turned to loving, they will find we are turned to hating."

FROM NELSON MANDELA, *"CRY, THE BELOVED COUNTRY."* MIRAMAX WORLD PREMIERE, MIRAMAX FILMS, OCTOBER 23, 1995

(online posting at http://archives.obs-us.com/obs/english/films/mx/cry/speech4m.htm)

Nelson Mandela's speech at the premiere of the 1995 film version of *Cry, the Beloved Country* is a tribute to Alan Paton—his understanding of the South African tragedy and his vision of the future. It also examines the roots of crime in South Africa.

Some time back I had a very cruel experience, and I have since become very cautious when I feel that I have made some impact on an occasion. As you know, I once practiced law and in my face [*sic*] at trial I thought that a brilliant lawyer had arrived on the scene who was going to shake at the foundations of the law. I collected almost every authority I knew as I went to the courtroom and paraded these volumes on the table and then the proceedings started. And at the end of them the magistrate said, "I am finding the accused not guilty," and I began swelling with pride, as I'm tempted to do after this warm applause that I have got. But the magistrate then added, "I have found the accused not guilty—not because, but in spite of you." And he said, "The authorities that you have quoted here are totally irrelevant, they have nothing to do with this case, and I must confess that your whole exhibition here has been a waste of time of the court." And I left the courtroom with my tail between my legs. And I hope that the end of these proceedings, my pride will not be deflated.

Chairperson and dear friends, I was hauled by Anant Singh and my bosses a few days ago to a theater to view a film for the first time in many years and I should say, I enjoyed every moment of it. Much of what is portrayed in *Cry, the Beloved Country* evokes such strong emotions about the terrible past from which South Africa has just emerged. *Cry, the Beloved Country,* however, is also a monument to the future. One of South Africa's leading humanists, Alan Paton, vividly captured his eloquent faith in the essential goodness of people in his epic work. A goodness that helped manage this small miracle of our transition, and arrested attempts by the disciples of apartheid to turn our country into a wasteland. An attribute that is at the foundation of our people's nation-building effort, Paton was right, in his time and circumstances, to despair at seeing no peaceful way beyond the oppressors (*sic*) denial of the humanity of the majority. Though he could not himself come to terms with the necessity of armed resistance, he recognized its inevitability.

When he gave evidence in mitigation in our trial he acknowledge that the accused had had only two alternatives, and I quote, " . . . to bow their heads and submit or to resist by force." *Cry, the Beloved Country* is a film that for my generation, will evoke bittersweet memories of our youth. Urbanization was costly and painful, but the sweetness of an emerging urban culture in the township and Sophiatown now and then overcame the stench of decay. Such was the case of both in social life and in the rudiments of working class and political and intellectual political organization. In a sense, *Cry, the Beloved Country* represents a tribute to South Africa's youth, for they bore the brunt of the dislocation that apartheid organization brought on our communities.

It is for this reason that they become the torch bearers under the most trying circumstances. When democratic South Africa was able for the first time to celebrate their bravery and affirm its confidence in them on June 16 last year, I took the opportunity to announce the setting up of our Children's Fund, thus we could help redeem our children's suffering by joining them in building a happy tomorrow. The Fund aims to contribute, in a humble manner to the elevation of the plight of young people who are homeless, those who have not had the benefit of formal education, and those in detention or prison.

At midnight one day, I came out of a well-known Cape Town hotel and a group of about 15 to 20 street children came running towards me and security, as it was their duty, tried to prevent them. I appealed to security to allow the children through. And the first question they asked: "Why do you love us?" There was a lot of meaning behind that question because they were saying, "We are outcasts of society, nobody gives us parental love, happiness and security. We have no future." I therefore took the question seriously and I said, "How do you know I love you?" They said, "When you got money overseas, you shared that with us." They meant the Nobel Peace Prize. I then said, "I am not the only person who loves you. Practically every South African loves you, including your mothers and fathers, wherever they are." But the problem is that they did not have the fortune that I had of getting some money without working for it, and I could therefore afford to share it with you. You have to see those children at midnight, with hunger written across their faces, their bodies, tiny bodies covered by rags, filth, but never-the-less as human beings. It is that situation which has made many South African's contribute to the Children's Fund, because they are aware that they have to contribute in order to make the future of these outcasts of society, the future of our country, to feel that they can play a positive role in serving the nation.

Today's premiere of *Cry, the Beloved Country* confirms once more our confidence in the future. . . .

TOPICS FOR ORAL OR WRITTEN EXPLORATION

1. To what extent has the end of apartheid alleviated the conditions of Africans?

2 Is it easy to change a political and social system? Explain.

3. On the basis of your readings, do you believe that the criticisms leveled at ANC are objective?

4. Research crime in South Africa. What are the reasons for the elevated crime in South Africa, and has crime diminished with the demise of apartheid?

5 Research the status of African women in the new South Africa. Now that their men are liberated, have they also achieved liberation?

SUGGESTIONS FOR FURTHER READING

Desai, Ashwin. *We Are the Poor.* New York: Monthly Review Press, 2002.

Mandla, Langa. *The Naked Song.* Cape Town and Johannesburg: Africasouth New Writing, 1996.

Worden, Nigel. *The Making of Modern South Africa.* Malden, MA: Blackwell, 2000.

WORKS CITED

Kabengele, E. Personal interview by author. April 2006.

Malan, Rian. "Book I. Life in This Strange Place." *My Traitor's Heart.* New York: Grove Press, 1990: 5–6.

Mandela, Nelson. *Cry, the Beloved Country.* Miramax. World Premiere, Miramax Films. October 23, 1995.

Nesvag, Stein Inge. "Street Trading from Apartheid to Post-Apartheid: More Birds in the Cornfield?" *International Journal of Sociology and Social Policy* 21, no. 3/4 (2004). Online at <www.openair.org/pub/IJSSP?Nestag200-htm>.

Paton, Anne. "Why I'm Fleeing South Africa." *London Sunday Times*—Dispatches, Sunday, November 29, 1998, online at <http://www.ourcivilisation.com/cry.htm>.

Saul, John. S. "Cry for the Beloved Country: The Post-Apartheid Denouement." *Monthly Review* (January 2001). Online at <http://www.findarticles.com/p/articles/mi_m1132/is_8_52/ai_70397123/pg_2. html>.

Tutu, Desmond, with Douglas Abrams. *God Has a Dream.* New York: Doubleday, 2004.

Index

Note: *CBC* will be used throughout the index in place of *Cry, the Beloved Country*

About the Author

NGWARSUNGU CHIWENGO is Associate Professor of English at Creighton University; her work has appeared in such journals as *South Atlantic Quarterly*, *Journal of Black Studies*, and *African Literature Association Bulletin*.